FV

St. Louis Community College

Library

5801 Wilson Avenue
St. Louis, Missouri 63110

MONTEZUMA

MONTEZUMA

LORD OF THE AZTECS

C.A.BURLAND

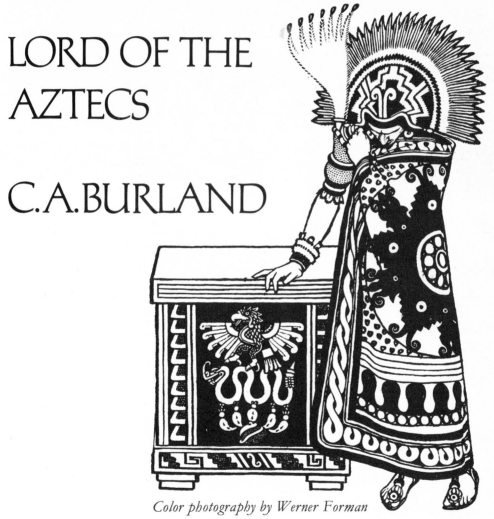

Color photography by Werner Forman

G. P. PUTNAM'S SONS
New York

Designed by Rod Josey
for George Weidenfeld and Nicolson Ltd
11 St John's Hill, London S.W.11.
Picture research by Pat Hodgson

SBN (United States)   399–11176–X

Library of Congress Catalog Card Number: 73–78633

Printed in Great Britain

CONTENTS

PREFACE

THIS BOOK IS A biographical study of a real person. Yet that real person is hard for the civilized mind to comprehend. Montezuma, as he is usually called today, was the product of a society radically different from our own. The cultural level of his people was that of a chalcolithic community at the very dawn of the use of metals. In some ways the Aztecs were great artists, accomplished poets, and deeply religious. Montezuma was by training and inclination a priest and dedicated himself to his patron, the god Quetzalcoatl, the Precious Twin, the Morning Star. (The name is often erroneously translated as the Feathered Serpent; but Quetzal refers not to *any* feathers, but to a rare and beautiful trogon with iridescent green feathers.) At times the book will seem to be an account of a world in which magic took precedence over reality. That is the simple truth; the ceremonial world shown in the few surviving books from ancient Mexico was the world which dominated the mind of the great ruler of the Aztecs.

The earlier part of the book dealing with the education and training of Montezuma is primarily derived from the great book of the missionary priest, Father Bernardino de Sahagún, where we find the Aztec training of young priests described in some detail. There are also details taken from the paintings in *Codex Laud*, where the preparations for an astronomer-priest are depicted. For the later part of the work we have a number of excellent Spanish sources, in particular the letters of Cortes, and the history written by Bernal Diaz del Castillo. There are also post-Spanish conquest accounts written in the Aztec language, Nahuatl, the best of which have been gathered together by Miguel Leon Portilla in his book *The Broken Spears*. There are of course contradictions and confusions in all the accounts, but I have chosen to lean on the accounts of Tezozomoc, because, although he wrote later than some other chroniclers, he was a prince of true Aztec descent who knew the tribal traditions of his people. In short I have tried to present Montezuma through Aztec eyes rather than Spanish.

The constant intrusion of a sense of fate and predestination through the sequence of time is truly Aztec in nature. Life was ruled very largely by the book of fate, the *Tonalpouhalli*. Montezuma was deeply obsessed with the idea that he was re-creating the glories of the long destroyed empire of the Toltecs. His dreams are recorded by trustworthy authors of the period of the Spanish conquest, and I have been able to correlate some of them with the appearance on the Mexican coast of the trading expedition of Solis and Pinzon a few years before the arrival of Cortes.

If there was an Aztec glory, it was the glory of a nation of American Indian warriors who were also farmers. They developed a city, seized upon the traditions of past Mexican civilizations, and in the space of two centuries became the masters of Mexico. They were a predatory tribe rather than colonists, which is why their hegemony broke up so suddenly under the impact of the Spanish invasion. But the qualities of their leader and his tragedy were personal expressions of Aztec culture at its highest.

The use of names has been conditioned by the need for simplification. Montezuma was really named Mohtecuzomatzin: *Moh* an expression of reverence, *tecuhtli*, the Lord, *zoma* the brave, *tzin* prince, one of noble birth, an honorific appelation. His city was called Tenochtitlan which means Beside Cactus Rock; we have used here the name Cactus Rock.

There is only one undocumented episode in this book: the dream of Montezuma wherein he saw the last Toltec ruler. It was a real dream, dreamed by the author on the eve of a visit to long-destroyed Tula, and now presented to Montezuma, for it is a dream which belonged to his nature and time.

We hope that this book will open to the reader not only a person, Montezuma, but some understanding of the world in which he lived, a world of strange beauty and much magic.

C. A. Burland
November, 1972

ACKNOWLEDGMENTS

Photographs were supplied by or are reproduced by kind permission of the following (numbers in italics refer to colour pictures).

Ferdinand Anton 13, 14, 16–17, 19, 42, 43, 114, 124, 132, 161, 177, 207, 237, 250, 255 below; Biblioteca Medicea Laurenziana, Florence (photos by Dr G. B. Pinateri) 48, 56 above, 63 above, 65 right, 81 top, 111, 147 below, 160 left, 167, 171 left, 172, 174 left, 180 right, 190, 198, 202, 203 left, 211, 214, 230, and Paul Hamlyn Picture Library (photos Guido Sansoni) 65 left, 252 left; Biblioteca Nazionale Centrale, Florence (photos Guido Sansoni) 23, 66, 92; Bibliothèque Nationale 239, and Paul Hamlyn Picture Library (photos Larousse) 56, 63, and Snark International 176, and Mathilde Rieussec 253 right; Bodleian Library, Oxford *28*, 40, 51, 52, 59, 62, 84, 120, 138, *245*, and Paul Hamlyn Picture Library 128; British Museum, 68, 113, 122, 150, 160 centre, 174 left, 175, 176, 180 left, 220, 244, and George Rainbird 81 below, 203 right, and Paul Hamlyn Picture Library 171 right; George Bunzl 261, 262, 264; Camera Press 35, (photo Martin Weaver) 209; City of Liverpool Museum 87, and Paul Hamlyn Picture Library 69, 78, 85; Dumbarton Oaks, Trustees for Harvard University, and Paul Hamlyn Picture Library 110; Werner Forman *25, 26–7, 53, 54, 71, 72, 89, 90, 107, 108, 133, 134–5, 136, 153, 156* top, *200, 217, 218, 235, 236, 246–7, 248*; Dr Gisèle Freund 130–1; Germanisches Nationalmuseum, Nuremberg 255 above, 256, 258, 259; Glasgow Art Gallery and Museum, Burrell Collection, 127; Paul Hamlyn Picture Library (photo Dr Pedro Rojas) 49, (photo Eugen Kusch) 104; Keith Henderson, endpapers, 151, 225, 226, 227, 228; Mansell Collection 169; Musée de l'Homme (photos F. L. Kenett) 18, 222, (photo Roger Viollet) 118, (photo Ferdinand Anton) 232; Museum für Volkerkunde, Basle, *154, 155, 182*, (photos Ferdinand Anton) 77 below, 91, 98, and Paul Hamlyn Picture Library 77 top; Museum of the American Indian, Heye Foundation, and Paul Hamlyn Picture Library 162; National Library, Vienna, 22, and Paul Hamlyn Picture Library 21; National Museum of Anthropology, Mexico, (photos Ferdinand Anton) 31, 34, 38, 44, 70, 75, 93, 95, 96, 105, 125, 139, 145 left, (photos Dr Gisèle Freund) 147 above, 178, (photo F. L. Kenett) 145 right, and Giraudon 32, 102, 115, 140, 149, 166, 185, and George Rainbird 79; Patrimonio Nacional and George Rainbird 191; Photo Bulloz 15, 100; George Rainbird 251; Mathilde Rieussec 241; Dr K. Stavenhagen Collection (photo Gisèle Freund) 142, (photo Ferdinand Anton) 164; Wurttembergisches Landesmuseum, Stuttgart (photos Karl Natter) *199*, and George Rainbird *156*.

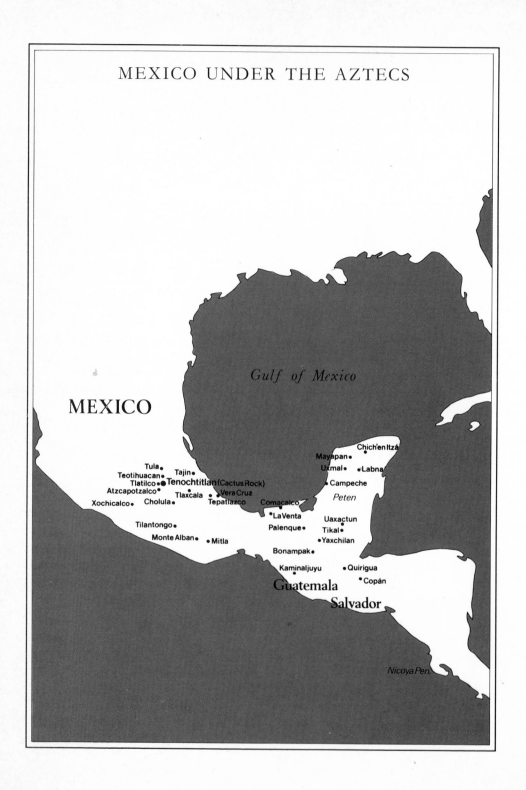

MEXICO UNDER THE AZTECS

MEXICO

Gulf of Mexico

Tula
Teotihuacan
Tlatilco
Atzcapotzalco
Xochicalco
Tajin
Tlaxcala
Cholula
Tenochtitlan (Cactus Rock)
Vera Cruz
Tepatlazco
Comacalco
Mayapan
Uxmal
Campeche
Chich'en Itzá
Labna
Peten
Tilantongo
Monte Alban
Mitla
La Venta
Palenque
Bonampak
Kaminaljuyu
Uaxactun
Tikal
Yaxchilan
Quirigua
Copán

Guatemala

Salvador

Nicoya Pen.

I

HISTORICAL BACKGROUND

ONTEZUMA WAS THE LAST 'Great Speaker' of the Aztec tribe of Mexico.
Behind him lay a long history of beliefs and traditions. Like all his people
he believed that they had been created long ago in Mexico, a land unmatched
on earth for its beauty and holy power. To them, the heart of this land lay in a valley
three days march north of their city of Cactus Rock, where two enormous pyramids
stood among a complex of overgrown mounds of a ruined city. This was Teotihuacan,
the 'Place where God is Adored'.

More than fifty thousand years ago, bands of ice-age hunters muffled in furs had
followed wild animals across the Behring Straits and, still hunting for their sustenance,
had passed through the ice-free plains to the east of the Rocky Mountains. Here
and there stone tools mark their passage. Camp sites, too, show the bones of the
animals they hunted, and charcoal from their fires. The migration was spread over
many centuries. Just a family or two at a time came over from palaeolithic Siberia
and found a new world. Their descendants had moved little by little over the whole
continent. They were the American Indians, a people with reddish-brown, cold-
resistant skin, eyes often with an epicanthic fold, and straight, raven-black hair. The
evidence points towards them having been an admixture of races even in the earliest
times.

By eight thousand years ago, among the hundreds of scattered groups of American
Indians, a few people living in what is now Northern Mexico and New Mexico had
discovered a plant which bore two edible seeds and which could be planted and
reaped with ever increasing yields of grain. Among them agriculture slowly extended
and their food grain turned into the first maize. No longer solely dependent upon
hunting for food, they were able to establish themselves in permanent village settle-
ments. The first stride towards self-sufficiency had been made and with it, the
development of civilization.

Agriculture gradually spread among many tribes until in the area of modern
Mexico there were no primitive hunters left. By about 2000 BC the country was lightly
populated by people living in villages widely separated from one another, but all able
to grow maize, beans and pumpkins as their basic subsistence. The villagers had tamed
the turkey, and some had semi-domesticated pigs. The dog was a companion of the
hunters who brought in occasional deer to add to the meals, and in the west it was

bred as a delicate article of food with highly succulent fat.

Near Mexico City burial mounds have yielded evidence about these people and their lives. They were typical American Indians – of small stature and, as their many little pottery figurines show, pleasantly-proportioned. They wore little, if any, clothing but were never without jewellery. They painted their bodies with bars and stripes apparently in some black dye, and dressed their hair in elaborate styles. The great numbers of female figurines tell us that they placed great value on young women as symbols of the fruitful earth. Their houses were made from sun dried blocks of clay and sand called adobes.

About 1200 BC, in a hilly district about fifty miles south of Mexico City, we meet with the first signs of a civilization. Here, among the rocks of Chalcatzinco, are relief carvings showing gods, a cave and symbols that have reference to ideas somewhat similarly expressed even twenty-eight centuries later. Associated with the villages in the valley of Mexico were new types of pottery, including large and beautifully finished figures of fat, baby-like humans with broad noses, high foreheads and high-set mongoloid eyes, features which may still be seen among some modern Mexicans. Whether they originated among the villages on the high plateau or not we do not know. A couple of centuries later we find the same physical type of people depicted in great stone carvings and enormous stone heads around well planned ceremonial courtyards in town sites on the southeastern shores of the gulf of Mexico. Because this was the country whence the later Mexicans obtained rubber, they have been dubbed, following a later Aztec tradition, as the Olmecs, which simply means 'the rubber people'. Because they were first detected on the coasts through their marvellous stone carvings and traces of symbolic writing, it was thought that they might have learned about civilization from some lost voyagers from Egypt of the time of Rameses III, but there is little solid evidence for this, and the earlier carvings at Chalcatzinco suggest that this first Mexican civilization was of native origin.

The Olmec culture starts about 1200 BC and lasts for about five centuries. Then it disappears. During its period of greatness the art of the Olmecs spread widely over Mexico, but we do not know if the local tribes in western and southern Mexico simply copied Olmec styles or whether the Olmecs were a tribe who spread their art styles by some kind of conquest of other peoples. Because they were such fine artists, working in stone and even in jade, we know a good deal about their religious beliefs from their carvings. The earth seems to be shown as a giant animal from the mouth of which the sun emerges carrying a jaguar child which may represent the planet Venus. In some cases the sculptor has used symbols for numbers, in which a dot represents a unit and a solid bar counts as five. It appears that they were the first people to use this numerical system as a means of counting days in a calendar which works like the

Opposite Colossal head carved in basalt. Olmec culture, from La Venta, Tabasco. Between 1000 and 600 BC.

time count used in later times by the Maya of Yucatan and all other ancient Mexican peoples.

The cultures which developed from direct links with the Olmecs were those of the Zapotecs in western Mexico, and the Maya in the south of the country and in Yucatan. They do not appear to have had any direct connection with the later development of the Aztec world, except that in 1498 the Zapotecs were overthrown by Aztec armies and forced to pay tribute. However, the Maya developed a high civilization of their own, with a remarkable calendrical system of astrology, syllabic writing, and a complex social system. It was not for several centuries after the disappearance of Olmec culture that the Maya took to making inscriptions upon stone, but the linkage between the two systems appears to have been a direct development. In later times the Aztecs left the Maya alone except for occasional trade missions. They did not consider them to be worthy opponents in war, and as sacrificial victims their loose living made them quite uneatable from the Aztec point of view.

However, in the second century BC at Teotihuacan in Central Mexico a very small

Opposite Small dancing figures in earthenware. Teotihuacan I. About 100 BC.

Above Clay mask of a god emerging from an eagle's beak, perhaps a sun deity. Teotihuacan IV. Soon after AD 600.

15

adobe pyramid and a typical highland village suddenly became important. Within a century a town was in being with a huge ceremonial centre. The arts of Teotihuacan were very distinctive and as the sacred city grew in importance its influence spread over all of the southern half of Mexico and very strongly into highland Guatemala. The arts of pottery, fresco painting, and lintel-and-post architecture reached remarkably high levels. The gods of later Mexico become important in Teotihuacan, which was mainly dedicated to the rain god, Tlaloc. It is clear that the Teotihuacanos had a glyphic system of writing, but so little remains that one concludes that any long documents must have been painted on perishable materials such as leather sheets or fibre paper. But the formality of Teotihuacano design, the layout of the great ceremonial centres and the evidence for widespread trade do suggest that the Teotihuacanos were of great importance to all later developments in central Mexico. Archaeological evidence makes it quite clear that the Teotihuacanos were traders and that the city was a holy city. There is little to suggest that the Aztec legends about a sun cult at

Teotihuacan were based on any local devotion to the sun god. The evidence of many frescoes in the ruins of the great city shows that Tlaloc, the lord of the rains, was the chief god, and that many other Mexican deities of later times were worshipped there. Although the art tradition and choice of colour are unique to the Teotihuacano civilization, there remains enough evidence to show that there was a continuity of many religious traditions in this great city which might have had nearly a million inhabitants.

But Teotihuacano culture, like all earlier cultures in Mexico, was doomed. In the middle of the seventh century of the Christian era the great city was devastated. Houses were smashed down, temples and palaces were burnt and the priestly area was beaten down to the ground, or at least to the level at which the rubble of destroyed buildings piled above the ground. Apparently the power of an enemy coming from the west was responsible. Yet for another century Teotihuacan civilization remained active in the much smaller town of Azcapotcalco near Mexico City.

Below Outer walls of a palace of the Zapotec kings at Lyoobaa (now Mitla) in the Mixtec area of Oaxaca. Possibly about AD 1000.

The reason for the destruction of Teotihuacan is not known. Even the identity of the destroyers is not clear. It is likely that these invaders were led by people who used an individual variation of the ancient Central American calendar, whose inscriptions are found in Guatemala in the fifth century AD and at Xochicalco in central Mexico in the seventh century. They have no history, and there is no trace of any historical tradition about the events which led to the disaster of the great civilization which had grown around the huge pyramids at Teotihuacan. The matter is one for the archaeologist rather than the historian. Nevertheless it is quite clear that around the great

Opposite Clay head of a deity arising from the serpent jaws. Possibly Quetzalcoatl as morning star arising from the earth. Before AD 1000. Totonac people of Vera Cruz.

Above Serpent columns of the Temple of the Jaguars at Chichen Itza, Yucatan, the last refuge of the Toltec rulers. About AD 1150.

city had crystallized much of Mexican theology, and that its ruined heart was still venerated for nearly a thousand years after the destruction. We do not even know the name of the people who built the city and carried its culture throughout civilized Mexico, neither have we any definite trace of their language, apart from the almost untranslatable name of the god Tlaloc, lord of all sources of water. We have some reason to suspect that Teotihuacan was ruled by a theocracy, not unlike the divine king of the Zapotecs who throughout Teotihuacano times, and until the Aztec conquest, ruled from Mitla in Oaxaca.

The next people of whom we have evidence in Mexico from native historical records were the Toltecs. In them we have the undoubted ancestors of Aztec culture, and Montezuma was concerned to prove a direct linkage between them and his own people in Cactus Rock. The Toltecs used the same calendrical system as the people who had come from Guatemala at the time of the collapse of Teotihuacan. Their language, Nahuat, ancestral to the Aztec tongue Nahuatl, was related closely to the language of the Ute Indians, a tribe of the southwestern USA who were typical Plains Indians. So there is reason for thinking that some at least of the Toltec population were of northern origin. The question at this point of time is not by any means answered, though Toltec origins may prove to be a mixture of new influences in Mexico. Certainly later stories tell of the Toltecs as a confederation of groups representing the four world directions, and the Mixtecs of the mountains of Oaxaca continued Toltec artistic traditions though their language was radically distinct from Nahuat. But although the exact origin of the Toltecs is cloudy to us, they were quite clear in their belief that their ruling lineage was descended from the god Quetzalcoatl, 'The Morning Star, the Breath of Life, the Precious Twin, the Quetzal-bird-serpent'. Not only do we have histories written in barest outline by post-Conquest Mexican historians, but also a painted book, now in Vienna and which Montezuma once owned, gives a short history, mixed with mythology, which confirms the belief that the Toltec power was theoretically sanctioned by the divinity of the much beloved god Quetzalcoatl who was traditionally first earthly king of the Toltecs.

The ruins of Tula or Tollan (the Place of Reeds), the Toltec capital, were first uncovered by De Charnay some eighty years ago, but only a small area was explored. The temple mound was not greatly impressive and it was assumed that this was a place of little importance. In fact many archaeologists in the first quarter of the twentieth century assumed that the Toltecs were a mythical people. However, later work revealed more and more of a destroyed city, and now Tula is seen to have been as large as Teotihuacan, but with an emphasis on palaces built around courtyards, and small temples with many carvings. The place is associated with Mazapan pottery known to be pre-Aztec in date. So in quite recent years the destroyed city has been revealed as a tragic ruin representing a great and powerful empire. The scale of the city amply justifies the legends, and there are still further areas to be explored. A few potsherds and a small pyramidal mound testify to later Aztec visits to the ruins of Tula. It may be that the mound was the small temple constructed for Montezuma in what he regarded as the home of his ancestors. Pottery of Mazapan type and associated 'plumbate' wares of the ninth and tenth centuries have been found widespread throughout Mexico and into the Maya area. The legendary 'empire' has at last

Opposite A page from the Book of Quetzalcoatl, now *Codex Vindobonensis Mexic. 1,* showing the descent of the divine king Quetzalcoatl to earth after receiving his attributes from Ometecuhtli the Supreme Deity.

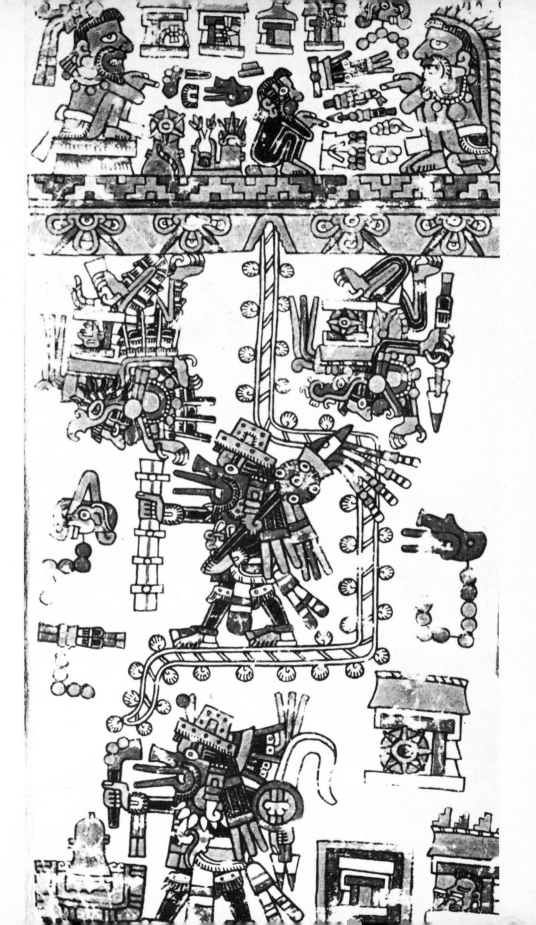

been found to correspond to an archaeological fact. The works of art, mostly sculptured walls found at Tula, show close parallels with the late Toltec-Maya art of Chichen Itza in Yucatan, said to have been the refuge of the last king Quetzalcoatl of the Toltecs. There is also a very close correspondence in style between the sculptured friezes at Tula and the painted figures in the *Mixtec Codices*. The linkage of legendary history and archaeology is very close indeed.

Montezuma was undoubtedly much concerned that his Aztec people, five centuries after the fall of the Toltecs, should restore the glory of the vanished empire of the past. In this no doubt he was assisted by the desire of his people to acquire roots in the distant past, long before their poverty stricken ancestors set out on their pilgrimage to Cactus Rock. An outline history of the Toltecs was certainly known to the Aztecs. The most important versions of it were written down in the mid-sixteenth century by the Tezcocan prince Fernando de Alvarado Ixtlilxochitl. His account is close to the painted story in the fourteenth-century painted document, *Codex Vindobonensis*, which once belonged to Montezuma.

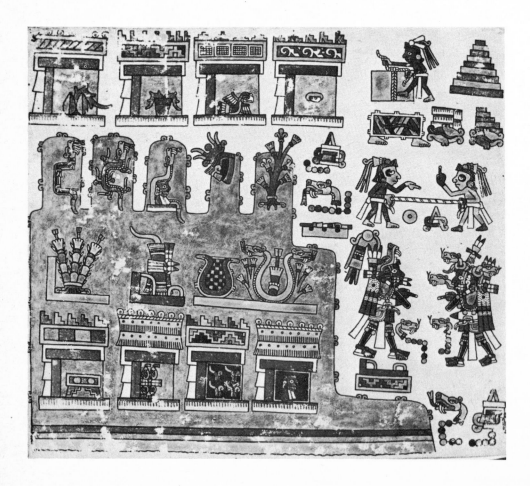

The story in this pre-Columbian book deals with the creation of the world, the appearance of the god Quetzalcoatl as supporter of the skies and as morning star. Then born of the earth goddess as a man Quetzalcoatl was given many blessings and eventually was taken before The Two (the Creator) in the highest heaven. There he was invested with his symbolic costume and given temples for his worship. Returned to earth the god became first lord of the Toltecs. He was both a priest and a civil ruler; he dedicated temples, constructed wonderful palaces, and then at a great ceremony he was overcome by the magic of the other gods. The witch-goddess tricked him into eating an hallucinatory mushroom and thus tempted him into sexual intercourse with her. Then, according to the legend, the god left Mexico in shame and sailed to the east. The Codex does not show the pilgrimage away from Mexico but it does show the final episode of the legend, where the heart of the god – represented in the Codex as *ce acatl* (one reed) – ascends towards the sun at midday and thus becomes the morning star. The Royal Observatory, when checking on data given in the Codex, identified this legendary description of a solar eclipse and visible Venus with

Opposite Page from *Codex Vindobonensis* showing the last remnants of the Toltec empire under Huemac in about AD 980. Painted about AD 1350.

Below Drawing of the Mexican patron deity, Huitzilopochtli (Blue Hummingbird on the Left) from *Codex Magliabecciano*, painted about 1550.

an actual total eclipse of the sun in Mexico in July of the year AD 650. We thus obtained a date for the departure of the first Quetzalcoatl of the Toltecs that confirmed the historical aspect of the myth.

The name Quetzalcoatl became a title, and there were eight other Quetzalcoatls of Tula. Of these eight lords, the names of two are exactly the same as those given by Ixtlilxochitl in his history. In each case, on his accession, the king is shown making new fire to signify the new king's era and carrying a bunch of sacred plants on his way to the city, where he is then shown causing new buildings to be erected. After each king is listed the temples and curative baths which he established. Some kings are shown with symbols which record towns added to the Toltec hegemony. In two cases there are symbols for a ceremonial mock-war which allowed prisoners to be taken for sacrifice on those years when no real war was taking place.

The last Quetzalcoatl to rule at Tula is depicted almost as if he is the returned god. The reason was that he shared the same birthday, and therefore the same name, Nine Winds. The page on which he is shown is covered with a symbolic layout of the mountains and cities of the Toltec Empire. His successor, Huemac, is shown beside another map with only a few mountains and towns. Tula has fallen, Huemac makes no new fire. He rules but a remnant of the former empire and that uncertainly. After him comes a sequence of individuals who appear to carry on the succession, though not as rulers of any empire at all. The record ends in the fourteenth century. Because each king is inaugurated on a specified day and year in the Toltec calendar, it is easy to count the reigns from the solar eclipse of 650. The Toltec rule in Mexico reached its end at about AD 980.

In Aztec times the history was interpreted in mythological terms, and although Montezuma possessed the *Codex Vindobonensis* and was well aware of the succession of Toltec rulers, he would have seen the end of the great empire as a recension of the end of the rule of the first Quetzalcoatl. The struggle was the combat of divine powers. Quetzalcoatl was replaced as the controlling power in Mexico by the great demiurge Tezcatlipoca (Smoking Mirror) who had originally drawn the earth up from the waters of chaos. Smoking Mirror was a strange being. He was thought to be the lord of the surface of the earth, 'the Prince of this World'; he was also the 'Tempter', the one always at the shoulder whispering ideas of savagery into the human mind. Naturally he was the god of young warriors. He was also a solar deity or at least he took different forms during the passage of the sun through the sky. In his eastern form he was a god of suffering and sacrifice for fertility, in his southern form he was the Blue Tezcatlipoca, the Blue Hummingbird, Huitzilopochtli, who was later to become the tribal patron of the Aztecs, and therefore important to their welfare. As ruler of

Opposite Carved wooden image of a falling deity with an animal snout, overlaid with mosaic of turquoise and shell. This may represent the evil twin of Quetzalcoatl, the god Xolotl.

the Aztecs Montezuma would have had to own the sovereignty of Blue Hummingbird over the tribe, even though he himself was dedicated to Quetzalcoatl of the Toltecs. Therein lay the dilemma which shattered him. Blue Hummingbird was Lord of Earth and Quetzalcoatl was Lord of Air; their contrast and conflict could be stated in terms of the alchemists. The conflict of the gods in the legend of Toltec destruction was archetypal. These great and mysterious powers conflicted in every human personality. In the case of Montezuma this resulted in his destruction. In most people the power of the shadow, which was the psychological aspect of Blue Hummingbird, had to be absorbed and integrated into the personality with the equally potent opposite force of life and wisdom.

However, the historical aspect of events was more clear. After the fall of the Toltecs there was civil war in Mexico. The many city states struggled for ascendancy; they sometimes established small empires, sometimes confederations of states to attack others. None however could seize power over the whole country as had been done by the Toltecs. The remaining Toltec families became aristocrats of little power during this period of political anarchy. The only continuity was that of the ordinary people all over Mexico; they cultivated their fields and carried on a quiet life except when the warriors laid waste their villages, or the young men were called to join the forces of their town and march out to devastate the fields of some neighbouring community.

By the thirteenth century in the high plateau of central Mexico the Acolhuas who ruled the city of Colhuacan, about twelve miles north of Mexico, became the dominant power of the area. Their power was considerable and they left a tradition so strong that when three centuries later the coastal people met the Spanish invaders they described the rulers of the country as the lords of Culhua Mexico.

It was in the thirteenth century that the Aztecs appear, although they were not called Aztecs until after the conquest by the Spaniards. At first they claimed that they came from a place called Aztlan, which seems in fact to have been called Aztatlan (Beside the White Heron). Their warriors usually wore two heron feathers in their headband as a crest, which serves to hint at the real name of their homeland. Their history is distorted. We are sure of this since one Great Speaker of the tribe, Itzcoatl (Serpent of Knives), had the historical records of the tribe's early days destroyed, and substituted a version more acceptable to the ruling clan, of which he was a member. The 'official' version of the Aztec beginnings is preserved in the *Tira de la Peregrinación*,

Previous page Itapan, site of a summer palace in the mountains where Montezuma could escape the hot humid summer of Cactus Rock.

Opposite The foundation of the city of Cactus Rock. The founding chiefs sit beside the waterways contemplating the vision of the Eagle on the Cactus, indicating the presence of their god Blue Hummingbird. *Below* Aztec warriors conquer the towns of Colhuacan and Tenayuca. *Codex Mendoza.*

a painting on a long strip of fig bark paper, now in the National Museum in Mexico. This claims that in the year AD 1168 the Aztecs left their homeland in Aztlan to visit a ruined temple nearby. There they heard a strange whistling coming from a carved stone head. This head represented the god Blue Hummingbird, who was singing a victory chant. He promised them that if they were faithful to him, they should conquer all of Mexico. They were to carry his stone head with them in all their journeyings until he should appear to them as a white sea-eagle sitting on a cactus springing from a rock. This would be their future home, the site of a great city called Tenochtitlan, which means Beside Cactus Rock.

The tribe set out and in the same year they settled at the Seven Caves. This was a famous place in Mexican history, since from there all the great tribes in turn left to find greatness. Here the history is obviously apocryphal, since the event is put by other peoples in a far distant past. It was at this place that the ancestors cut down a sacred tree and incurred the displeasure of Blue Hummingbird. He appeared to them and condemned them to an unspecified period of wandering and poverty until they should find their glorious destiny. Later, as they marched on their way, they came across three human bodies lying on their backs over huge cacti with their chests torn open and the hearts extracted. Thus the Aztecs learnt how human beings were to be sacrificed to appease their gods. The whole of this introduction can be found in earlier documents. It was probably the change ordered by Itzcoatl in later times. However, it assured the Aztecs that their origins were no less divinely inspired than those of other peoples.

After the preamble the Codex records the migration of the Aztecs. The tribe is always represented by the Council of Four, who were governors chosen by popular discussion. The places of sojourn are marked by glyphs which can be read as place-names. Here for four years, there for ten, and so on, the roads between being marked by footprints, and the trail of time marked by squares containing the signs for years. Eventually the ancestors reached the hill of Chapultepec, and, still driven by the will of their god, they settled near the spring. This land was already controlled by the Acolhuas, who did not care for the arrival of these miserable ragged wanderers. Their young men were sent to attack the Aztecs; the victory of the Acolhuan army was never in doubt, but for the Aztecs it seemed a final disaster, and a betrayal by their god. They were dragged before the Lord Coxcoxtli, ruler of Colhuacan (Twisted Hill). He was a Lord of Toltec descent with a right to rule over men, and he proceeded to enslave the Aztecs.

Shortly after this event a neighbouring town sent its messengers to Colhuacan with a formal declaration of war. The Acolhuas prepared, and Coxcoxtli planned to send the Aztecs to meet the enemy on the trail across the hills. He reasoned that it might delay the enemy, and at the same time the Aztecs would be killed and a nuisance removed from his town. The Aztecs, armed with stone knives and wooden clubs, arranged an ambush and attacked with cries of victory for their god Blue Hummingbird. The enemy was seized upon. Many were made captives, the others

Above Stone figure of a Tlaloque (called a
chacmool) who in the form of a storm cloud
carries a bowl for sacrificed hearts. The
stone-knife symbols on his sandals indicate
that he is a spirit of destructive hailstorms.

slain. Immediately the Aztecs cut out hearts for their god without waiting to go to
Colhuacan. They then cut the right ear off each dead body and wandered back to
Colhuacan. They arrived in the square before the palace and the temple. The inhabitants of the city jeered at them and the Lord Coxcoxtli derided them as cowards who
had failed to bring a single prisoner; that they remained alive was proof that they had
run away from the battle. In reply the Aztecs stood forward, each man with a basketry
hamper on his back as if he was a porter with merchandise on his back. Then at a word
from their war chief they unleashed their packs and poured a torrent of human ears
over the feet of the terrified Coxcoxtli.

After this episode the Acolhuans decided to send the Aztecs to settle on a swampy
islet a mile or two from the shores of the nearby Lake of the Moon. The Aztecs
paddled their flat-bottomed canoes through the waters, knowing they would be hard
put to grow enough maize in the swampy soil to pay their tribute to Coxcoxtli as well
as to feed themselves, even though the lake seemed full of fish and water fowl. When

they landed, the priests were astonished to see a stream flowing with red and blue water, which was their symbol of victory in war. They followed its path to where it flowed from under a rock, and there on the rock was growing a cactus, upon which perched the white sea-eagle of Blue Hummingbird. In its talons it gripped a serpent, symbolic of the taking of life from the earth for the gods. It was the sign promised to them. They knew that in this place beside Cactus Rock they should have a habitation and a base for the conquest of Mexico.

They discovered on a nearby islet the ruins of an ancient Toltec temple, whereon was sculptured a procession of gods of which the central figure was the god Tezcatlipoca, one of whose most powerful aspects was as their own war god Blue Hummingbird. But they built their own temple at Cactus Rock, making a mound of beaten earth and placing on it a hut of reeds like their own huts, and within it they placed the singing stone image of their god.

The first settlement in Cactus Rock (Tenochtitlan) is given various dates, all within the fourteenth century, by different authorities. The official Aztec account is probably that copied in 1553 on *Codex Mendoza*, now in the Bodleian Library at Oxford. This document was compiled for the Spanish Viceroy, Don Antonio de Mendoza, and includes a copy of the tribute-list of Montezuma, an account of daily life among the Aztecs and a concise history of the Aztec rulers. The history is confirmed, with minor variations by several sources, and can be accepted as an authentic record.

In those days the Aztecs were led by the Council of Four which consisted of the Speaker for the tribe, the High Priest, the Market Controller, and the army leader who was distinguished by the title of Serpent Woman. The Speaker was the acting chief. The first Speaker in Cactus Rock was, according to the legends, named Tenoch which was practically the name of the town. He is said to have ruled from 1325 to 1375. The Aztecs claimed to have captured the two great cities of Tezcoco and Colhuacan during this period, but the truth is probably that they made successful raids and returned with plunder, and it is possible that the rule of the Speaker Tenoch was largely a fiction. What is certain is that the early Aztecs went in fear of Tezcoco and continued to pay tribute to Colhuacan. One fact belongs to the period and that is a calendrical occasion. In 1351 the Aztecs made the ceremony of 'tying up the years, and making new fire'. This great ceremony took place at intervals of fifty-two years and marked the point in time when it was thought the world might come to an end. The past 'bundle' of fifty-two years was symbolized by a cluster of fifty-two wooden rods which were ceremonially burnt to ashes. For twelve days the people made no fires,

Opposite Mictlantecihuatl (Lady of the Land of the Dead). A protectress of souls in the underworld, which is a place of song and dance. Her dancing skirt is decorated with feathers and fringed with shell rattles. Carved in basalt. Aztec about 1500.

Above Quetzalcoatl, as Ehecatl, Lord of the Winds. This is one of a row of similar figures which supported an offering table. Aztec, about 1500.

Opposite The *coatepantli* (serpent wall), of the Aztec pyramid at Tenayuca. About 1450.

and fasted on bread and water. Then came the day when the star Aldebaran passed over the zenith at midnight. All Mexico watched. If the star stood still, the end was at hand. But it moved on, and amidst cries of rejoicing a victim was killed and the Fire-Priest kindled a blaze over his heart. From this torches were lit and sent to all the temples in Mexico from which the people obtained fire for their domestic hearths. Thereupon the women started to make new pottery and clothing to replace the things destroyed twelve days before, and life went on with the assurance that the world

would continue for another fifty-two years. The ceremony of 1351 was the fourth one celebrated by the Aztecs, and the first to take place at Cactus Rock.

Tenoch died according to the records in 1375, and was succeeded as Speaker of the Aztecs by the previous war leader, Acamapichtli (Handful of Arrows) who reigned until 1396. He was of some importance because he was the son of a Toltec princess of Acolhuacan. He is said to have captured four important towns around the shores of the lake. This does not imply permanent conquest; only that the Aztecs were able to force the people of those towns to pay tribute. It must have been a considerable gain of wealth because these were ancient and rich cities including Cuernavaca and Xochimilco. But the Aztecs were forced to pay tribute to another city, Azcapotzalco (In the Ant Hill). Perhaps it was as warriors in the employ of Azcapotzalco that they had obtained their revenge in a raid which deprived their ancient enemies of Colhuacan of their power. However, Handful of Arrows died in 1396 and was succeeded by his son Huitzilhuitl (Hummingbird-Feather). He was a good choice by the Council of the tribe, since he was a successful diplomat. His first wife was a Toltec princess even more important than his mother. She was of the ruling family of Azcapotzalco and was greatly respected. Her father altered the tribute which the Aztecs were forced to pay to the 'peppercorn rent' of two ducks and a basket of fresh fish annually. The Aztec Speaker Hummingbird-Feather took a second wife, also a diplomatic alliance because she was a princess from the great city of Cuernavaca south of Cactus Rock. Huitzilhuitl had many children of whom the most important was Montezuma Ilhuicamina (The Mighty Prince, Who Shoots at the Stars).

In Huitzilhuitl's time the Aztecs progressed further by diplomacy than war, but they still needed victims for sacrifice to their gods, and these they obtained by 'Wars of Flowers'. Two cities would arrange for their young warriors to meet for a cere-monial combat until each side had captured enough prisoners to make an acceptable offering to their gods. Then they separated to make the offerings without demanding any tribute from either side. It was a friendly way of fighting of some antiquity, since we know the convention was also used in the days of the Toltecs. It was particularly important for the Aztecs in 1403 when the years were again bundled up and burnt before the making of New Fire.

In 1417, on the death of Hummingbird-Feather, the Council met to elect another Speaker. They chose an active warrior who had earned his name Chimalpopoca (Smoking Shield), but who as Speaker spent the ten years of his rule in a series of difficult negotiations with the people of the north of the lake, the Tepanecs, who controlled the hill of Chapultepec. The trouble lay in the fact that the drinking water in Cactus Rock came from wells and was brackish since there was an insufficient flow of water out of the lake to dispose of the salts. Meanwhile on Chapultepec hill there was a splendid perennial spring. The Tepanecs had no intention of helping their island neighbours to become more powerful, and fought off Aztec people who came in canoes hoping to take back huge pottery jars full of fresh water. The struggle was not successful, but in view of this continual provocation the Aztec people were constantly in readiness for battle and plans for war were ready when Smoking Shield died.

The council chose Itzcoatl, a child of Acamapichtli by a slave girl, as the next Speaker for the Aztecs. His name meant Serpent of Obsidian Knives and he was of an aggressive disposition and a brilliant fighting man. The Council abandoned their class feelings concerning his parentage because they knew that here was the man to capture the water supply for the city. Cactus Rock was becoming important, the houses were of stone and the temple was a fine pyramidal construction covered with painted slabs of rock. The population had grown to the point where the water from Chapultepec was a matter of life and death. Serpent of Knives knew well that there was no way out, apart from a planned war against the Tepanecs. By constant minor attacks the Tepanec chief was provoked into starting a march on Cactus Rock. The tribespeople, afraid of the apparently invincible mass of warriors advancing against them, asked the Speaker and the nobles around him to make peace at any price, for they feared their city would be destroyed. Serpent of Knives and the great warriors asked the people to agree to a plan to break the stranglehold of the Tepanecs, and after some debate the people agreed that if there was a victory in the war they would serve the noble leaders and their families and give up their ancient right to take part in the election of the Speakers of the tribe. It was a move of desperation on the people's part, but the nobles took their chance and Serpent of Knives called the young Tlacaelel to take command of a group of warriors who would ambush the enemy. Meanwhile diplomacy was not neglected. Envoys were sent to towns around the lake seeking for an alliance. The town of Tlaltelolco on an island beside Cactus Rock refused any help and sent messages to the enemy. However, the great city of Tezcoco led by the famous chief, Hungry Coyote, allied itself freely with the Aztecs. As the Tezcocan warriors came in canoes to protect the Aztec centre, a spearhead of warriors went out to meet the advancing Tepanecs. All day the battle raged, and it was largely determined by a well-timed flanking attack by Tlacaelel. The Tepanecs were totally defeated, and the Aztec people accepted their subservience to the war leaders of their nation.

The Aztecs, allied with Tezcoco and the small town of Tlacopan, now controlled the whole of the lakeside and the mountain valleys in which they had lived from the beginnings of their history. Serpent of Knives gathered in all historical records for destruction, and altered the past of his people. On the face of it the plan was to state that the Aztecs were of an origin as holy as any other tribe in Mexico, and that they had a manifest destiny to rule all the country. He himself, through his Toltec ancestry, was a descendant of Quetzalcoatl and was sure of his own social rights. He had prepared a basis for Mexican political advancement. The power he wielded was formidable, and used for the aggrandizement of Cactus Rock. The defeated Tepanec were forced to pay a special land tax in grain and cloth, which was used as a fund for building a more splendid covering for the great temple in Cactus Rock. The god who had given victory to his people was honoured with a more glorious home and many sacrifices.

Serpent of Knives next turned his forces against neighbouring Tlaltelolco. The challenges and formal demands were made and refused, then the Aztec warriors attacked. They swept through the town, burning houses and taking prisoners for sacrifice. The chief, Moquiuix, was terrified and fled. The Aztec chief personally sought for him, and routed him out from a sacred sweat-bath in the temple courtyard. The two great warriors fought but Moquiuix escaped and dashed up the steep stair-case of the temple. Serpent of Knives followed, calling out his war chants, but before he reached him Moquiuix threw himself from the top of the building to dash himself to death on the ground beneath. The Aztecs were horrified. For a warrior to refuse combat was unheard of. The local people were shocked and the body lay on the stones for some days before somebody piled wood over it and burnt it. So Cactus Rock became one city with Tlaltelolco just at the time it achieved control of all the Valley of Mexico.

There were other wars. One against Cuernavaca was led by Tlacaelel with an army composed only of boys from Cactus Rock. They began by destroying the enemy canoes, and attacked with such gusto that the enemy broke and ran, leaving prisoners behind for sacrifice. Then, at the south of the lake, Coyoacan surrendered easily, but at Xochimilco there was a battle and siege lasting eleven days. The punishment laid upon its people was that they should build a stone causeway across the lake to Cactus Rock. This twelve-mile causeway still stands beside the modern main road running south from Mexico City to the lands beyond the volcanoes. The rule of Serpent of Knives came to an end with his death, but he was ever remembered for his mighty fight to establish Aztec independence.

The Mighty Prince, He Who Shoots at the Stars (Montezuma Ilhuicamina) was chosen by the Council to take over the government. He was not consecrated as Speaker, but took the title of *Ueitlatoani*, which means Great Speaker. This indicates that he spoke not only for the Aztecs but for many another tribe who paid them tribute. His coronation was a grand affair. Many prisoners were sacrificed to Blue Hummingbird, and then, as the rituals were completed, the new chief, seated on the basket-work throne, was crowned with the turquoise diadem, the Fire Crown, by his trusted friend Hungry Coyote, Lord of Tezcoco.

37

Left The young goddess, Chalchi-huitlicue (Lady Precious Green) wearing the serpent girdle of Mother Earth. Aztec about 1500.

The new chief was a wise man of commanding personality. He was also a very modest man who preferred not to take all the perquisites of his high office. His palace was simple and spotlessly clean, he spent much time in discussion with wise friends, and took only a few wives. On the diplomatic front this king formally cemented the alliance between Cactus Rock, Tezcoco and Tlacopan by a decision that all spoils of war should be divided into five parts, one of which was to go to Tlacopan and the rest to be divided equally between the other two partners.

In 1443 there was a great festival commemorating four times twenty years after the founding of Cactus Rock. Fine new buildings were erected in the city. But the gods were chary of rewards, or perhaps they wished to toughen their children. Four years of drought came with much sorrow to the people. Many families walked away in search of food in other lands and many died. Nevertheless, the Aztec armies were employed in wars. The town of Coixtlahuaca was captured and its chief was strangled.

In 1455, after the period of disaster, the calendar had turned again to its beginning, and there was the fast and making of new fire once more. It was fated to occur only once more in Mexico before the greatest change in the history of the nation. Much of the glory for the Aztecs was yet to come. In 1458 Montezuma led his armies into the province of Panuco and defeated the Huaxteca, an important victory for the Aztec armies because, for the first time, the borders of their empire had reached the sea. In 1461 the armies returned and moved southwards to capture the rich lands of the Totonacs in what was later Vera Cruz. They continued round the swampy southern coast of the Gulf of Mexico and subdued the people of Coatzocoalcos, where in later times the lady Ce Malinalli, later Doña Marina, who played such an important part in Montezuma's history, would be born. In 1465 the armies went westwards and subdued the Chalca. The Aztecs had become a power comparable with the Toltecs, as their chiefs well knew. The city of Cactus Rock had become the beautiful heart of a predatory empire and was growing fat on the plunder of conquered lands, and the annual tribute which they sent to glorify their conquerors.

In 1469 the Great Speaker Montezuma Ilhuicamina died and the Council of the nation asked the famous Tlacaelel if he would lead the people, since there were no brothers of Montezuma Ilhuicamina left. It was a wise choice because Tlacaelel had been war leader in every great victory of the Aztecs and had been the director of the policy of striking to control the whole country as had been prophesied by the divine Blue Hummingbird. But the Council pleaded in vain. Tlacaelel was now an old man and he set his face firmly against personal power. Instead he joined in the debate and suggested in his place the lord Axayacatl, a cousin of the dead chief. He was the grandson of the famous Serpent of Knives, and son of Prince Tezozomoc. His personal name, Axayacatl, meant Face of Water, a symbol of constant fruitful change. He was self-effacing but with a splendid war record. He was a poet and lover of female companionship, but it was clear that he would glorify Mexico not only by his sense of beauty but also by his undoubted military ability. So he was chosen by the Council and the announcement was greeted by popular acclamation.

But two years before this event, in the year *ce acatl* (1467), the year of the Morning Star – Quetzalcoatl, the baby prince Montezuma Xocoyotzin, the subject of this biography, had been born to the lord Axayacatl. (Montezuma's parentage as given here is that described in *Codex Mendoza*, which appears to have been copied from Aztec archives of importance, perhaps from the palace records. However, it should be noted that some authorities describe Montezuma II as the son of Montezuma I born just two years before the death of the old Great Speaker of the Aztecs. While this is possible, and indeed it would explain some of the personal qualities of Montezuma, it is the less probable of the two alternatives.

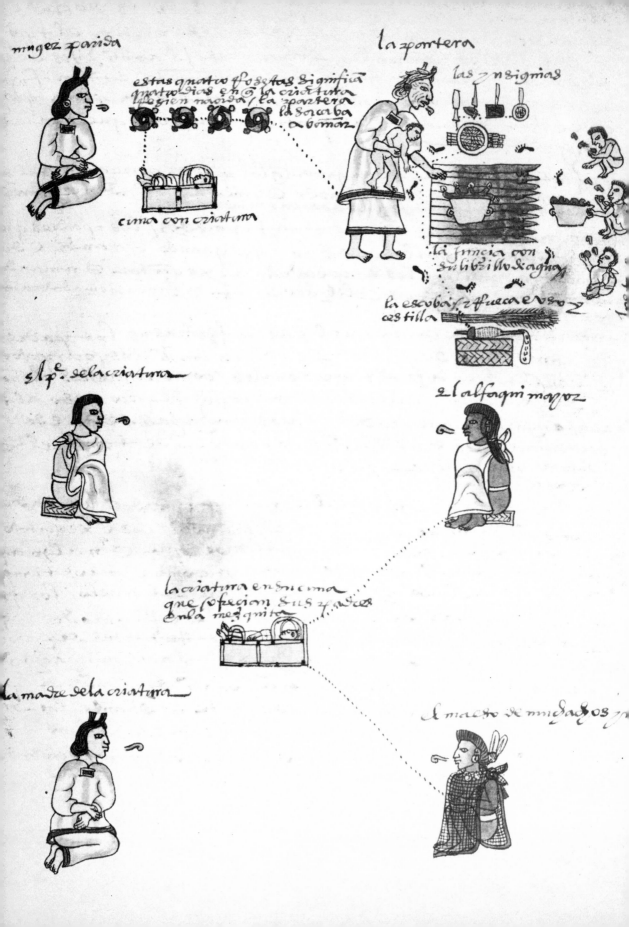

muger parida

la zportera

estas quatro rrosetas signfica
quatro dias en que la criatura
ste gien naçida / la zportera
la socaba a comer

las ynsignias

cuna con criatura

la fruçia con
su libri llo de agua

la escoba se fueca en so
castilla

s p. de la criatura

2 l alforqui mayor

la criatura en su cuna
que so fecion sus padres
en la mesquita

la madre de la criatura

l maesto de muchachos

2
CHILDHOOD

THE GREAT CITY OF Cactus Rock, the birthplace of Montezuma, was built on an islet in the large shallow Lake of the Moon, the centre of a huge valley surrounded by mountains. The pyramidal temples of the city towered high, and below them clustered thousands of houses, arranged in regular rows, with court-yard palaces in the centre and single room houses around them, all with their own gardens. Causeways led across the lake to the city but the main traffic was by means of canoes.

In the year of Montezuma's birth, the city was the hub of the powerful Aztec empire, a busy commercial centre whose canals served as streets and were filled with slowly moving canoes. In favoured areas the houses of nobles had been built on high foundations to stand above the smaller houses. Many of the buildings were colour-fully decorated but none had windows; doorways were covered by light screens and were never closed.

In 1467 the palace of the lord Axayacatl, Face of Water, would have been the scene of the celebration of the birth of the prince Montezuma; from its doorway would come the sound of flutes and singing for this lord was famous among the Aztecs for his love of music. It was not the most splendid of the palaces but to the small boys playing in the street by its walls on this particular day it would appear awesome and they would no doubt have been frightened by the appearance of two warriors with painted faces and feathered shields who approached them from the courtyard, which was normally closed to the people. The fear was increased when the warriors ordered the boys to accompany them into the palace. But here they were met by the smiles of young women and they were told that they were called to a feast given by the Lady Cotton Flower for the fourth day. The boys then knew that this was the naming of a new baby and that they would be asked to perform the traditional Aztec duty of calling out the new child's name before the people and the gods.

Opposite The ceremonies of naming a baby. Four days after birth the midwife presents the child to boys who call out his name. Later the relatives meet to admonish the child and call blessings on him. *Codex Mendoza* painted about 1552.

Overleaf left Pottery vessel representing a Zapotec musician beating a rhythm on a tortoise shell. From Monte Alban, Oaxaca, about AD 500–800.

The laughing young women led the boys up the steps and through the red-painted portal; through a dark narrow room and then outside into a courtyard, over which a coloured cotton canopy tempered the brilliant sunshine with a glory of decoration. Seated on a basket-work stool was the princess, her face painted yellow with red signs of the wind god on her cheeks. Her shining hair was braided with coloured ribbons, and she wore a head-dress of painted paper and flowers. The baby lay on a thick cotton cloth, on which were also laid model weapons – a club, spear and shield – all of gilded wood. The boys bowed before the princess and her new-born son; then they ran round them four times. Once they stopped at the east and called the name of the prince's birthday; once again they stopped at the south and called, once more at the west and lastly to the north, this time with a different intonation for the north was the direction of the darkness.

Their duty done, the princess signed to her maids to take the boys inside, where they were presented with gifts; to each a cloak, a loincloth of fine white cotton and sandals of plaited rushes. A low table was placed in front of them on which were clay dishes of honey and baskets of maize cakes, on which the boys feasted.

For the family much more was to come. The relatives had all gathered. Face of Water made a long oration calling on the child to be faithful to the gods and to be brave throughout the adversities of life. Uncles and cousins all made long speeches and finally elder-cousin Montezuma spoke gravely of the way of life and sufferings which all must face and accept as their personal gift to the Lord of Life, the fire god who gave the soul its existence. Like a butterfly sweeping through the field of flowers, it would stop here and there to savour happiness and bring delight; yet before long it would be gone and no one would remember anything except that once it shone brightly in the sunshine.

The festival was magnificent. Feathered warriors danced in the courtyard, stamping their feet and singing of glory for the new prince. Their faces were painted in black and red but those who were priests also wore the bars of black and yellow of the great war god and patron of the Aztecs. The girls and young women, with flowers in their hair, danced in a round dance, lifting garlands of flowers in their hands. The golden bells fringing their skirts tinkled in rhythm to the wooden gongs and skin-covered drums. Flutes, trumpets and rattles created a rhythmic pattern through which the melody of the singing ran like a string of jewels.

In the small temple across the courtyard the black-painted priests sat poring over the pictures in their books of magic. Their hair was tangled and they wore black robes embroidered with symbolic human bones. Only the high priest wore the high helmet and the red, black and blue costume of the god of wisdom, Quetzalcoatl, to whom this year of *ce acatl* (1467) was dedicated. Finally, after much deliberation, the priests acclaimed the baby boy as a future great ruler and a high priest of infinite wisdom. As the younger son of a younger son he might seem unimportant but his future was to follow the path of wisdom and greatness until it reached the eventual glory of dying for the gods. Such was the life of Quetzalcoatl on earth, and such a life would weave itself around the baby Montezuma as he grew up to glory.

After these deliberations the banquet followed, with dishes of fruit and freshly-made tortillas dipped in honey and spices. The elders were regaled with fermented pulque made from the juice of the agave (plant related to the cactus). Only those men or women who were grandparents were allowed to taste intoxicants. A young Aztec must never be intoxicated for a stranger might see him and report that the Aztecs were weak-willed and their army not powerful.

As Montezuma grew up he learned the strength and glory of the Aztec empire. He learned to walk to the sound of music, amid the joyful people who danced at the ceremonies every twenty days, and sometimes threw flowers at one another in the festival processions. At other feasts when captives were sacrificed, they ate human meat and small pieces of finger were given to the baby boy as a delicacy. He was told that they held magic power from the gods and would make his spirit strong and brave when he grew up.

He was not taken as a baby to the great temple that overlooked the square of palaces in the heart of the city of Cactus Rock. However, he saw the life of the town when he was allowed to roam among the flower gardens on the roof of his home. These gardens were on top of the two-storey palace building and were filled with all the beautiful flowers which thrived in the sunshine and dry air of this city on the high plateau. Vanilla orchids scented the air, hibiscus and jacaranda grew there, and in some of the shrubs there were honey bees. Lizards ran around in the sun darting after the flies, and sometimes found their way to the edge of the walls where they immediately slipped off because of the polished plaster. In that way the child was taught caution. He was taught to respect butterflies which came in swarms of colour, because sometimes they were souls visiting the earth from the land of the dead.

When Montezuma was five, he was weaned and could no longer find life and love from the dark nipples and golden breasts of his mother or her maids. Yet this love of physical beauty remained in his mind all his life. He was not stinted of beauty in the palace for the Aztec nobles took several wives and many beautiful girls became second-class wives. Their children became his playmates, although they could have little chance of becoming leaders among the princes. The girls wore their glossy black hair long, sometimes adorned with a wreath of flowers. They wore only a wrap-around skirt until they were of marriageable age. However, girls did not make very interesting playmates for the boys because they were taught to be excessively modest, and at an early age learned to walk with small steps and never to look a boy in the eyes. Boys soon learned to run and wrestle and the little prince would race around in his soft rush sandals wearing only a cotton loincloth with feather fringes. In the colder season he had a cotton blanket woven with splendid patterns which he wore knotted on one shoulder.

For a little boy life in a minor palace held many delights. Montezuma learned to sing and recite poems, and to know the days and festival dates of the year. Although food might sometimes be short, the children received the best that was available. At the end of the dry season when fresh food was always scarce, the children would wait at the palace doors for their great 'uncle' Montezuma to hand out food from the royal store-houses to all the people of Cactus Rock. This great occasion taught the young of the duty of a ruler to look after the welfare of all his people. In return for their hard work he provided food to help them over the hard month before the rains made Mexico fruitful again.

Almost as soon as he could stand, Montezuma was taken to see the great dances in the temple courtyard. These were happy days when the whole place was crowded with people. The nobles, among whom was his father, were able to lead their dependants away from the crush to places on the lower pyramids in the great courtyard. Everyone was carefully placed in order of rank so that the young Montezuma and his mother never had a very important place. He watched the dances of the warriors or the ring dances of the girls throwing flowers in the spring festival. He heard music everywhere: the rattles and wooden gongs, the pottery flutes and whistles and the soft blasts of the shell trumpets calling the people to worship. He watched the strange ballets of the priests moving gracefully up and down the hundred steps of the pyramid, and saw the sacrificial victims dance to their glorious death. Sometimes he was afraid as the gigantic drum at the temple top throbbed deep notes like the beating of a heart. He knew that sometimes children were sacrificed. But he was taught that the sacrifices were to help the world and the sun to live so that people should have life and happiness in this world and glory in the other. Those warriors whose blood spurted so beautifully over the stone of sacrifice would fly up to the sun and ever afterwards dance with him as they lifted him into the sky every morning.

When the old emperor died, young Montezuma attended the beautiful funeral procession, after which the body was covered with logs of scented cedar and burnt, and the ashes placed in a beautifully carved stone box. Unknowingly fate was working for young Montezuma. After the death of Montezuma 'who shoots at the sky', the tribal nobles gathered to choose a new ruler from the men of the leading families, as was the custom of the Aztecs. The brothers of the old emperor were all dead and his direct descendants were still young, so they considered the cousins. One was pre-eminent for his bravery and skill in conducting campaigns. This was the shy, quiet cousin of the old chief, who had always been as modest as he was brave, and generous to those who came to him for help. His family life was above reproach even by the strict puritanical code of the Aztecs. The Council thus chose to abandon the direct line and elect the lord Axayacatl, Face of Water, to the rank of *Ueitlatoani*, the Great Speaker.

This was a great honour for Montezuma's father, though in some ways it was a painful one. A new palace would be built for him in a new place. He would have to make a ceremonial appearance in the great temple before the people, and then spend a year secluded in a special building in the temple courtyard, where the great offering bowl with the ocelot head was kept. There he would fast and meditate on the gods, but would also be available for public business. Young Montezuma would not see his father for a year.

When he was five years old Montezuma was allowed more liberty and with his companions and elder brother, accompanied only by one or two well-armed young men, he visited the busy town outside the palace. The boy saw the canals of the city lined by pathways along which people came hurrying towards home or market. It was usual for the men to go everywhere at a jogtrot. Women and girls did not hurry because it was considered immodest for them to take broad steps in their wrap-around skirts in case they should show their knees. Everybody would be carrying goods obtained in the markets. Sometimes loads were carried in small bags, but people usually carried bundles on their backs supported by tump lines stretched across the forehead. Sometimes the boys came across vendors carrying huge wicker crates containing pottery for trade. In other places would be low tables beside which sat the sellers of pop-corn or sweetmeats. It was a busy city and always provided interest for the children.

In the market convoys of merchants would arrive from distant lands. Some were Mexicans returning with gold, turquoise, feathers and fine cloth from the distant coast

and mountain tribes. In other places the boys were amused by the Huaxtecs who sold fine cloth but went entirely naked and by the Tarascos who sold fattened puppies for meat and who also went naked. Girls went past these people quickly and were expected to look away in shock. In the city there was always travel news, strange things for exchange and a gentle hum of musical voices, but it was a quiet city with no rumble of wheels or clatter of shoes, only the soft plop of paddles as the flat-bottomed boats glided past, and the shuffle of sandals and bare feet.

There was never a time when Aztec Mexico was at peace and Montezuma from his earliest days heard stories of battle and of the bravery of the glorious warriors of Cactus Rock. He learned to pronounce the names of the gods and in particular that of Huitzilopochtli who was the war god and the sun in the mid-day sky. He knew that the name meant 'hummingbird on the left' and it suggested that the hummingbird was blue. But there were many more gods in Mexico and above them all was the creator whose name meant The Two because creation needed male and female powers together. The boy was fascinated by the carvings and paintings of the gods of his city. He saw the mysterious painted books which told the history of the people of Mexico and the legends of the gods. The tales were told to him and he associated them with the pictures on the pages, which were so strong and brilliant that it was easy to understand their meaning and remember it.

The boy was delighted when he was told that he would soon leave home to go to school. He was especially glad that he was to go to the temple school, the *calmecac*, where he would learn more about the gods and their worship. By then he knew that the *calmecac* would provide a hard training and that one had to be brave to face the austerities which were demanded of the students before they could become even the lowest kind of priest. The boy knew that he would later train to be a brave warrior as well. But first his father wished him to be a priest.

At the temple the high priest interviewed the boy and his parents at length, asking many questions of them. Long speeches were made and the child was made to understand the importance and hardship of the priestly life. At last the great priest, strange in his black paint and brilliant feathers, retired to meditate. Any boy might go to the *calmecac* whether poor or powerful, and no favour was shown to the nobles. Montezuma was accepted because he was considered the right sort of boy for this training, and thus his life took on a new aspect.

3

THE TEMPLE AND MILITARY SCHOOLS

YOUNG MONTEZUMA WAS born of a noble family and was a great-nephew of the high chief. It was proper for such a family to see that its sons were educated in the war schools to make them strong and insensitive to pain and hardship, like all Aztec boys. But there was also a duty to see that the boy learnt the science and magic of the priestly class. The priests alone could foretell the future and read the prophecies of the stars. They alone had the knowledge to read the *Teoamoxtli*, the sacred book of fate, and to divine from its pages the ways of the gods in their progress through time. Some of the boys would grow up to become sacrificing priests who would offer human hearts to the gods; others would be soothsayers, and others, distinguished for their delicate skill, would become the painter-scribes of books and would learn the true forms of the divine images and the proper ordering of the yearly rituals.

The system of training was harsh and indeed amounted to a rigid conditioning of the mind. Boys were brought to the *calmecac* by their parents and handed over to the high priest in a ceremony accompanied by the long speeches so much beloved by the Aztecs. They were given to serve the lord, the god of the temple, and to suffer in his sight. Their suffering was not only a training, but also an offering of themselves to influence the gods to have mercy upon the people. The legends had told how the gods had faced extremes of suffering when the world was new, and how mankind was blessed through them.

The first duty of the boys was to help the priests by keeping the temple precinct clean. Hence Montezuma swept the courtyard 'in humility' as an old Spanish chronicler relates. The boys were not pampered, and lived on a diet of two tortillas a day and a cup of water, with little in the way of vegetables and meat. They were hardened by being made to sleep on the bare stone floors of the temple buildings, and during the night, which can be cold in Mexico on the high plateau, they often had no covering at all.

The first great test for the boys was the 'night journey'. They had already progressed from cleaning the holy places to helping to prepare the magic paint for the bodies of the priests. This was compounded of strange materials: the calcined bodies of scorpions and other stinging creatures, the leaves of certain sacred plants which were used to cause hallucinations, and the greasy remains of burnt rubber offered as

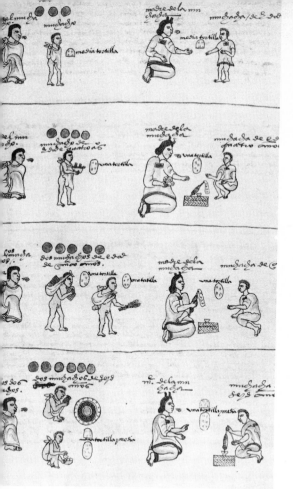

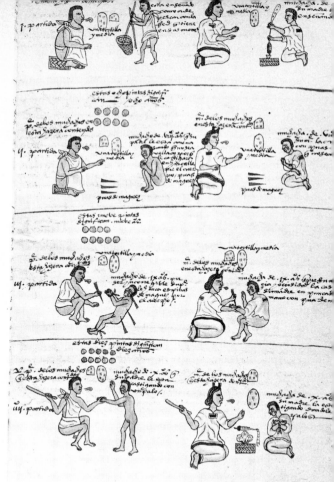

incense. The 'night journey' was made to collect the ingredients at a magical time when the powers of darkness were awake and the mass of the people asleep. Who knew what terrible creatures haunted the darkness, lurking in trees and behind rocks? Even human ghosts of those who had died unlucky deaths might be encountered. But, while the ordinary people huddled indoors in dread, the boys from the *calmecac* went out, padding along silently on sandalled feet, sometimes wearing only a loincloth. Each group was led by a priest who knew the laws of the passage of time and could recite the necessary charms to dispel spirit threats. But even so the boys must have trembled with fear during their first journeys into the chill night under the shimmering silver sky.

Montezuma, like his companions, carried a gourd in a cloth bag into which he put the scorpions and spiders which he caught. Picking them up with a twig made into tweezers was quite a feat. A boy might be bitten and, even if he did not die, would suffer great pain. But this misfortune would not arouse pity for it was a sign that the boy had been rejected by the gods. He would be sent home in disgrace before he went on to the compulsory military school. However, nothing untoward befell young Montezuma. He passed through his ordeals like a young stoic, and each night during

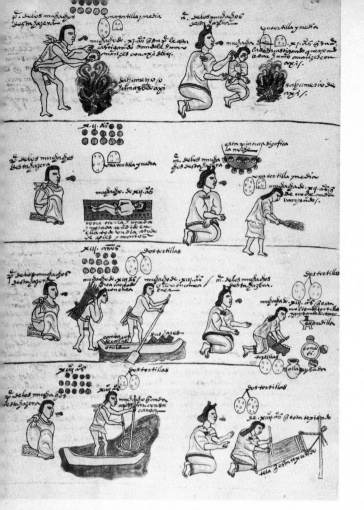

Left and previous page The education of children from the ages of three to fourteen years. From *Codex Mendoza* in the Bodleian Library, Oxford. Prepared for the Viceroy Don Antonio de Mendoza by native informants.

The age of the child is shown by the row of blue circles in each picture. The left hand column concerns boys, the girls appear on the right. The pictures show the duties performed and the punishments which might be inflicted. This basic code of behaviour applied to all children of whatever social rank.

Opposite Cacao vase carved in calcite. The rabbit was a symbol of erotic fertility. From the coast of the Mexican Gulf in the Totonac region.

Overleaf Pottery plaque, about 25 cm square, representing the water goddess. The flow from her mouth may represent turbulent streams.

the period of night journeys he brought in his quota of dangerous insects and helped to roast them and grind the calcined shells into the magic black powder. He knew the magic power of his work but he was still too young to know the reasons for the mixture which the priests prescribed. The body paint marked the priest, but it also contained drugs which helped to deaden pain and to produce a state of exaltation in which the sacred dances on the steps of the temples could be performed. Under their influence the priest would cut out the hearts for the sacrifice or hold the dancer impersonating the corn goddess on his back while her head was sliced off with a bamboo blade. To be a sacrificing priest was hard work and the performer needed the strength given by the magical paints and sacred drugs.

Montezuma must have graduated to the first stages of the priestly training, and he was certainly skilled in reading the great painted books of magic. His training was that of an astronomer-priest but after his year or two as a neophyte his family would have sent him to the normal school where the young men trained as warriors.

For an Aztec boy the military school was a place of glory. All he knew about the history of his nation centred around the way in which the war god, Blue Humming-bird, had led his ancestors from their primitive poverty to exercise authority over the

whole of Anahuac (the central American isthmus between the Atlantic and Pacific Oceans). They now ruled the lesser tribes with a strong arm. If there was a revolt or a failure to pay the tribute demanded by the Great Speaker of the Aztecs there would be a war, and more prisoners taken to be slaughtered on the sacrificial stone. Plunder and glory were the mainstay of the society. Montezuma was a junior member of one of the three families from which the war leader of the nation could be chosen and so for him these were matters of deep concern. The military school was less rigorous than the *calmecac*, though even here the boys had only a grass mat as a bed, and a thin cotton cloth as a covering. The exercises of young warriors were aimed at developing agility and the ability to suffer pain without murmuring. They leaped over ropes, learned the military dances and went on long marches carrying heavy loads. Their clubs and lances were of wood without the glassy blades of natural obsidian which were so deadly in war. The boys fought in groups with great bravery; many suffered broken limbs and a few were killed, because the mock combats were honourable ways of gaining a reputation as a ferocious warrior. Normally they were dressed only in a loincloth and an open-netted cloak. This was to inure them to the chilly atmosphere of the high plateau of central Mexico. Sometimes they inflicted penances upon themselves, piercing their tongues with bone awls and cutting the calves of their legs with agave spines in order to appease the gods by these offerings of pain and blood. (These practices were not confined to the military but were followed by the whole population.) It was a very useful training in the traditional American Indian virtue of stoicism.

The boys followed the army on expeditions. They acted as carriers of bundles of sandals, war clubs and spears to save the warriors from such laborious tasks. The expeditions to the lowlands were important because the youths learnt how to withstand the languorous heat and heavy air of the forested coasts. An Aztec warrior must be able to fight anywhere, except perhaps in the mountain snowfields which were sacred to the water gods. On the battlefield the boys saw rituals performed to discover the propitious days for a battle; they saw the commanders send out spies and advance guards to explore the enemy defences. These were called the ocelot warriors. Then they saw the eagle warriors lead the main attack to slash and batter down the enemy soldiers. If possible, enemies would be captured, bound and carried on the backs of the victors to the city, where they would in due course be offered to the gods.

Each year in the summer there were festivals for the warriors, when the boys, dressed in cloaks of cotton netting and the crane feathers of the Aztecs, performed chain dances and competed in climbing a greasy pole to obtain war flags and symbols of honour. It was rough sport but they thoroughly enjoyed it. They showed off before the people, and spent a lot of time singing and dancing. Montezuma, of course, would be taken to meet the older army commanders to learn strategy and the arts of command. In particular he was allowed to visit the ancient warrior, Lord Tlacaelel, a distant cousin who had three times refused to become Great Speaker of the Aztecs because he wanted to lead the forces to protect the nation. This must have been an important event in life for the young nobleman. His ancient relative had seen the

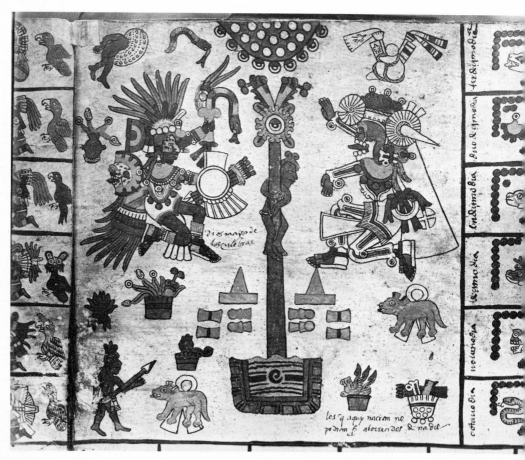

advancement of Cactus Rock from a small but respected town controlling most of the shore of the Moon Lake to the ruling power in a trio of cities which had by military means come to control all Anahuac. It was Tlacaelel who had led the war parties across the mountains to capture foreign cities outside the plateau, as described on pages 36–7. The old warrior was a true American Indian, quiet in his strength, filled with the glory which came to great war leaders. His wisdom had been called upon by four Great Speakers of the Aztec people. He had advised them in matters of policy and counselled the army leaders so well that there had been continuous victory. When he met the young prince he was seated on his basket-work throne, wrapped in beautiful feather blankets. His iron-grey hair was still tied into the high tuft of the 'master of cuts' (a title awarded to the warrior who had slain three foes in single combat and the greatest distinction he could win). On the walls hung his feather-work decorations and the shields of his many army commands, and set in his nostril was the turquoise fire-stud allowed only to the greatest and bravest commanders. (This decoration signified also his great wealth because to wear it meant that he had had to give a great feast to his peers and distribute many gifts to the Aztec tribespeople.) From his old lips young Montezuma learned much statecraft and learned too that even the mightiest prince was but human. The old man died while Montezuma was still a boy but his impact upon him must have been great. He had sat at the feet of the man who had made the Aztecs great in Anahuac. That the wisdom of the ancient hero sank into his heart, his later actions reveal.

It is hard for us to picture Montezuma at this time. He must have been like so many growing boys, full of hopes for his future glory. The rigours of training had hardened him to cold and hunger. The young warrior who carried the sandals of his betters knew well that he was fitted to equal the best of them when his time came. He did not know that he would become *Ueitlatoani* (literally 'Great Speaker' or emperor) in Mexico, only that he was a nobleman who would surely become a leader of warriors. Yet the boy was a dreamer. We are told that he was always devoted to the mysteries of religion. He knew the songs of the gods and was aware of the mysteries of time and sought to learn more of them. He might have been strong and brave, and a good talker, but his heart was always turned towards god and the mysteries of the universe, so that he would inevitably become an astronomer and watcher of all the phenomena of the natural world which symbolized the will of supernatural beings. Though they were unseen, he knew them to be so close that, like the war god Blue Hummingbird, they were 'just upon his shoulder'.

Opposite top left Boys are brought by their father to the school for warriors. From Father Sahagun's *Historia de las Cosas de Nueva España*.

Opposite top right Boys and their instructor, a distinguished warrior. They reply to his questions. Any error would be punished by the cactus thorn which he carries. Sahagun's *Historia de las Cosas de Nueva España*.

Opposite below Between the gods of Fire and Death, at midnight beneath the stars, the boy aspirants for glory climb a pole. They symbolize the planet Mercury which ascends to a limited height in the sky and then descends. *Codex Borbonicus*.

Before Montezuma graduated as a warrior he had again to change his way of life and he returned to the *calmecac*. This was not as a personal honour, for he was to follow the traditional path observed by the sons of noblemen. This was the way of the ruler: to alternate social duties with religious understanding. His education must make him an adept in magic as well as a healthy fighting man.

It was with a natural and very personal delight that Montezuma returned to the temple. He accepted willingly the need to paint his whole body black and to sleep on the floor with only a thin grass mat under him. The offering of his own blood in penitential rituals at every sunrise was simply a small return to the gods for the pains they had suffered for the Mexican people. He was no masochist, but accepted what his people knew to be right and necessary. The ceremonies with their dances and flowers would delight any young man, especially one who loved poetry and music. The element of bloodshed was all part of the sudden reversals of fate which were so important to his religion. There was beauty in the sacrifices of humans; and we have evidence that Montezuma became a sacrificing priest, but he was never among the simple ecstatics drawn by the gods to the madness in which prophecy babbled from their lips.

His early duties included the offerings of quails at sunrise. This little bird, whose black plumage was speckled with white-tipped feathers, was a symbol of the starry sky of night, the 'four hundred stars of the north and south', which were slain at the birth of Blue Hummingbird, who was a form of the sun god, lord of fate. So at the moment of first light he slit open the quails and placed their hearts in a bowl before the god. Then followed the magic but inaudible roaring of the ocelots on the eastern hills welcoming the advance of the sun. The young priest pierced his ears and tongue to offer his blood to the rising god as he appeared over the horizon. To dazzled eyes the bright sun appeared a fire-stone of turquoise blue, the magic colour. So it was right that the high-flying sun of midday should be called Blue Hummingbird, even though he was at the same time the white eagle, leader of brave warriors. Every day this ceremony was repeated.

In such a world of contradictions and magical correspondences, young Montezuma grew up. He learned to read and memorize the great books of the temple, written in the complicated Aztec system which was a mixture of pictograms, ideograms and phoneticism, with the use of colour in addition.

But it is clear from all accounts of his life that Montezuma was most interested in reading the book of the heavens. His life would have been that of the astronomer-

Opposite The initiation and training of an astronomer-priest. The day signs at the bottom of the series indicate the passage of time and not a total period of 20 days. At first the initiate sings hymns to the stars and has learned to ignore the sexual desires indicated by the red serpent. Then he visits a deserted ball-court, and makes offerings on the mountain of Tlaloc. Finally after making offerings in a ruined temple he acquires the knowledge which enables him to wear the mitre and white body paint of the qualified astrologer. *Codex Laud.*

priest, and the training meant much arduous study and lonely meditation. One may see an outline of the life he must have led painted in the pages of *Codex Laud* in the Bodleian Library, Oxford. The pictures tell the story of a young student's life. He sits in the temple singing songs to the gods, and subduing his natural sexual desires; he offers his pain to the altar of magical power where the witch-broom will sweep away earthly desires. He gazes at the stars to perceive their wonders, so that his powers can be strengthened and the ghostly footprints of the ancestor spirits rise from the jaws of earth which have been opened where the offering of a heart has been laid on reed brooms in readiness as a burnt offering. He goes at night to make offerings under the starry sky of the magic brooms and a stone knife in a deserted games court (the *tlachtli* or the ball-game court, was near the temple; the game itself had a religious significance). He climbs the mountain of Tlaloc, the rain god, to make offerings at the snow line. He repeats these offerings again in the eerie silence of a ruined temple. From them will come a sign in the black smoke of burning magic. Then he will have been accepted by the gods and before the mountain of life he will make offerings, and wear his white mitre as he respects the face of earth and commands the knowledge of the stars. So the ancient book tells the training which the young prince underwent.

The astronomer-prince had to perform all these duties and go out fearlessly among the ghostly terrors of the Mexican night. The rejection of sexuality was also a terrible ordeal in the puritanical society of Aztec Mexico. Any indulgence, even simple mas-turbation, would be construed as an offence against the powers of the war god. Its punishment would be dismissal from the temple, and beatings and such torture, from being forced to inhale the fumes of burning pepper pods, that a transgressor could hardly escape with his life. Only adultery was treated more severely, with death by stoning. The growing prince thus had to face inhibitions of terrible force. Yet through all this Montezuma survived with honour, so completely absorbed by his studies that he was later regarded as a great priest even more highly than as a war leader and *Ueitlatoani* of the Aztecs.

However, Montezuma was not permitted to stay in the temple even though his heart might have desired it. He must follow the custom of the nobles and once again turn to secular life as a warrior. He remained a priest, which meant he wore his priestly coat of magical black paint even when involved in battle. But, in addition, he was expected to learn fencing with clubs and spears, dancing with shields and feather ornaments, and power in singing. Also, as he grew into a young man, he learnt the elegancies of civilized life: to wear fine clothes with distinction, to know which stamped patterns he might wear on his face, and to speak the Nahuatl language with an elegant upper-class accent, rather high-pitched and somewhat nasalized. The young Aztec fledgling grew into an aristocrat, literally in fine feather.

4

THE WARRIOR-PRIEST

W AR WAS NOT STRANGE to Montezuma. From his infancy he had seen the warriors going out and returning with prisoners for sacrifice. He had heard captive chiefs pleading with his father that their people should not be despoiled of all their possessions. At the age of six when he was beginning to understand what it meant to belong to a noble family among the Aztecs, he heard of the disgraceful behaviour of Moquiuix, lord of Tlaltelolco, who when defeated had, instead of surrender, committed suicide and thus cheated the gods of their feast and brought disgrace to the enemy.

That act must have impressed the mind of the growing boy. He had admired his father's bravery when he chased the enemy to the top of the hundred-foot-high staircase of the temple, and shared the disgust of all Mexico at the outcome. He felt with his brothers the glory that came to the Mexicans with the final defeat of Tlaltelolco. Once more the whole island was united as one city, and the glory of the Aztec people was wonderfully enhanced. The Aztec chief had shown personal bravery in that mortal combat and reaped honour in the eyes of the world and his family. Montezuma was resolved that when he grew up he would be equally noble, and like all noblemen, he accepted the disciplines of the temple school.

In Montezuma's school days the palace was always busy and brilliant with flowers and people. His father had many wives, so that Montezuma was always surrounded by many brothers and sisters. But his mother, a daughter of the old emperor Montezuma I, was somewhat withdrawn and considered herself the great wife of the polygamous chief. It pleased her that her son was also somewhat reserved and interested especially in the religious schooling. She encouraged him to understand for himself the painted histories which told of the marriages and descent of their ancestors. Through her mother she was a direct descendant in the female line of the royal house of the Toltecs, and this was counted a very honourable distinction even four and a half centuries after the fall of great Tula.

When the young neophyte was nine years old he first experienced the hush which fell on the city at an annular eclipse of the sun (this is an eclipse of the sun by the moon, which nearly covers the sun, leaving only a ring of light visible). The sun became crescent-shaped like the moon and then for a while it had a black heart fringed with brilliance. The whole place felt cold. The priests had foretold this mysterious

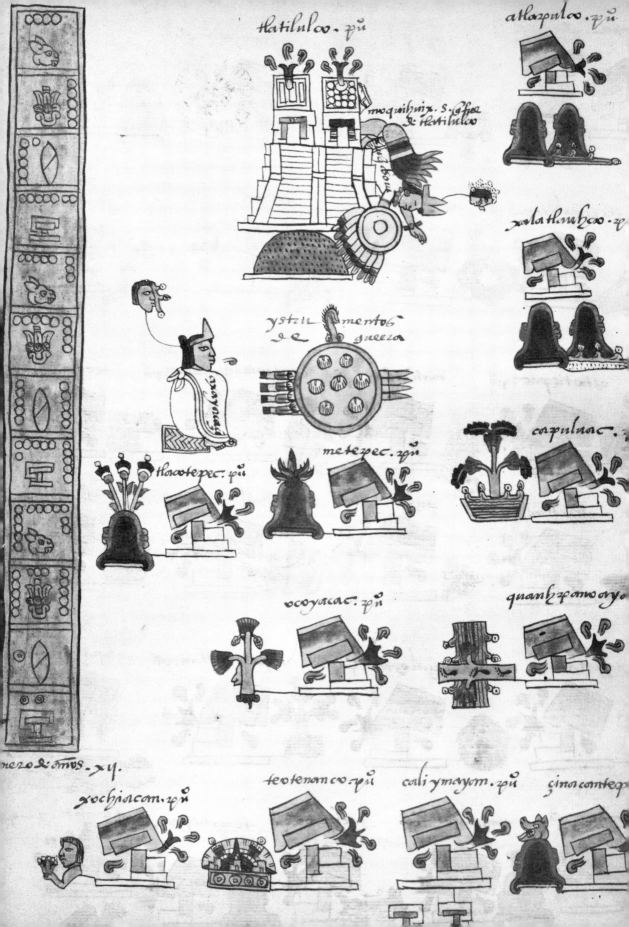

Opposite The reign of Axayacatl. On the left the column of years of his reign. The burning temples mark towns he captured. At the top the chief Moquiuix commits suicide at Tlaltelolco. *Codex Mendoza.*

Right Musicians, acrobats and hunchbacks perform for the pleasure of the Great Speaker. Sahagun's *Historia de las Cosas de Nueva España.*

Below The magical signs of a warriors' festival. On the right is Blue Hummingbird, as the war eagle, on the left the witch-goddess Tlazolteotl, who, as the moon lady, is repeatedly giving birth to herself as the new moon. Note the skull-rack below. Above, the planet Mercury as the young warrior-prince descends behind the moon. *Codex Borbonicus.*

event, and to avert the shadow of disaster from the face of the sun they had gathered dwarfs and hunchbacks for sacrifice. In Aztec eyes these people were regarded as clowns and jesters. They were selected in childhood and trained as jugglers and singers. They lived in the Great Speaker's palace and were kindly treated until an eclipse of the sun occurred, when they were sacrificed. The Aztecs believed that they would ascend to the sun, there to make merry and entertain him so that the shadow would be removed from his face and danger of the eclipse would pass away. The happiness of the slain cripples in the sun's world would be greater than ever before. They would always have an appreciative audience of warriors and ladies who accompanied the sun on his accustomed roads singing and dancing through the sky.

Like all Mexican boys Montezuma was sent to the 'house of young men' for war training when he was about twelve years old. He was already inured to hardship in the temple school, and had acquired some knowledge of the art of picture-writing. His family had taught him to be well-behaved and graceful in movement, and he had been continually reminded that as one of the nobility he must be gentle and courteous to other people. It became quite natural to him. Every year he had seen the armies go out and return with captives to be offered to the gods. Every year he had seen the processions of tribute bearers bringing their loads of treasure to add to the riches of Mexico. His grandfather had made the alliance with the neighbouring cities of Tezcoco and Tlacopan so that they together dominated all the valley in the heart of the country. Now the armies were capturing the towns of the mountain passes and sometimes beyond, even to the sea. These were glorious days for the Aztec people. Blue Hummingbird was leading their warriors from victory to victory. It was clear that he would keep his promise and give them dominion over the whole of Anahuac.

So the young warrior went to the battle school to learn to be a brave man who would help the god in the task of giving dominion to the Aztec power. He knew that the patron god of the year of his birth was in many ways opposed to Tezcatlipoca, the god of the night sky; but all Mexicans accepted such situations. The gods were neither good nor evil. They kept a balance of nature and their influences were asserted through the calendar. The power above them all was the giver of life, but he allowed all to co-exist. Good and evil were not real concepts; the rules of behaviour for the tribe were correct, anything else was to be punished. It was good, to the Aztecs, that their warriors should destroy towns, bring home captives and exact tribute; it was for the glory of Blue Hummingbird and his people.

Montezuma learned to handle the war club, edged with obsidian blades. He stamped with his sandals so that his feet should not slip in the blood on the ground, and he learned how to press down an enemy shield so that he could slice the flesh from an enemy face and shoulders. In the process of learning there were real battles with sharp weapons, and he did not escape serious cuts which would leave scars all his life. These were the marks of a brave fighter and showed that he had not run away to have them sewn up immediately. The schools were strict. All boys were given the same training. Attendance was compulsory and no allowance was made for social class.

Dress and hair styles of Aztec girls and ladies. The two with their hair in two rising locks are married; the style indicates their desire for children. From Father Sahagun's *Historia de las Cosas de Nueva España*.

Children take part with their mothers and the young women in a family feast and offering of food to the fire god. From Father Sahagun's *Historia de las Cosas de Nueva España*.

The process was aimed at making the young Aztec into a man who would face danger in a disciplined way. The great terror instilled into the minds of the boys was fear of cowardice. To run from the face of an enemy was a terrible thing. It was nearly as apalling as the suicide of Moquiuix in Tlaltelolco. In the schools the boys were divided into groups which were taken on training courses in difficult terrain, and which were sometimes involved in actual fighting if they were caught in the territory of a rival city. Sometimes the boys were taken out to see battles and sieges in progress. They might take bundles of weapons for the warriors. (Most of the business of supplying food, clothes, and shields fell to the women who went with the armies.)

It was at the 'house of young men' that Montezuma first came into contact with women. Sex in that natural society was not hidden and he, like most boys, had experienced sexual desire. But as an Aztec he had learned that early marriage was frowned on because it weakened the warrior. As with most of the boys, he had refused opportunities for homosexual pleasure, and had accepted the dreams sent by the gods as being healthier than masturbation. But here, in the house where he trained, there was a weekly dance to which the duennas brought girls. This was part of the training in good social manners. The girls were always clean, scented and well-dressed. They wore their hair long because they were yet unmarried, and their faces were painted

Young warriors from the schools preparing to
climb the pole to capture the image of Blue
Hummingbird. An annual ceremony. *Codex
Magliabecciano.*

yellow. They did not wear sandals because this showed that they did not have to go to
the market but worked at home weaving and cooking.

The dances were very gentle performances which consisted mostly of walking in
a ring holding bunches of flowers and swaying as the dancers sung hymns to the
goddesses. The boys danced too, standing in a ring and jumping rhythmically with stiff
knees, so that the rattles on their leg bands made a rhythmic clatter. Each sex had a
chance of seeing the other, though conversation was frowned upon as being a little
too tempting. The girls learned to dance with their eyes gazing on the floor and not
into the eyes of the boys. The mixing at these formal academies was important, and
introduced young people in Aztec society to the duties of social life at an age when
otherwise the sexes would have drifted unnaturally apart.

However well-bred the young Montezuma was, like all youth he enjoyed excitement and display. A very special occasion every year was the feast of Xocotlhuetzi,
'the falling of fruit'. It fell in the latter half of August in the time of high summer when
the fruit ripened and was dedicated to the fire god, who was the earthly aspect of the

creator. At this time the boys from the military academy came out to dance. They wore the crane feather of Aztec warriors and were clothed only in openwork net cloaks tied on one shoulder. In the midst of the courtyard before the great temple was a greasy pole some forty feet high and rubbed over with a black oil from the petroleum deposits on the coast. At the top of the pole was an image of the god, made of a mass of dough thoroughly mixed with amaranth seeds. Attached to it were golden ornaments arranged in a diadem. On the day of the feast, while the fire pits were being prepared before the house of the fire god, the boys came in singing and raced round the pole. At a signal they rushed at it and struggled to climb it. Some dragged the leaders back, others climbed over the backs of their friends trying for a higher vantage point. Montezuma had the advantage of his physique which was thin and light, and one year he did especially well. As he had considerable strength, he managed to climb quickly over his scrambling mates to gain a good start up the pole. Clawing and slipping, by persevering he managed the ascent, toppled the image and snatched the golden crown. This he donned as he slid down into the fracas below where the other boys were engaged in a magnificent rough and tumble, each striving to grab the largest portion of the idol of amaranth seeds. It was a rare honour for a nobleman to win the golden prize, for it was fairly won by superior enterprise and strength. The honour enabled the young prince to help in the sacrifice which followed, and for which he was well fitted through his priestly training.

The prisoners for the fire god were painted red and yellow and spattered with white eagle's down in patches like stars. They came singing in a row, staggering and rolling about from the effects of the morning-glory seeds which had been fed to them in abundance to make them insensitive to pain. They were lined up beside the great stone pit in which the mass of blazing logs had now degenerated into a heap of white powder glowing red at each breath of wind. They were cast into this and writhed scorching. When the skin began to burn but before they died, the priests thrust poles with copper hooks into them and dragged the scorched writhing creatures to the high stones of sacrifice. There Montezuma was allowed to hold a limb of one of the prisoners, together with four other junior priests, while the high priest of the lord of fire cut open the blistered breast with his chert-bladed knife and snatched up the heart of each victim. When all were sacrificed, the bodies were burnt.

This was all quite natural to the young prince. Every year the sacrifice was performed, and the souls of the victims went to the fire god who could alone return them newly born to live again on earth. A young priest, as he now was, knew these things and felt a glorious exaltation as the sacrifice was consummated.

In the year 1479 of our calendar, the prisoners for the fire god sacrifice had come from the Chinanteca tribe. Montezuma was twelve years old. Already brave and wise, he was now being prepared to go into battle against the tribes and towns which had refused to pay tribute to the all-conquering Aztecs. For the rule of the Aztecs was not always continuous. Many conquered tribes revolted and had to be suppressed by increased use of force.

CAP.º 32.º

CAP.º 33.º

Each group or tribe was more or less autonomous, but they accepted the principle of overlordship. By the late fifteenth century there was a general concensus of opinion that this overlordship was inherited in families of true Toltec descent. After the ghastly catastrophe of Tula at the end of the tenth century, families of the invading Chichimeca, who swept into Mexico from the north, all endeavoured to find Toltec princesses to become mothers of a ruling clan in each tribe. Hence many towns had as good social claims to overlordship as the Aztecs. However, legitimacy was confirmed by power, and the wars of the elder Montezuma had reached the coasts and even overthrown the civilized Totonacs. In any case the Aztecs never incorporated a defeated people into the Aztec State. Each city remained quite independent to govern in its own way and to worship its own gods. But the indispensable condition was that they met the demand for tribute and paid the Aztec tax collectors regularly. From the records it seems that many people must have had to denude their resources in order that Cactus Rock might be glorified.

The boy Montezuma was well aware that through his mother he had inherited a double strain of Toltec blood. He was a lineal descendant, on the maternal side, of the divine Quetzalcoatl. The horoscope of his birth year confirmed him in the idea that he would one day be like the great priest-king who had made the Toltecs the bearers of civilization in Mexico. But the Mexican rule was elective within the family councils, so there was no reason for Montezuma to expect the sacred power to fall on his shoulders. He felt indeed that his purpose was more and more the study of religion, for although inspired by his school to high military ambition, he aspired in his heart to a future which might lead him to be the Quetzalcoatl Totec Tlamacazqui. This was

Opposite Above: Axayacatl, Montezuma's father, sits in judgement. Below: Axayacatl and his Aztec army defeat the army of a mountain tribe. From Diego Duran's *Historia de los Indios de Nueva Hispaña*.

Below The Lord Tezcatlipoca (of whom Blue Hummingbird is one aspect) as ruler of all thirteen-day periods in the magical calendar. The god is devouring the delicate flesh of the palm of a sacrificial victim. *Codex Fejervary-Mayer*.

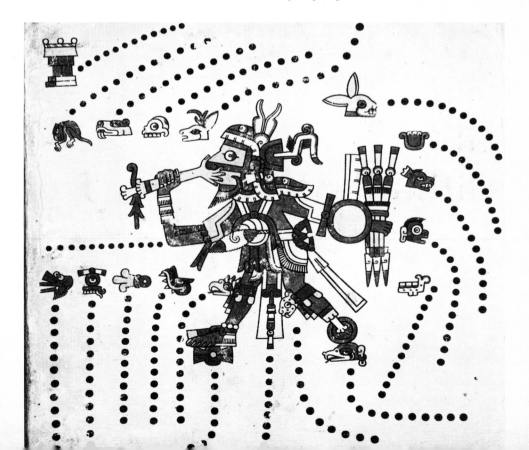

Below The dedicatory jade for the great temple at Cactus Rock (Tenochtitlan). The date at the bottom gives our year 1487. Above, the Lords Ahuitzotl (left) and Tizoc (right) offer blood from their ears for the gods.

Opposite Stone figure of Xipe-Totec, The Flayed Lord, showing the skin worn by a young warrior.

the name given to one of the two high priests who reigned together over religious life. He was in charge of the worship of Blue Hummingbird, and the other was concerned with the worship of Tlaloc the rain god.

But among the Aztecs even priests must fight, so the prince was quite happy to learn the techniques of battle. In a sense the warrior was also a priest. His greatest glory was not in the slaying of men on the battlefield but in the capture of prisoners to be taken for sacrifice to the gods.

In 1480 a warning came to Mexico in the form of an earthquake. Everyone knew that the rule of the present sun in the heavens was to be ended by an earthquake, and that it would probably be the end of all creation, but none knew when the event would fall. Hence all earthquakes were recorded in the books of history. Montezuma saw the dust clouds, the leaping of the lake and then the violent shocks, and the damage inflicted. He heard of people swallowed by Tlaltecuhtli, the earth god, before they were prepared for burial. There was the roaring and breaking of earth and a great outburst of smoke from the volcanoes ringing the lake. Some houses caught fire on the outskirts of the city, where most of the construction was of wood and reeds. The priests raised a great outcry, beating the drums and calling people with their conch-shell trumpets. Many surged past the palace and into the temple courtyard, which at least offered a safe open space protected by the gods. People cut their ears and tongues to offer blood, and the priests hurriedly slew a group of captives. Then as the roaring passed away the earth was still and there was a silence. Some of the stone houses had been cracked open, others beside the lake had been breached by waves. Although they too were terrified, the nobles in their splendid feather garments walked calmly among the people and soon their calmness was echoed by others. For Montezuma it was a sign of the great power of the gods, and a chance to prove himself a strong prince by his own calm.

After the earthquake damage had been repaired, Axayacatl called a conference of the nobles. He explained that the great temple deserved even greater splendour. The gods who protected Mexico were honoured, but the temple was not yet the finest in the country; it could hardly compare with that of their allied city, Tezcoco, and was much smaller than the ancient temple at Cholula where Quetzalcoatl was worshipped. He questioned all the local governors about the areas where stones might best be obtained, and the Council decided which towns were to provide stone and where labourers were to be recruited for the holy work of rebuilding the great temple. It would soon be the time for celebrating the sixth group of twenty years since the founding of Cactus Rock, and the best way to honour the god who made the Aztecs powerful in those distant days was to make his temple even more glorious and magnificent than before.

Opposite above Carved wooden *teponaztli* (two-toned xylophone) representing a warrior blowing on a shell trumpet. From western Mexico, early 16th century.

Opposite below Aztec goddess in the form of a rattlesnake. It symbolizes the eternal poverty of our mother, Earth. Diorite carving. Aztec, 16th century.

73

No one in the city refused the extra contributions of cloth, wood and labour which were laid upon him. A few outlying people objected to bringing stone for their Aztec masters, and some of the messengers were killed by the mountain villagers. But the warriors were sent out, and Montezuma saw the skirmishing, even joining in some of the fighting, where he showed some courage in attacking the enemy. He enjoyed the change from the city, although at times in the high mountain air he felt tired and slow. When the fight was over, the defeated villagers had to beat and hammer the rough blocks of hard stone into shape, and then help to drag the bigger ones over rollers, and to carry the smaller ones in slings upon their backs. After much toil, the blocks were floated on rafts and canoes, and were brought to the great square in front of the old temple. They had to come from some fifty miles away, because the temple was to be built of fine hard stones, and not of the soft local reddish lava, *tezontli*, of which the houses of the citizens were built.

As the months went by the great piles of stones grew, timber beams were stacked up, and the foundations were prepared from large stones which were laid in a wide trench completely surrounding the ancient building. Below the stones were beams which in their turn rested on brushwood mattresses. The new structure was to be a thick skin of splendid stone right round the old buildings on the sacred place where the Cactus Rock was discovered. Among the greatest of the works done for this temple was the bringing of the great sacrificial disc, known to us as the stone of Tizoc, from the chief who actually finished the work on it. This enormous mass of porphyric rock was cut, levered on to a cradle and dragged over rollers little by little along the track from Coyoacan to the sacred square in Cactus Rock. The journey was not long (Coyoacan is a suburb of modern Mexico City) but for the progress 50,000 men were employed. There were not only the hauliers pulling on ropes and laying rollers, but also great crowds of singers and dancers, priests waving their incense bowls, and groups of young people, such as Montezuma, dedicated to war and the gods.

However, the god had already frowned on his people with the earthquake and worse was to come. Only a week earlier, the lord Axayacatl had consulted his elders with a view to sending an expedition to the untamed tribes to the northwest, in what is now the State of Michoacan. Not all were in favour of this scheme, but nevertheless a favourite brother of the high chief was chosen to be army commander leading the expedition. Montezuma saw them set off, the soldiers moving at their regular jogtrot, carrying shields and clubs, the feathered warriors dancing around the litter in which the war leader was carried, and then the numbers of women and boys carrying the back packs which included spare arms and clothing for the warriors. It was a brave sight as they went singing to fight in the wild mountains and bring back captives to

Opposite Detail from the Stone of Tizoc showing the Aztec Great Speaker seizing an enemy chief. The Aztec chief is shown as the god Tezcatlipoca. In this case the victory was really achieved by Ahuitzotl.

sacrifice to the gods. When the time came for the ceremony, a few Chinantec captives with their long copper-headed spears were sent back for the sacrifices. Then there was silence. It was seventeen days before a small group of wounded warriors came slowly back to Cactus Rock. They brought a few captives and the news of disaster. Trapped in the barrancas and ravines of the mountains, the army had been destroyed. They had assaulted fortresses and found themselves attacked from other mountains beside and behind them. They had stormed up the sides of barrancas and found themselves falling down the dusty slopes under a barrage of boulders. Amid the rocks the feathered nobles had been smashed to death by the ball-headed wooden clubs of the mountain peoples. The long copper spears had pushed rows of men over the edge of cliffs. The rout was terrible and the army commander had been found killed with a ring of dead enemies around him. Those who escaped had no chance of bringing back the dead bodies because, for the sake of honour, they were bound to bring back what live prisoners they could so that there would be the proper sacrifice before Blue Hummingbird. The hearts of the prisoners were placed in the bowl before him. But the distressed High Chief was afraid and promised his god a still finer offering bowl of stone.

Mexico fell into mourning. None of their conquered neighbours dared attack the Aztecs because they were still far too strong, but in the streets the women were weeping. As they went to the temples, untidy and wearing ragged clothing, they offered blood from their ears. The men let their blood flow freely, sorrowing at the anger of their god turned against them. Great offerings of clothing, jewels and slaves were made, and a group of sculptors and masons were sent to carve out the huge white marble sacrificial bowl which Axayacatl had promised the god. They made it in the form of a gigantic ocelot watching for the sunrise. In his back was a great opening which would be filled with hearts. It was moved into the building where stood the old bowl, and where the chief's successor must one day pass the year of meditation and penance.

Axayacatl was heart-broken. His offerings of stones for the new temple had been rejected. The gods had taken his favourite brother from him and broken an Aztec army. So, smitten in the midst of his glory, the chief sickened and died. He died, not on his sleeping mat, but on the basket-work throne, wearing his diadem as if in a last assertion of kingship. Thus Montezuma at the age of fourteen lost his father.

The funeral was carried out with the honour traditionally due to an old chief. The body, wrapped in hundreds of precious mantles and fastened, according to Aztec custom, with the knees drawn up to the chest, was carried in procession to the funeral pyre, where the battle honours which had adorned the body were broken, jewels were scattered over it, and a thick wooden crib was built around it. The pyre was then lit by the fire-priest; thick smoke, scented with cedarwood and herbs, rose high into the air, the pile flared a little and after a while became white. Eventually a glowing heap of white ashes and a few chalk-white bones were all that was left. The sad music of conch shells and drums which accompanied the dirges came to an end. The high priest

Above Jadeite sacrificial bowl for human hearts. The symbol inside represents the day Olin (earthquake) in the midst of the sun, a day on which the earth would end.

Below Base of the sacrificial bowl, showing the earth god Tlaltecuhtli with the skull of the victim. Aztec, about 1507.

Above Tlauixcalpantecuhtli, god of the totality of the planet Venus, with his ceremonial offerings of incense balls burnt on a small temple platform. The number below is $7 \times 9 \times 3 = 189$. *Codex Fejervary-Mayer.*

Opposite Reconstruction by Dr Ignacio Marquina of the sacred square at the heart of Cactus Rock.

reverently placed the ashes in a beautifully carved and painted stone box. Then the great nobles, heads of confederate cities as well as Aztecs, formed in procession to take the ashes to the temple.

Montezuma was allowed to be present at the great council of the three ruling families from whom the next leader of the nation would be chosen. There was much speechmaking. The council sought the advice of Tlacaelel, the oldest among them and the possessor of the highest military dignity. It was he who had saved the nation in many wars, and who had always avoided personal power apart from his military role. As a preliminary he was asked to accept the honour himself, but all knew well that he had refused such honour three times before and, as was expected, the ancient warrior refused again. He then went on to discuss the brothers of the dead chief. He stressed the bravery and good fortune of one of the more religious among them. This was Tizoc, whose name glyph is of a leg pierced with cactus spines, thus indicating his devotion to the gods by offering his own blood at every festival. The weight of the old man's opinion swayed the choice and Tizoc was chosen to be the national leader.

Montezuma was glad that one of his well-disposed uncles was now in charge of

Mexico. But he returned to his strict school. His father's old palace was closed up, and many of the treasures, including the feather shields and head-dresses and masses of golden regalia were walled up in a chamber which was sealed by small stones set in fine polished plaster. The stone masons and carpenters were set to work to build a new palace for the new emperor on the farther side of the square in front of the great temple pyramid.

Tizoc was installed with great ceremony. He was invested with the blue war jacket, leggings of gold, sandals of ocelot skin, and then the blue mantle and turquoise diadem. His nose was pierced so that he could wear a decorated bone with hummingbird feathers, and his lip ornament was replaced by one of rock crystal bored to contain a blue kingfisher feather. Thus Tizoc, lord of Cactus Rock, was placed on the basket-work throne, and then carried out for the acclamation of the people. All this was accompanied by singing and music. The whole city swayed to the rhythmic tone of drums, trumpets and the joyful rattles of the dancers.

The first action of the new ruler was to pledge the people to proceed with the building of the new temple to Blue Hummingbird so that the nation could be reunited with its divine leader. The recent period of disaster was like an illness which must be cured. Tizoc was then seated in the hall of meditation whence he would rule for a year. There he found, already installed, the gigantic offering bowl in the form of an ocelot, which his brother had had made to appease the god.

Montezuma was now of an age to fight in earnest and he was sent with his com-

79

panions to the country of Tzinancatepec to capture prisoners to be offered at ceremonies during the year 1483 (in our calendar) when the first terrace of the new facing
of the temple should be completed. It was a longed-for adventure in which danger was
sought and found. The hill town was reached after a week of trotting along the dusty
tracks of western Mexico. On the last day they had travelled more slowly so that the
ocelot warriors could creep out among the rocks to spy out the land. In the evening
the boys hid among the rocks and scrub. All was quiet, and they prepared the fine
clothes and the splendid feather insignia for their leaders. As dawn came the ocelot
warriors climbed up the hills and howled like wild cats to welcome the sun. And after
they had called, the eagle warriors in their bird costumes danced their welcome in
turn. Perhaps by night their souls would be dancing with the sun as he went down, or
perhaps they might have sent some of the enemies to him.

Montezuma assisted his elder cousins to tie on their splendid panoply of painted
paper banners and coloured feathers. Then they marched solemnly and openly to the
entrance to the unwalled town, for war among the Aztecs was not a sudden assault
on an unsuspecting enemy. They were met by the war chief of the district and his
officials. The Aztecs demanded that a tribute should be paid to the Great Speaker in
Cactus Rock, and that the chief of Tzinancatepec should be replaced by an Aztec
governor. Furthermore, the town was to send twenty men annually for sacrifice to
the gods of Mexico. The chief replied courteously with much bowing that his people
were free of foreign rule, and that they would wish for friendship with the great Tizoc
but that none of their men should be sent for sacrifice. Evidently this was to be a real
battle – the challenge had been made and accepted, and both sides parted.

At high noon the warriors came out of the town, their leader with a great feathered
sun on his back. The small army spread out at a steady trot in two wings with their
war clubs sharp-edged and ready. They whistled and screamed to intimidate the
Aztecs who appeared to be moving slowly to meet them. The central group of Aztecs
gathered tightly. Some of those at the back spread out on either side. They seemed
few and their enemy expected an easy killing. But then they heard a sound all knew:
the howl of an ocelot. The Aztec scouts had been separated from the main body and
now came shouting and whistling from behind the flanks of the enemy. The battle
began. Warriors leaped at one another, trying to batter down shields and weaken the
enemy by cuts of the sharp obsidian club blades. If a man stumbled and fell he was
likely to be seized, tied with a leather thong and dragged away. Montezuma saw some
people fall, but suddenly he was parrying blows from a tall man much older than
himself. He dodged and the two danced around each other. Then came a glancing cut
which hurt, but the prince suddenly dived as his enemy towered over him for a final
slashing blow. He swung his shield to deflect the blow and thrust the blunt end of his
club under the ribs of the warrior. As the warrior doubled up in agony the boy swung
his club, and just in time remembered to turn it to stun and not to cut. Then slinging
his shield to protect his neck in the mêlée he whipped a leather thong from his loincloth
and tied the hands and feet of the unconscious warrior so that he could later be carried

Right Prisoners of war kept in cages pending sacrifice. Sahagun's *Historia de las Cosas de Nueva España*.

Below Sacrificial knife of chert, with mosaic figure of an eagle-spirit on the handle.

off for sacrifice. He let out a shout of triumph and then saw two of his companions chasing another warrior towards his corner of the field. He slashed at the man's legs as he came near, but instead of tripping him, his foot was cut through, releasing a stream of blood. The warrior fell in a pool of blood on the floor. He would be no use for sacrifice so they slashed his throat and cut off an ear as a trophy. Then passing a pole through the thongs binding the captive they shouldered him and took him back to the corral where the prisoners were kept.

When he came round he groaned at his fate, but once with the other prisoners he submitted to the slave pole tied around his shoulders. It was a point of honour not to try to escape the glorious destiny of the captive. As with the Aztecs, some soldiers were killed, but a few were captured and they knew that when they had been fattened up they would be sacrificed and afterwards their bodies would be eaten. Made holy by the gods they would bring strength to those who ate them.

However, the enemy was defeated. The chiefs of both sides met. No exchange of prisoners was made, for that would be considered dishonourable. The captors demanded the death of all the towns-people, the losers offered tribute and then both sides haggled until a tribute was fixed which was to be paid twice yearly.

The young soldiers did not know until they had assembled to return to Cactus Rock that the new Great Speaker, Tizoc, 'Jewel of the Sun', had planned this raid as part of a general move of the Aztecs and their allies in which nearly a quarter of a million warriors attacked the tribes west of Mexico. The Aztecs were victorious everywhere. They lost a thousand or so men, but ten times that number of prisoners were taken.

It was clear to all the Aztec people that Blue Hummingbird had relented and was once more favouring the work on his great temple. There were parades in Mexico and great dances of feathered warriors stamping and chanting in bright coloured circles in praise of the great war god.

Tizoc called groups of warriors before him and granted them symbols of honour, shields, bunches of feathers and, to the leaders, cloaks indicating high rank. The boys from the military academy were highly praised. Now they would be allowed to cut off the lock of hair, the *piochtli*, to show that they had captured prisoners in battle. (When they were ten, the boys had their hair cut, with a lock of hair left on the nape of the neck. This lock, the *piochtli*, could not be cut until they had succeeded in taking a prisoner in battle.) Some, including Montezuma, who had captured prisoners single-handed, were given necklaces of jade beads and garlands of flowers. Their ears were stretched to take still larger ornaments, and they were allowed to wear netted cloaks as a sign of prowess.

The victory brought all the Aztec people into the city for a great festival of singing and eating. Most of the prisoners were put in wooden cages for fattening, but a hundred were taken for sacrifice on that one day. Flowers, feathers, songs and blood were mingled in the great festival. The lord Tizoc was delighted that the god had approved of his people. He set about organizing the building of the first great stage of the reconstructed temple.

Montezuma went on further raids into border towns, and at length caught three prisoners in single-handed combat. One he sacrificed himself on the circular stone of Tizoc on which the chief recorded the conquests of his brother Axayacatl under his own name. (Montezuma was displeased to see his father's victories claimed by his uncle.) As was the custom, the prisoner was tied to the stone and armed only with a wooden club. He fought desperately but was no match for Montezuma who, dancing and leaping around him, slashed at him with his obsidian-bladed club. Eventually the prisoner collapsed and his heart was ripped out. Thus the gods were honoured by the young prince and his honour as a warrior was confirmed.

But during the next two years, while half the population was busy building the lower platform of the great temple, Montezuma returned to his priestly duties, and took up the study of magic and religion as painted in the temple books. This was his natural world and the two years were pleasant ones for him.

5

THE STUDENT OF THE
STARS

WHILE TIZOC WAS KING, there was a short respite for the peoples of Mexico. For two or three years wars were either small raids or glorious 'wars of flowers' which were agreed between the Aztecs and the barbarous Tlaxcalans, and guaranteed a supply of prisoners for sacrifice in times of peace. This human harvest was usually gathered some months ahead of the time of taking the sacred tuna flower (the human heart) to the eagles and Blue Hummingbird. The prisoners were kept in stout wooden cages, given little exercise and fed the best that could be found for them.

The arrangement for the wars of flowers was undertaken at the highest diplomatic levels. It was an advantage to the towns taking part in them because they thus avoided the expense and destruction of real war, and it was fortunate that Tlaxcala was close enough to Mexico to make it easy for these struggles to be arranged. The Aztecs never set out to conquer Tlaxcala but reserved this small nation in its mountain fastness as a source of food for the gods in times of peace. The situation remained so until the fateful year when Montezuma celebrated his fifty-second birthday.

The three years of his uncle Tizoc's reign as Great Speaker were good ones for Montezuma. Except for an occasional border raid or a war of flowers, he was able to spend them in study in the temple. It was always his preferred way of life. This lean ascetic young man was a brave warrior but the austerity of the *calmecac* was his chosen milieu. In this place he even escaped the attentions of the girls who were quartered with the young warriors in order to absorb the sinfulness which torments young men. Montezuma was not destined to be a celibate. His social position required that he must eventually father a family. He was not allowed to destroy his sex life as the higher priests did. These ascetics would thrust a bone pin into their urethra and slit the tube open. When they experienced desire their penis would open like a red leaf from some tropical flower. It was beautiful and, of course, painful.

As a young warrior in the schools, however, Montezuma was allowed to associate with certain specially chosen girls in order that the strain of continence would not tell too much on him. These girls had been selected by fate because of the gods ruling at the time of their birth. Their function was to be slaves of Tlazolteotl, the witch goddess who ate the evil which tainted humanity. Her images wore black face paint to show that she was the 'eater up of dirt'. These girls were pampered, taught dancing, singing and the arts of seduction. They wore bells and pretty feather ornaments, their

Above Education of a young priest. The neophyte carries scorpions for the young incense-bearing priest. The priest who sings to the stars, the skilled astrologer. *Codex Mendoza.*

Opposite The four directions of time: a calendar in which the 260 days of the magical time count are divided into the luck of the four directions, east at the top, south on the left, west at the bottom and north on the right. The 4 days on which years can start are marked by birds. Each quarter has its patron gods, and in the centre is Xiuhtecuhtli, Lord of Fire, who is the earthly surrogate of the Creator. Mixtec, 14th–15th century. *Codex Fejervary-Mayer.*

skirts were shorter than other girls' and showed their knees, while their capes were so short that they revealed their firm round breasts with the nearly black nipples. Their faces were usually painted yellow with a black circle round the mouth and if they wore bands round their hair they were made of raw cotton. Their function was to serve the pleasure of the young warriors in the 'houses of youths'. When they showed signs of becoming feeble or were taken ill with venereal sickness, they were invited to a dance and there suddenly strangled. But because they had absorbed so much evil by their magic sexuality they could not be sent to the other worlds, so, neither cremated nor buried, the bodies were thrown into the reeds. Before long the *zopilotes* (vultures) would scent them, and, slowly flapping their huge wings, they would hop around and snatch the flesh from the bodies until only a tumble of white bones was left.

The discipline of the temple, however, was strict and while Montezuma was there he would have little opportunity for free speculation, certainly no chance of gaining a knowledge of the universe outside the accepted philosophical system of Aztec learning. The day in the temple began at sunset; after the symbolic sacrifice the boys would go to sleep in the dormitory on their sleeping mats on the stone floor. As midnight approached, all were awoken and joined in a procession to the upper platform of the temple. Here hymns were sung, self-inflicted torments were offered up, and priests explained the position of stars and planets to the neophytes. At these times the youngest neophytes were sent naked into the darkness to bring back those scorpions and spiders which Montezuma remembered so well. For him now there was a period of meditation which ended in sleep until first light. The whole company then attended

84

the morning sacrifice and sounded the shell trumpets which symbolized the ocelots calling in the hills. The quails symbolizing the starry night were slain, a human victim yielded up his heart, and the sun rose. The lord of fate spread light over Mexico for the second half of the day. The sounds of talking and singing came to the temple walls, and from them the trumpets and drums echoed back reminding all that the day was alive, that the sun was marching to victory, that at his highest point in the southern sky Blue Hummingbird would be incarnated in him, the god who was protector of Mexico and of all young warriors.

During the day there were ceremonial dances, prayers and long sessions of learning from the professors of astrology. Learning was imparted in songs and in the painted

symbols around the images of the gods. All this required mathematical skill because it was important to be able to calculate the numbers of days and understand the way in which the movements of the planets combined into recognizable patterns.

None of the courses of study was passed through without supervision and questioning. The priests watched over the candidate and allowed him to advance only at a gradual pace. After a series of advances he was bound to spend some time in revision and seclusion, although he must never miss a period of ceremonial activity. There were the sacrifices and dances, the changing ritual of the eighteen major festivals of the year (one for each month as the Aztecs numbered eighteen months in the year) and the series of penitential periods of fasting and self-inflicted pain. The neophyte had to face constant criticism. He must be obedient to his superiors and suffer whatever pains they inflicted, even for such offences as dust on a piece of firewood. Every day he passed a bone awl through his tongue and cut his ears with agave spines to offer blood. His legs and arms were spotted with the scars he made with such spines. After the great fasts lasting eighty days, when only a single tortilla and a bowl of water a day were permitted, the prince looked like a moving skeleton, but his mind developed enlightenment and understanding. Curious phenomena occurred around him; sometimes when he moved quickly blue sparks scattered from his dry skin, sometimes he seemed to see round the corners of space and become aware of other beings. The gods appeared in all the glory and terror depicted in the books. The visions seemed real and it did not occur to Montezuma that they were but manifestations of his own personality. He was a natural shaman and, with his ascetic training as an astronomer-priest, he also suffered from the experiences which befell the priests, who were painfully given to trance and hallucinations.

The prince rose rapidly within the temple, and he was finally initiated as a sacrificing priest. His spare wiry frame was strong enough to withstand the effects of austerity, and his arm was capable of slashing the heart from a living man for the morning offering of life to the sun.

In addition to his duties as a priest, his uncle Tizoc would order him from time to time to take a small expedition to subdue some local rebellion on the outskirts of the empire. Montezuma never sought personal glory, but his bravery in combat was beyond doubt. The three prisoners he had taken in single-handed combat brought him into the class of honoured warriors. At a gathering in the temple courtyard at midsummer on the festival of Blue Hummingbird, he, together with one or two companions who had also achieved this military distinction, was brought before the Great Speaker and knelt while the war chief ordered slaves to shave the back and sides of his head (a rather painful process even with sharp obsidian blades). The hair of the noble youngster was that of a priest and had never been cleaned from the clotted blood of sacrificed victims which had spurted over it. But now a tuft of hair was all that was to be left on top of his head and this was bound with a red leather thong so that it stood up like a stiff brush. He was also, as a nobleman, given a new and longer stud to wear through his lower lip. Thus honoured he had become a *tequihua* or

Above The Two, Ometecuhtli, the Creator as the Supreme Duality. Mixtec, 14th–15th century. *Codex Fejervary-Mayer.* (They place the fire-butterfly of the soul into the otherwise lifeless skull.)

'master of cuts'. Montezuma had early fulfilled the dual nature of his personality. He was a leader among men and at the same time his knowledge of secret learning and of meditation enabled him to maintain one side of his character remote from human contacts.

Yet he was never free from a certain passion for the mysterious past. He was obsessed with the Toltec image. The ruins of Tula, two days' walk from Tenochtitlan, had become his wilderness, to which he would retire to meditate on the glories of the ancestors. It was a place of visions for him and in its loneliness it had something in common with him. In those days no archaeologist disturbed the ruins, starting up from the dusty scrub and remains of burnt timbers and crumbled, fire-crazed stone. It was a place of sadness and desolation. Here and there a mighty Toltec face gazed from the dust towards the sun, whose butterfly shield he wore across his throat. Faint traces of colour showed still on those stern Indian faces. The broken wall had still its procession of ocelots. From the mound that had been the temple of the feathered serpent and an astronomical observatory Montezuma could see the movement of the planets and constellations and figure out the shapes of the gods in that gleaming tracery. Down below lay the outlines of the ruins and on one mound, once the holy 'house of the frog', he had a vision of the last Great Speaker of the Toltecs, the unhappy Topiltzin. The sadness as the figure turned away towards exile over the ruins of the city was ever in his mind.

It was no doubt Montezuma who petitioned his uncle to allow the priests to erect a small temple within the ruins of the ancient city. There in a corner of the steps of the destroyed temple a little oratory was erected and offerings made to the lord Quetzalcoatl and to Blue Hummingbird the Conqueror. But it was a small place and very lonely in that tragic field of ruins. The charcoal of the burnt palace and the adobe dust of the ruined houses blew in the wind. The haunting sadness of the place crushed the heart, and people were prone to see visions. Yet Montezuma as he prepared to sacrifice the occasional hare or coyote knew that the blood of the ancient kings flowed in his veins. He wept and sometimes brooded, for he knew that to restore the glories of Quetzalcoatl of the Toltecs was a great task and already his horoscope told him of the ambivalence of his position as a warrior of Blue Hummingbird and a priest of Quetzalcoatl.

Montezuma knew the history of his people better than anyone else of his time. He had found among the books of his father's palace a leather volume bound in wood and set with jade. It recalled the history of the god Quetzalcoatl, and told of the creation of the world and of the coming of Quetzalcoatl to earth. The founding of Tula was described together with a short history of the nine high chiefs, his ancestors, the Quetzalcoatls of the Toltecs. On the other side was painted a history of the Mixtec tribe, who had preserved it because they were descended from the Toltecs. His uncle, Montezuma I, had captured it from them a generation before his grandson was born. But now that grandson, trained in the wisdom of the priests, could read the book, and he treasured it greatly, awaiting the return of Quetzalcoatl. He knew the ancient legend and as an astronomer knew a great deal about the synodic movements of the planet Venus. The disappearance and the return of the direct influence of Quetzalcoatl as Morning Star and his opposite, the twisted creature Xolotl as Evening Star, were all very apparent. He also, as one of the inner circle of the nobility of Toltec descent, knew that one of their number was selected and slain in the 'House of Fear' when the planet Venus was invisible at the periods of inferior and superior conjunction. This was a very secret ceremony which took place in the circular building with a door in the form of an open serpent's mouth.

Montezuma knew that on his fifty-second birthday he would have to face the consummation of fate when once again his birth year *ce acatl* appeared in the Aztec time span. In our calendar this was to be the year 1518. But there was plenty of time for study and preparations yet before him. He was only seventeen when his uncle Tizoc had completed the lower stage of the rebuilding of the great temple.

The walls of the pyramid rose high and magnificent, laid with smoothly-shaped stones. All around there were inset panels with stucco figures carved and painted with

Opposite The most complete surviving Aztec temple, at Tenayuca. The two braziers at the top of the staircase were kept blazing with pine logs all night. Aztec, early 16th century.

Opposite Gigantic stone head of an eagle warrior, possibly representing the Sun god. Aztec, early 16th century.

Above Small wooden figure of Xolotl, the spirit of the evening star, the evil twin of Quetzalcoatl, the morning star.

35

Above The image of the vegetation and song
deity Five Flower (Macuilxochitl) is carried
in procession by young warrior-priests. The
leader blows on a conch-shell trumpet.
Codex Magliabecciano.

Opposite Colossal stone head of the Moon,
Lady Golden Bells (Coyolxauhqui), sister of
Blue Hummingbird. Aztec, early 16th century.
From the temple enclosure in Cactus Rock.

images of the gods. The beautiful stone-work was covered in fine plaster with brilliant
colours set against a white background, so smooth that it glistened and reflected the
sunlight. The shining white building was coloured with pictures like brilliant jewels.
The main staircase was flanked by great carvings of rattlesnakes with open red jaws
and white teeth. At the top of the steps was that great, circular, greenish stone slab
which commemorated the victories of Axayacatl under the name of Tizoc. But
although Tizoc had his own hieroglyph on the figures, they were dressed as Blue
Hummingbird so that the glory was given to the god rather than the man. Down the
middle of the stairway ran the great spine dividing it into two, one side dedicated to
Tlaloc, lord of the rains and all sources of water, and the other to Blue Hummingbird,
high sun and patron of the Aztecs. The brilliant decoration of the temple reflected the
feathers and jewels of the nobles and the bright flowers beloved by the Aztecs.
(Everyone grew flowers as well as food in the city of Cactus Rock.) Now their great
temple was to match the beauty of the land it guarded.

Montezuma served in the temple, apart from short military expeditions, for three years. He played his part as a young warrior both in one important campaign and in the minor forays to keep the frontiers intact; yet few people knew him. His natural habits of withdrawal made him uncommunicative, his voice was notably soft and his mien was aloof and aristocratic. This young philosopher prince was respected and envied, but people found it hard to love him.

Now that the great festival of the consecration of the temple was drawing near, Tizoc sent his embassies out to call on all the cities of Mexico to send their princes and warriors to come in friendship to take part in the ceremonies and to share the sacrifices. For Montezuma it meant that the years of study were to be curtailed. He turned, almost for the first time, to look beyond the reed screens to the new building and found himself gasping at the beauty of the great mass with its bright colours and the contrasting simplicity of the upper part of the old temple.

He passed the courtyard and turned right behind the temple pyramid towards the

93

barracks where the prisoners lived. They were cheerful enough. Most of them were allowed to go out to the city without the shoulder bars of the slaves, for they would not think of trying to escape. Montezuma passed a few friendly words with them, especially those whom he had captured himself. He knew from the magic books that the sacrifices would go well for them and for Mexico.

His route then led him through a narrow passageway to the palace of his uncle. Montezuma was not then a very important member of the family, but his duty was clear. He must be completely available for the service of the lord Tizoc at this time. His duties as a priest were now relatively light and he could perform them at the palace, since it was easily possible to keep the watch on the stars from the palace roof at night, and the morning sacrifice of quails was performed there regularly.

His duty as a *tequihua* was to be with other distinguished warriors escorting the visiting noblemen to the palaces and rooms where they and their entourage would be quartered. He called slaves to lay the bed mats in correct places and arranged for the rooms to be kept clean and cool. When the watchers on the temple roofs reported bands of men approaching, the warriors would go out to meet them. The lords were carried on litters of gilded wood decorated with brilliantly-coloured plumage. Some of them were welcomed personally by the lord Tizoc. Others were escorted all the way to the palace by the company of warriors. These were the trusted friends and allies of the Aztecs. Among them Montezuma found many distant relatives and friends of his childhood. Important among them was old Nezahualcoyotl of Tezcoco, now so old that he was usually carried everywhere by servants in a special basket-work chair. In cold weather he was wrapped in a mass of cotton-wool to keep him warm. He was much attached to his young cousin because of his devotion to the gods. He was also a great and famous poet and from him Montezuma learned much of the formal beauty of Aztec poetry which he loved to hear and sometimes recite.

All Cactus Rock was full of people. Householders gave shelter to provincial relatives. The subject tribes sent groups of warriors and dancers. Even the surrounding peoples who would not acknowledge the Aztecs as their overlords had been invited by the lord Tizoc. Trusting in his word, they came to join in the celebrations and no doubt to spy out the land to find some hoped-for weakness in the Aztecs. However, the purpose of inviting them was to impress them with the greatness of Mexico and the glory of its patron god Blue Hummingbird. There was no weakness to be seen, no drunkenness, no outward sign of poverty. All was planned and orderly.

The market place was busier than ever, the million people who lived in and around Cactus Rock had trebled in number for the occasion. All manner of strange foods and decorated pieces of cloth were to be found and the workers in feathers and leather were assured of brisk trade. Only the armourers had been restricted. All the Aztecs' weapons were stored in a special hall near the temple which was closed to all strangers and those arms in the hands of the Aztec warriors were not to be handled by other men. So the brilliant city, with its canals glistening green and the footwalks always swept so that no single speck of dust was visible, prepared for fiesta. The gardens were full of

Above Gigantic stone head of a rattlesnake,
which once stood at the foot of the stairway
of the great temple in Cactus Rock.

flowers. Coloured bark-paper rosettes and chains swung from the houses. Every wall
was newly plastered and burnished, and the people were dressed in their best clothes
and ornaments.

When all were gathered in the city the High Chief consulted the High Priests of
Tlaloc and Blue Hummingbird. They chose a day, and then they opened a pit on the
terrace in which they placed a stone box of jewels as a foundation deposit to mark the
holiness of the new building. They covered it securely and then began the great dances.
The whole of Mexico seemed to be dancing to flutes, whistles and drums. Even the
great drum, twice the height of a man, from which came the mournful call for sacrifice,
was throbbing to new rhythms. All was alive in honour of this festival for the dedication of the first platform of the new temple building. It was three years since the
foundation had been laid and one hundred and twenty years since the first stones were

brought to Cactus Rock to build the first little temple to Blue Hummingbird. Since then, as the god had promised the ancestors, Mexico had prospered. Now he was to be thanked for his protection and given the promise of yet more glories to come as the rebuilding of the temple continued.

It was the function of Montezuma as a young member of the leading family to lead some of the dances. He was decorated with feather head-dress and cape, brilliant and glistening in all colours. In one hand his light dancing shield of cane displayed the symbols of his name. In his other hand he held a nosegay of scented and brilliant flowers arranged in a cone. At the same time he represented both war and beauty. His face was painted with the black of his priestly rank, as was his body, but across the face were two wide bands of brilliant yellow. This was the mask of the god Blue Hummingbird in his disguise as the power of the darkness and the north. Behind the young noble came a row of young men, all born in the palace, all related. Their dance was a circling, stamping, bowing rhythm which revealed their muscular bodies. Their feather ornaments swayed as their shields were raised and lowered. In the centre were the drummers and flute players, but everyone sang. Everywhere there was singing and drumming.

Running hither and thither among the throng were the grotesque jesters whose function was to make people laugh and be joyful so that the ceremony should show the god how happy his people were. These sacred clowns were often cripples and hunch-backs who knew all manner of amusing tricks. On such occasions they were naked and the men joked and the girls laughed in a rather shocked way at the sight.

Then came the procession in which the great company of prisoners marched. They had now reached the climax of their lives. They were chanting a war song as befitted brave men. Each was painted with red and white stripes, symbolizing blood and bones, the signs of a glorious death, and they were covered with spots of white eagles' down representing stars to show that they would ascend to the sky. At the platform of the completed building stood the enormous Stone of the Sun, brilliant with fresh colour, and before it stood the sacrificial stone. Relays of priests wearing the insignia of the gods were there, and their acolytes, painted black and dressed in simple white headcloths and seamless shirts, were ready. As each prisoner reached the top step five acolytes seized him, holding arms, legs and head. They slung him back over the stone, perhaps breaking his back, but stretching the chest taut so that the sharp sacrificial knife of chert should burst the flesh, separate the ribs and cut straight through the aorta and other blood vessels. The slash completed, the priest lifted the leaping heart, still writhing and spurting a spray of residual blood, to offer it toward the sun and then put it in the great bowl. The acolytes drained the blood from the chest cavity into a gilded bowl. As each victim died an acolyte bearing the blood would run up the steps of the old temple and deposit it on the image of Blue Hummingbird in

Opposite An Aztec worshipper. The stone figure
still retains its stucco coating. 16th century.

his sanctuary. One after another the victims marched to their doom. It took many hours for the work to be accomplished, but the sun shone the more brightly as the hearts were offered and the souls of the sacrificed warriors came to dance among his eagle spirits in the sky.

One after another the bodies of the victims were thrown bumping down the steps at the side of the procession, and at the floor of the temple the priests cut them up. The glorious heads were put on one side. The torsos and offal were piled up for the beasts in the menageries attached to the palace. The limbs were carefully cut into small cubes. The god had entered the bodies and each piece of raw flesh now contained magic power and was holy. One by one they were given to the singing people. The delicate hands and soles of the feet were given to the nobles. But all the time the singing and dancing went on.

There were thirteen days of rejoicing. At night lords and commoners went to their homes for feasting and drinking; there were entertainments and dancing. But the priests continued their sacred offices. Montezuma left the court to ascend to the roofs to watch the stars at the appointed hours, and read the movement of fate for the Aztecs. Among his uncle's stars there was some unusual clouding. He knew its meaning but it was not for him to speak. In another part of the palace Tizoc also was watching the stars, and he pierced his flesh many times to offer his blood to the gods. But he knew too that before very long he would be joining his ancestors.

When the dawn came again the trumpets and drums sounded and rejoicing continued. After the appointed time the visiting chiefs departed with their retinues, and the Aztecs returned to their daily round. Supplies were low, and more food must be prepared, more work done in the fields, and trade resumed. There was also work for all the citizens in sweeping the streets clean, dredging the canals and plastering and painting the streets of one-storey houses. The garden plots were straightened, and the flowers on roof-gardens were made trim again. Once more the city was itself, brilliant and clean with the temples in each quarter shining in the sun. In the distance the volcanoes rested serene and snowy beyond the foothills. The gods had been honoured and the valley of Mexico was at peace.

Montezuma returned to his duties in the temple, but like all the people of Mexico he felt that the time must soon come for the further growth of the Aztec empire. More captives would be needed for the completion of the temple, and not just those from the annual war of flowers with the Tlaxcalans. He knew that he must soon assume new responsibilities on the military plane. His time as a priest was coming to an end.

Opposite Statue of the young sun god (Tonatiuh) as an Aztec warrior. The discs on his headdress symbolize heat.

6
THE LEADER OF WARRIORS

Not long after the celebrations had ended, Tizoc died. There was great consternation among his people, although it seems that Tizoc himself had foreseen his death. He had commanded that a wooden figure of himself should be carved and adorned with his garments ready for the funeral ceremonies. The cause of his death is unknown but it may have been a ceremonial slaying, for this philosophic king had not been distinguished in war. On his great stone, as already mentioned, conquests of his elder brother are attributed to him, possibly because, apart from the forays to obtain victims for the dedication of the temple platform, there was no war in his short reign. For Montezuma the change meant that he must finally assume the responsibilities of a leader of warriors and leave in abeyance his priestly duties.

Runners went out to summon all lords of towns and the great allies of Cactus Rock, the lords of Tezcoco and Tlacopan, to the royal funeral. Again the city was filled, but this time with lamenting crowds. The great nobles assembled, and the priests in the costumes of the gods came to take away the body. It was clothed in fine garments with all the decorations of a great king. A red dog was slain in front of the body so that it could conduct the soul of the dead ruler to his abode in the other world. A crib of fine logs was built around the body and the whole carried to a platform at the feet of the terrible idol of Blue Hummingbird. The torches set it afire, and a great column of scented white smoke ascended into the clear sky, until nothing was left but a fine white ash. This was placed into the customary box, beautifully painted and carved with the symbols of the dead king.

On the next day the kings of Tezcoco and Tlacopan called the council of the lords of Cactus Rock. All the family were present including Prince Montezuma. Following Aztec custom long speeches were made about the dead king, and the state of the nation, before all went in procession to the palace which sheltered the ancient protector of the nation, Tlacaelel. The harsh cracked tones of extreme age were listened to with special attention. The seer told of the past glories of the kings he had known, and

Opposite The warrior's soul, ascending as the eagle of the Sun. He carries bouquets in either hand, and below his mouth the symbol says that his breath has departed from him like a golden song. Below are the waters of war and the shields of Blue Hummingbird. The *huehuetl* (war drum) of Toluca, Mexico.

assessed the qualities of the younger men who were present. His advice was to seek the brilliant in battle, the bravest and most generous of the princes who would lead the men of Cactus Rock to victories after the sad period of unwanted peace. The Aztecs must expand and expand. Long ago their god had promised the ancestors that their power should cover all Anahuac, the land between the two oceans. Now was the time for war to spread and bring glory with the fulfilment of the prophecy. Who would be the leader to choose? There was a quiet moment and then one name was murmured and rapidly agreed upon. It was the youngest brother in the ruling family: the brilliant and brave Ahuitzotl.

The ceremonies for the new emperor were magnificent. He was carried in a special throne to the priest's house before the temple, and he stepped out onto a path of fine, coloured cotton blankets, his arms supported by great nobles. Then he was clothed. His basic dress was that of an American Indian brave: a loincloth, and a blanket, but these were made of finest woven cotton, and decorated profusely with shining hummingbird feathers. His blanket was dyed sky-blue to match the high diadem set with turquoise which adorned his head. Special jewels were set in his nose and ears, and he was seated on a basket-work throne covered with jaguar skins. Then his feet were washed and he was shod with golden sandals; his long black hair was combed and oiled and his face was painted in black and blue bars in honour of Blue Hummingbird.

Messages had been sent to all the peoples of Mexico to send gifts to Cactus Rock for this great ceremony. Most of the towns and confederations had thought it wise to comply for fear of what might happen if the Aztec armies came to plunder them. Eight, however, had sent refusals. They knew the consequences but hoped that through the help of their gods they would make some break in the constant encroachments of their predatory neighbours.

This time, to the joy of the nation, the Great Speaker Ahuitzotl, after his coronation, himself organized the gathering of the armies to punish the recalcitrant tribes. They were long in coming together. Some came from the distant tributary nations, some from the coasts of the sea and some from the mountains. The core of the army was the Aztec militia, consisting of all the young men between eighteen and twenty-two who were conscripted for war. They had been trained for battle, and lived in the hope of honour in taking captives. They were so drilled in their social obligations that they were dedicated to death or glory. Among them in command of a hundred men was Montezuma.

The young chief was well respected. He was brave, as his hair bound in a crest with a red leather thong showed. He was bold in battle and led his men well. Yet nobody

Opposite Ancestral warrior, a statue from
Toltec Tula representing a warrior wearing the
fire-bird symbols of the ruling clan of the
Toltecs. The cavity in his chest once held a
heart of jade. 10th century.

Above Figures from a sculptured wall at Tula, the Toltec capital. These creatures represent the two military orders, the Eagles and the Ocelots. About AD 900.

Opposite Symbol of the Ocelot warriors, the scouts of an Aztec army. Mexico city.

really knew him. There was a mysterious side of his personality which could not be gauged. It was his training as a priest which made him a quiet and thoughtful young man who was often observed looking for omens or going out alone at night (considered a very daring act in that time) to watch the position of the stars, which gained him a somewhat sinister reputation.

When the armies were finally gathered together they attacked first the peoples in the east. They conquered them and exacted a vast tribute, after which Ahuitzotl turned his attention to the mountains in the west, where they fought on more difficult ground. Hill forts had to be stormed under a shower of boulders from the defenders, and there was constant fear of ambush. The Mexicans were skilled fighters, however, and by a series of sudden outflanking forays they were able to invest every fortress and eventually capture it. The ceremonial niceties of war were always recognized: before an attack both sides met and terms were offered. Sacrifices and offerings were then made and the chiefs and priests made speeches. There was a code of chivalry in this which insisted on giving fair play to the enemy. Sometimes the negotiations resulted in a surrender which provided a small tribute and a few captives for sacrifice. But if there was a chance of resistance there was usually a battle. Even after a victory the terrible Aztecs would often reduce the demands for maximum tribute. The real grievance, however, which rankled in conquered cities and tribes was the demand of a regular tribute of young men and women for sacrifice.

In many of the negotiations the soft spoken Montezuma had taken a minor part, but people were already beginning to realize that he followed his uncle's policy of vigorous conquest because he believed that after five centuries the ancient *imperium* of the Toltecs would be re-established. However, the young priest must be prepared to fight for the Aztec power. He must help personally by fulfilling his duty as a warrior

in facing danger and bringing back captives for Blue Hummingbird. Only in that way could one be sure of the continued protection of the war god who was also the lord of this world. So Blue Hummingbird must for a time supplant Quetzalcoatl, the Precious Twin, in the mind of the prince.

The steady growth of the Aztec dominion had rendered marches of up to a thousand miles necessary and that made two moons of constant travel. In the mountains it was cold and airless, towards the coast it was humid and oppressive, but all must be endured for the glory of Blue Hummingbird, to whose protection the Aztecs attributed all their present glory.

War was well organized among the peoples of Mexico. In this they resembled the brave warriors of the Plains Indians of North America. There was the same care for formality in challenging and beginning war, the same bands of selected warriors who sought the privilege of being first to touch an enemy, and an even greater determination to seize prisoners for killing later. However, the ceremonial of war and the command structure was much more developed among the Aztecs than among their more primitive cousins on the prairies. Montezuma knew nothing of such comparisons. As far as he was concerned the wars followed strict tradition. He had seen them depicted in ancient pictorial histories, and among the ruined sculptures at holy Tula.

Sometimes the war leader was the Great Speaker in person, but more often he was a great nobleman who had served as Keeper of the Arsenal and who held the curious title of *Ciuacoatl* (serpent woman), referring to his role of provider of food to mother earth who devoured the slain. Under him there were group commanders, youth leaders, and great masses of conscript warriors. Confederate armies from many tribes were usually led by generals of experience who could work together amicably. There were two special orders of warriors, the Ocelot warriors and the Eagles, and these were especially chosen to be members of the two ritual societies. They had to be dedicated to the service of the sun and to be sponsored by warriors of proven valour in the society. Membership gave one a lesser likelihood of surviving in war, but if one recked little of the joys of life and desired to dance with the sun in the heavens for eternity, then the dangers were but golden keys opening the doors of glory. The Ocelot warriors were mainly scouts who usually fought against the flanks of the enemy, and the Eagles were often nobles whose duty was to attack from the centre of the army against the centre of the enemy. The ordinary conscripts engaged in a general mêlée in which one army or the other was gradually pushed back until their losses became too heavy and their leaders came to parley on terms for surrender. Then

Opposite The Fourth Sun, porphyry slab, 4 metres in diameter, which stood at the top of the staircase of the great temple in Cactus Rock. The central mask is the sun god, Tonatiuh, ever burning and thirsting for refreshing blood. Around him is the glyph Olin (movement) which prophesies the end of the present world in a great earthquake.

Around are symbols of days, of the sun rays, and the cosmic serpents. The symbols can be used for calculating solar eclipses.

there were a special group of heroes chosen from the Masters of Cuts – those who had taken in one battle three enemies alive for sacrifice. They were all volunteers and affiliated to the two military orders. They were prepared to take captives alive or to die in the attempt. Many of them died because they carried neither war club nor shield. They rushed into battle naked apart from an open cloak made of strong rope netting. This they hoped to cast over the enemies facing them and then to carry them off. Many of them who were not disabled for life carried the most horrible scars as testimony to their gallantry. They were allowed many social privileges, and indeed were somewhat feared as beings who were dedicated to magic. However, their social prestige and their glory when they joined in the dances before the temples were so great that there was never any lack of young men, especially from the families of noblemen, hoping to be recruited into their ranks. The *macehualli* or commoners were held back by other ties. They had to care for the land by which the people were fed, and they were expected to marry when their period of military service ended. The age for marriage was between about twenty-two and twenty-four, and after they had reached this age they were not recruited for the army except in times of extreme danger.

Montezuma had some part in each of the many wars under the leadership of the brilliant Ahuitzotl. He had joined in the punitive expeditions to western Mexico against the tribespeople who had murdered a company of Aztec merchants, and once he marched to the Atlantic coasts into the warm stony lands near the Maya border. On another occasion he marched towards Guatemala in the hopes of destroying a highland town where another convoy of merchants had been surrounded and threatened with death. Only one of their messengers had been able to slip away into the forests and, guided by stars and well-known mountains, had come with the bad news to Cactus Rock. Montezuma, now a young army commander, prepared to lead the punitive expedition to assert the rights which went with Aztec power.

The journey was a long one lasting perhaps a quarter of the year. With the army went long trails of porters carrying extra weapons, equipment and supplies of dried meat and maize. They also took some trade goods for exchange with the merchants of towns they passed through. Thus they could advance without leaving hostile people behind them. All was well with them as they entered lands beyond the towns which paid tribute to Cactus Rock. This was highland country with a climate like that of their homeland, but the land was more forested and the ground more broken, so that they found it hard work climbing among the ravines. However, they found that stream beds helped them because at that time, before the rainy season, they were relatively dry.

Opposite The goddess Coatlicue, Mother Earth, also the mother of Blue Hummingbird. This was one of a pair of gigantic statues (1.70 metres high) which stood in the courtyard of the great temple. Aztec, 1507. Mother Earth is shown as the lady who gives life in return for suffering and struggle. The skull of the dead refers to those who return from the sunlight to repose within her.

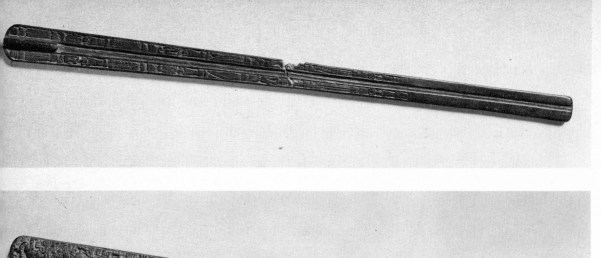

Above Carved and gilded Aztec spear-thrower (Atlatl).

Opposite Montezuma honours warriors with presents of fine clothing. Sahagun's *Historia de las Cosas de Nueva España*.

When they had been in this area for some days, they heard a great shouting in the distance. Immediately the army was on the alert. The Ocelot scouts went forward among the rocks; the mass of the warriors mounted the usual ambush on either side of the path. They were busy tying on sandals, slinging shields into position, and painting their faces. All was done quickly and ·without fuss. The Eagle warriors formed up in full costume, with the war leader Montezuma in their midst, splendid in the full regalia of his order. All of them held their spear throwers ready to launch their bone-headed darts among the advancing enemy. The plan was for the Eagles to advance, and their war shouts would then be echoed from the Ocelots who would have positioned themselves behind the enemy. The main body of warriors would then leap in at the sides, and with any luck a good number of prisoners would be taken in the first assault. All was ready when a couple of the Ocelot warriors ran back with astonishing news: the company advancing was a body of Aztec traders. At once Montezuma led his chiefs forward to give greeting. It was a splendid sight as the gloriously bedecked nobles met the victorious merchants, tired, hungry, wounded, but joyful. Many of them had grown black beards during the long siege they had endured, many were scarred from the fighting. But they had withstood the robbers, seized their town and after a long siege finally sallied out to win a victory with the arms they had found in the enemy town. Now they came with captives and slaves to bring victims for the gods, and to gain wealth in the markets they would pass through in the long journey back to Cactus Rock.

The two groups sat down with the fresh warriors forming a protective screen around them, but they had nothing to fear. There was a great feast, for which the woods in the neighbourhood were almost cleared of game, and long speeches were made by the leaders. But true to their instinct the merchants were mostly engaged in watching the soldiers to see if there would be any opportunities of disposing of the captured weapons for other useful things, such as personal ornaments, which could be exchanged profitably in the markets of the border towns.

Rejoicing in the victory, Montezuma sent his best runners back with the news. An army detachment went with the merchants to see them safely to the first tributary town. The army then swept in a wide arc taking local prisoners from the Quiché towns, and carrying away fine textiles and jade. Many towns were thus brought into subjection.

By the time the soldiers rejoined the merchants, an ample vengeance had been taken. No one in that part of the country would act against merchants or the Mexicans while the memory of that dreadful suffering was alive: villages burnt, the fields robbed, dead men and helpless women left to suffer the plagues which followed. The chiefs who had to organize the payment of tribute told of a young Mexican commander who could read the pictorial records of their scribes and who spoke in a soft

calm voice to the interpreters suggesting that half the wealth of the province must be given to Cactus Rock in honour of the god who had defeated the Quiché. He threatened, still gently, to kill the entire population if they did not submit, and explained that such a death would end in an inglorious after-life in sad Mictlan among the shades. There was no way to avoid his demands. The defeated brought the supplies demanded, and gave a tribute of their own people as slaves to carry back the loot to the distant city of the conquerors. They did attempt to bribe Montezuma by a present of attractive girls, but this austere conqueror said simply that they were not fit to eat and sent them away. The victorious leader warned the chiefs to be punctual each year in sending their tribute to Cactus Rock. Then came a ceremonial leave-taking, very polite on both sides, and the Aztec army went on its way, leaving fear among the ruined villages.

The army had not needed to save the merchants, but they had avenged them. So both parties, rejoicing in the success they had achieved, marched back to their homes. At Tenochtitlan the people flocked out along the western trails to meet the returned heroes. There were sacrifices of captives and prayers chanted at each temple-mound on the way back. They then assembled in the painted courtyard of the great temple of Blue Hummingbird and Tlaloc the Rain God. A million people took part in the rejoicing, dancing and throwing of flowers. As Montezuma was quick to note, the work on the great temple pyramid was now on the point of completion.

As for the merchants, they tied their staves together to form the symbol of their god Yacatecuhtli (He Who Goes Before), and made offerings of their own blood and a few captives. This god demanded a sacrifice of slaves and the merchants gave him the older, worn-out ones. He would restore them in the other world, but meanwhile they were goods bought in honest trading. Then at night when most people were indoors fearing the spirits of the darkness, drumming and singing could be heard coming from the courtyards of the merchants. Behind those plain walls the people knew that fantastic ritual dances were going on. The merchants brought out hidden jewels; they burnt powerful foreign incense before the god and absorbed the fumes until they saw the gods, who appeared as beautiful humans with long and glossy hair. They wore gold and feather insignia that Ahuitzotl had presented them with in honour of their great victory. They listened grimly silent to the accounts sung to them of the expedition, its hardships and victories. Among the merchants the girl slaves were sent to dance. Behind the walls of the houses, which looked so poor, they danced naked except for their adornment of jewels for the pleasure of the guests, who responded and drank rough-ground cocoa as an aphrodisiac to lift them to a higher plane of eroticism. Sexual intercourse took place openly in the sacred courtyard, for the god of the merchants travelled in many lands and was not offended by this breach of Aztec convention. The girls gloried in their possession by the spirit of the great witch-goddess, Tlazolteotl, and took the men in a free embrace which they believed to be divinely inspired. With the adoration of sex, conventions slipped away and the orgy became a holy ecstasy of half-conscious joy in the presence of the gods. But in the

morning an onlooker would have seen the houses dull and drab again. The treasures
had vanished. The image of the god was adorned with fine cloth; a scent of incense
hovered around, and the merchant families and their slaves were very decorously
eating a meal of gruel, before the visitors took to their canoes to paddle back to their
home compounds.

The merchants comprised a special group in Cactus Rock. They were despised by
the nobles because they were not fighting men, but they were the bringers of jewels
and carriers of news, and so they were treated with cautious respect. Montezuma
understood their importance, and he relied on their information. Because he was a
priest he was able to forecast propitious days for their enterprise. He protected the
members of the *Pochteca* (merchants' guild) and the result was an increase of the
materials of trade made available to Cactus Rock as the power of the Aztec armies
spread ever wider throughout the land.

Xochipilli (Flower Prince) god of song and
beauty. Aztec 16th century sculpture.

In the second year of the lord Ahuitzotl the great temple was finished and finally dedicated. A stone slab was erected on the stairway showing the date of the year, *chicuei acatl*, 'eight-reed' (1487 in our calendar) and depicting the image of the sun radiating light while the two Great Speakers of the Aztec nation – Tizoc who commenced the work and Ahuitzotl who completed it – offered blood from their ears. Indeed they did shed blood from their own ears, and no doubt the spirit of Tizoc was with the sun. But Ahuitzotl determined to offer more blood than had ever before been presented to the Sun. He had sent out the armies on a series of campaigns in the mountains of Oaxaca to capture sacrificial victims, and they had been only too successful. Two Mixtec tribes were practically exterminated, for every grown man was made prisoner and destined for sacrifice.

At the announcement of the occasion the allied chiefs of Tezcoco and Tlacopan had been invited to the celebration of the feast of the War God of Cactus Rock. They came, but Nezahualpilli, King of Tezcoco and a wise man like his father Nezahualtoyotl, told the Aztec Speaker that so enormous a sacrifice was not necessary. The magical number was twenty, and that was the right number to offer the gods; but Ahuitzotl was offering them a thousand times that number. To offer so many

Right A man of the Aztecs, carving with no attributes, probably Ixtlilton the lieutenant of Blue Hummingbird.

Below The steps of the Aztec temple of Teopanzolco. After sacrifice the cadavers were thrown down the steps to soften them for cutting up for ritual eating.

prisoners, the whole manpower of two tribes, was to offer the destruction of men to the god, to drench him in blood and yet not to nourish him or bring happiness to the people. Montezuma was of the same opinion but being a minor prince he did not openly question his uncle. Nevertheless he knew that the books enjoined the offering of sacrifices in small numbers, and that there was no precedent for a holocaust on such a scale. It seemed only too clear that the popular Ahuitzotl would follow his own path without thinking of the consequences, for nothing moved the Great Speaker. To him this year *chicuei acatl* was a time for a great demonstration of warlike power. He had no knowledge that fate was moving and that in Spain Hernando Cortes was now three years old and that the Genoese Christopher Columbus was pushing ahead with his plan to sail round the world. In these people the Other was to manifest itself against the powers that Ahuitzotl was arousing.

There was a great rejoicing in Mexico that the god was to be honoured so splendidly. This was a double occasion for the War God and for Tlaloc, the Lord of Water, who shared the same temple. It began in song and sunshine. The people came to celebrate and thank their god for victories. At eight temples the sacrificing priests worked hard slashing the hearts out of the victims as they moved up in slow queues one at a time. The blood sang to the gods, and the noble skull racks were filled. The people were gorged on human flesh, and the animals in the zoological gardens were filled with bones and offal. The god accepted the sacrifices, as the priests, weary and drunk with the smell of fresh blood saw visions. But in other places people questioned fate. The tribes who were forced to pay tribute to Cactus Rock trembled for fear that all their men might also be slain one day. The outlying people were terrified of being brought into the Aztec military machine. A chill settled on the soul of Mexico. This was the greatest triumph of the demonic Blue Hummingbird. So the bodies accumulated and the Great Speaker ordered the unwanted carcasses to be thrown into the lake. The gods had their fill but mankind could not devour men at such a rate. It is said that even the ever-watchful *zopilotes* were gorged and could not clear away the carrion. So great was the glory of this occasion, so splendid the offering, that the Aztecs were sure of blessings, but they were a little shaken by their excess. Montezuma was concerned. He did not know what would come from a king usurping the privileges of the gods, and turning them into propaganda for terror.

The great sacrifice alienated many tribes and roused among them fear and hatred for the Mexicans. There had always been an acceptance of war and sacrifice, for it was the normal process of life. History showed the growth of powerful cities which achieved widespread dominion and then collapsed. But people who were not Aztecs nor of the confederation wondered if they would ever have a chance of revolt. It seemed that nothing could topple the power of the Aztec Great Speaker.

So, secure in their belief that the gods had accepted the sacrifices, the Aztecs continued on their traditional path.

7

THE PRINCE AT HOME

MONTEZUMA WAS AT ONE remove from ordinary life because of his social eminence. As a child he had naturally been protected from ordinary contacts with the mass of the people of the city. As a young man his schooling had been in the temple and training colleges. He had, of course, seen much of Cactus Rock, and knew the way of life of its citizens, who after all were his fellow tribespeople, but apart from ceremonial occasions he had little opportunity of mixing with them. In his day the Mexican way of life was far removed from the primitive democracy of an American Indian hunting tribe, though some of the Aztec customs had obvious connections with that long-past way of life. Montezuma was living in a powerful city state which had imposed its will on a great part of Mexico. It received tribute from subjugated tribes who could be numbered only as many millions of people.

Since the time, three generations before Montezuma, when the people had surrendered their democratic rights into the hands of three leading warrior families, this ruling oligarchy had become an elective monarchy. The holder of the ultimate controlling power, the Great Speaker, had, however, to combine the sometimes conflicting claims of the other three chief administrators in the ruling Council of Four, the High Priest, the Supervisor of Markets and the Chancellor or *Ciuacoatl*. Other high administrative posts were held by members of the ruling family, of which the most important was that of supervisor of the national arsenal and of military training, and all military commanders were approved by the Great Speaker and the Council. Since it was the obligation of the Great Speaker to marry several wives in order to cement diplomatic friendships with other tribes and since most members of the ruling family had two or three official wives, it was almost as if the ruling family was a tribe within a tribe. They divided themselves into groups called *calpulli* according to their descent: the people also were divided into *calpulli* but these were determined by which quarter of the city they lived in.

Montezuma was one of a great many young people who were descended from former Great Speakers of the Aztecs, but he was of the ruling group and so separated from the great body of the people. As a young military man he had a fairly large house built on a stone platform two layers of stone above ground level. It was by no means a palace, although it was carefully built and limewashed until it shone. The lintels were painted red in contrast. Inside it was dark and cool, with mats on the floor and paintings on the plaster of the walls. The furniture was simple: some wooden chests and a sleeping mat with a cotton coverlet. Since he was not a commoner he was allowed to sit on a small circular cushion, and not on the floor. Family slaves were responsible for cleaning and cooking his simple meals.

Most Precious Flower (Xochiquetzal) goddess of the flowering surface of the earth. Basalt carving. Aztec, 16th century.

In effect his small house and garden patch was an apartment in the huge complex of buildings which made up the palace square of Ahuitzotl. However, Montezuma was often away, sometimes performing priestly duties of ritual sacrifices and dances, sometimes on far-away expeditions with the army. As the power of the Aztecs expanded, the distances to be covered by the army continually increased. Everywhere they journeyed on foot. It was his army service that acquainted Montezuma with the geography of Mexico. He knew the rivers, mountains and the coasts of the seas, and made note of the temples and gods who inhabited them. To him all this beautiful land was alive. It was the mother of mankind, and its clouds sheltered the rain spirits which brought fertility.

On the mountains were the sacred abodes of the gods, but it was in the sky that the gods had their homes. His knowledge widened as he studied the forms of clouds, and the kinds of rain. The rainbow and the dust devil had a message. Mexico was indeed a mother to Montezuma and as his learning increased, his reverence for the divinity of the earth grew.

In the years of his early manhood he was an optimistic prince, looking always for victory, secure in the patronage of the two deities, his relative Quetzalcoatl, the lord of the breath of life, and his master Blue Hummingbird. He knew that the balance of his life would alter, that Blue Hummingbird would desert him and the wise Morning Star would be closer to his innermost heart. But what was the fate of the earthly Quetzalcoatl? To have to abandon his power, step by step? But as yet Montezuma had not been given power and he had little inkling of the kind of power that the Council might assign to him.

By the time that Montezuma was in his early twenties it was the wish of his uncle the Great Speaker that, as befitted a nobleman, he should marry. Naturally Montezuma had thought of this step in life. He was not supposed to know who the family had chosen for him, but already he was prepared with a knowledge of possible young princesses who were of good Toltec ancestry. He felt that no other would do for him and there was no doubt that Ahuitzotl had similar ideas. It was now quite obvious that the ruling clan of the Aztecs as a whole was determined to emulate the Toltec rulers, and that its members had deliberately sought divine sanction by forging as many links with the ancestors in Tula as possible. This was done by marriage, so that each suc-ceeding prince had more Toltec blood than those who went before him. This might have eventually alienated people and rulers but, apart from an occasional food riot in bad years, there had never been any open division. Perhaps the Tezcocans felt that their greater claims to Toltec descent should be more regarded, but they had to submit to being junior partners in the alliance because the less cultured Aztecs were clever politicians and militarily powerful.

Montezuma was delighted to hear that the marriage brokers had been sent by his uncle to consult a noble family about the lady Tezalco, who by any count was beautiful. Poets had described her as the 'gliding jewel' of the palace. She was of ancient lineage and being of the ruling clan was not unknown to Montezuma, nor he to her. But all

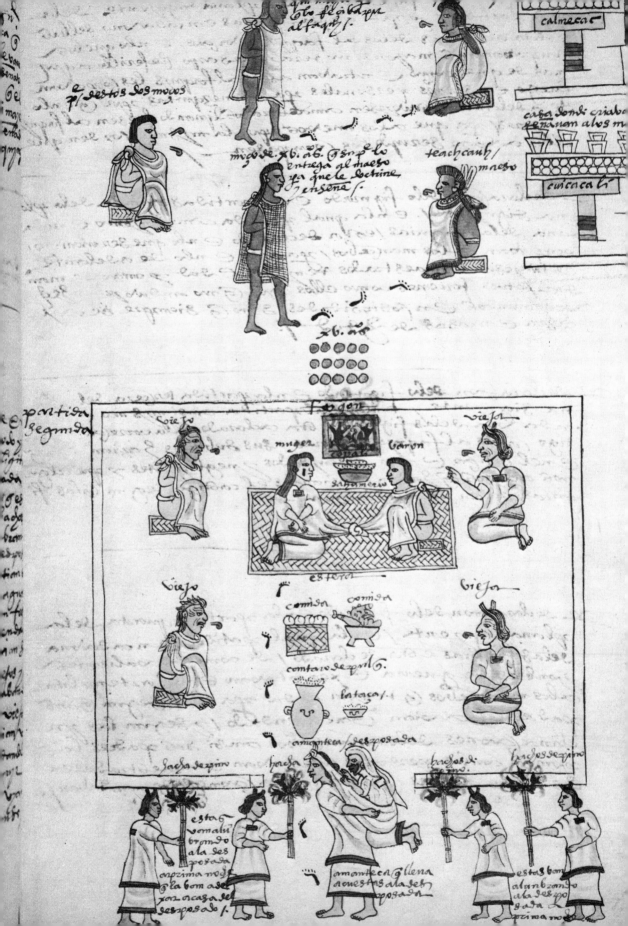

the proper rituals had to be conducted. Montezuma no doubt would have preferred to be married under the ancient Toltec custom, in spite of the discomfort of being sat naked with the bride under a mat which was then drenched with cold water!

However, the Aztec ceremony prevailed, for this was very binding in form and in fact. The occasion of Montezuma's marriage was naturally a festival. The amount of gifts on either side had been discussed by the marriage brokers, and these were now on display: heaps of finely embroidered clothes, jewels, feather-work, and tools for gardening and weaving. There were frothing bowls of *pulque* for the older guests, and scented juices for the younger. Meat, spices, maize, tamales and tortillas were being prepared by the servants of the family, all working together and singing as they worked. The hall in the palace was prepared with special mats and a low bench for the young couple. All around were the round cushions for the noble witnesses and a throne backed with glittering turquoise for the lord Ahuitzotl himself. Priests were there, not to make the marriage but to call blessings on the young couple. In the centre Montezuma sat alone and uncertain, hopeful that now he would achieve a new social status. He was aware of the strict Aztec laws which would tie him irrevocably to the service of the Wife of the Mat (that is, the principal wife) who would soon be placed beside him.

There was music and singing outside, the rattles were sounding a slow dance rhythm. Then came a procession of young women carrying torches, all looking straight in front of them with expressionless faces, taking tiny steps so that they seemed to glide; next, a powerful woman accompanied by the elderly marriage brokers. On her back the large lady carried a slender bundle wrapped in fine white cotton and secured by a broad strap across her forehead. She approached Montezuma and kneeling slowly she released the binding and revealed the Princess Tezalco. She was wearing her glistening black hair in a long, loose tress down her back; her face was painted yellow with a red flower on either cheek. Her clothes were of spotless white, embroidered in jewel-like colours. She wore the most gorgeous ornaments of which the chief were large golden ear-rings with pendant bells, and the jade and shell-encrusted ornament which, hanging from the septum of her nose, swung over her lips. There were necklets and armbands, flowers and scent so that she seemed a veritable garden of flowers. Her husband to be was worthy in her eyes too. His face was painted black except for the two yellow bands which denoted his worship of Blue Hummingbird. His head-dress was a bandeau with the two crane feathers of the Aztec warrior, while his hair was in a tuft on top tied with a red leather cord. In his lower lip there was a simple stud of translucent obsidian. His ear-rings shone with symbols of

Opposite Aztec life. Above: young men going to their training colleges, above for priests, below for warriors. The age is 15 years. Below: a high-class marriage. The bride is carried into the house with four married women as sponsors. The young people are married in the silent presence of the fire god by knotting their garments together. At the feast the relatives make speeches. *Codex Mendoza.*

the sun, and his loincloth was embroidered with hummingbird feathers to show the symbols of the god Quetzalcoatl. The wiry strength of his torso and the elegance of his thin features were set off by necklet and armlets. His body was also stained a bluish-black because he was a priest, and from his ears there hung drops of dried blood which showed that he had offered a little pain to the morning star that morning. Over his shoulders a cloth was draped for that special occasion. The noble relatives came into the hall and sat according to their rank. They were dressed accordingly. The High Priest made a long speech on the sanctity of marriage; the bride's grandmother did likewise. They were couched in the classical poetic style of the Aztecs, full of similes and parables. The young couple felt intensely honoured that such perfect language should be uttered on their behalf. Then came the moment of marriage; the old lady who had been marriage broker tied the girl's cape to the cloth around the shoulders of the groom. The symbolic joining of lives was thus made in all solemnity.

Then the music broke out: small drums, flutes, rattles and conch shells made rhythmic harmonies and the singers, lifting their heads high, sang out the honours of the pair and declaimed the poems wishing good for the future. Next came more speeches; relatives of either side came to praise the young people and delight in the alliance between the families. Bride and bridegroom sat steadily through the hours of

Painted pottery drinking cup from a high-class
household. Aztec Mexico, after 1507.

speeches, bowing from time to time as they recited short verses of gratitude and acceptance. For everybody there the long sessions of poetic speech were the greatest pleasure of the occasion. Montezuma gently lifted his nosegay of small bright flowers to smell the lower end, and hoped the butterflies might come to perch on the top, for they might incarnate the souls of his father and the ancestors. He noticed a beautiful black one come to his wife Tezalco, and thought of the Toltec ancestors, perhaps of the priestly Quetzalcoatl.

The musicians continued with gayer rhythms as the formal speeches ended. Food was brought by the slaves and offered by the younger members of the family. All had maize and spiced tamales, turkey with mole sauces, and wonderful sweetmeats of fruit and honey. For drink, there was herb-flavoured water and honey, and to the delight of Montezuma, his uncle the Great Speaker brought them lacquered gourd bowls filled with frothed and spiced cocoa. They knew it was an aphrodisiac, but it was also a scarce and valuable drink which only nobles could afford. They drank it through wide drinking straws of gold.

At last the speeches and poetry were over. The musicians were sent to the royal guest rooms to entertain the visitors there. Montezuma and his bride put aside the knotted capes and parted for their three days of meditation before the consummation of the wedding.

Eventually they were brought together again and the women declared Tezalco to be a virgin. The priests declared that their young prince had led a good religious life abstaining from women. So the couple were placed on their sleeping mat and a sheet was laid over them. Tezalco knew well that young warriors were given the duty to have intercourse with the serving girls, and she had heard how modestly the young chief had conducted himself. She was pleased and yet a little afraid. But soon she learnt that his experience had taught him to be gentle as well as strong. As he took her she felt the steady pressure and sudden pain, then a wild delight seized them both until after only a minute or so they both surged together in total forgetfulness. It was the delight of life for Tezalco and for Montezuma a moment free from all he had known, a kind of wordless consummation of happiness. Then folding the stained cloth they had lain on, Tezalco gave it to her maid for display at the feast that evening. Now she would need to have no baskets broken. For in those days if a girl was not a virgin, the young man would arrange for festival tortillas to be given to the guests in baskets which had no bottom and which therefore dropped the food on their laps. The girl would be disgraced, and her family made to pay compensation and take her away. However, many a young man in such a predicament would cut his penis and add some blood for love and honour.

For the ordinary Aztec, marriage would mean the end of military service, but for the nobles it meant a higher degree of social responsibility. War was never ending for the dedicated servants of Blue Hummingbird, even though, like Montezuma, they were also priests of other gods. His fate was not that of the *macegualli* who dug the family plot, carved the furniture and decorated gourds. He must do greater things,

Above The young water goddess, Lady
Precious Green (Chalchihuitlicue) as a bride.
Aztec, 16th century.

Opposite Statue of Huehueteotl (the Old, Old
God) Lord of Fire. The patron of the home
and of childbirth. Aztec, 16th century.

even beyond his knowledge of religious ceremonial. Yet each year he must take part
in one day of ceremonial tilling of the land. He and his wife must share in the breaking
of ground in the fields which were allocated for their upkeep by the Council. So with
digging stick and seed bag they planted a few token maize hills to the music which
always accompanied Ahuitzotl through his years as Great Speaker. He too went to
the fields with his relatives and as the bards sang his praises and called on the maize
god to bless Mexico, he dug his plot of ground and piled the first maize hill.

In his home life Ahuitzotl was a sybarite, and no doubt Montezuma wondered at
the royal extravagance of the palace. It became ever more elaborate and beautiful.
The gardens had more scented flowers than had ever been seen in Cactus Rock before,

124

the painters decorated the walls and the palace women made beautiful wall-hangings and rugs. There was always music in the building and the sound of trickling water. There were always women too, beautifully painted, and many of them wearing only skirts, as twelve-year-old girls did, or with short versions of the *quechquemitl* (poncho) which revealed their dark nipples whenever they lifted their arms. It was a palace of sweet scents too, for the ceilings were of cedar, and incense of many kinds was burned. It was a paradise, a deliberate attempt to create an earthly kingdom for Tlaloc, the God of all sources of water, and his consort, the ever-youthful lady 'Precious Green'. Yet in all the happiness, and echoed too in the poetry, was the Aztec sense of impermanence before the powers of nature. There was fear also, for Ahuitzotl was much given to killing and omitted nothing from the sacrificial rituals. His reign was a long catalogue of captures of towns and sacrifices of inhabitants. His army commanders did most of the fighting, but the Great Speaker was not above campaigning in person. He was a brave man, and a poet, yet for all that his name remains a synonym for cruelty even to this day.

For Montezuma the reign of his youngest uncle was a happy period. He was in contact with priests and seers and at the same time the young chief was involved in many of the war expeditions sent out by his uncle. In 1489 there was an expedition into Guatemala. The chronicles simply tell us that prisoners were brought back for sacrifice. We can wonder how the army endured the long journey on foot over the mountains and back, a round trip of three thousand miles. In 1491 and 1492 there were wars in which the Tlahuica and the people of Uexotzinco were conquered. In 1493 the wars against the Mixtecs and Zapotecs continued. The capital city and magical heart of the Zapotec nation fell when Mitla was captured in 1494. In 1495 and 1496 Aztec power continued to expand, and encompassed the rich mining country to the east. But on 8 August 1496 the warriors trembled and dwarfs and cripples were sacrificed because of the eclipse of the sun. To Montezuma this was a portent. He feared that the earthquake of the previous year had been a preliminary sign of divine anger. Even earlier in the reign of Ahuitzotl there had been mysteries from the sky. In the winter of 1489 the agave crops had been damaged in a sudden snowfall, and hail had beaten down the maize. There was a great hunger after these events. But in the next year a strange comet shone in the sky, a *xiuhcoatl* with a long trail, the fire serpent in the heavens. For the Aztecs it might warn that the drought had reached its height, but for the Zapotecs it had a sinister meaning, for it heralded the first skirmishes that were to lead to the destruction of their power after fifteen centuries of independence. To us it would have been Père Pingre's comet on one of its periodic visits to the skies of earth.

However, the wise young man and his beautiful wife continued to rise to high position. Prowess as a warrior gave Montezuma much honour, and he had slain his captives and ceremonially wept for them in his position as a sacrificing priest. But it was his reputation for learning linked with wisdom which determined his rise to ever higher military commands. Soon after he was thirty he became Leader of Men, that is to say, Army Commander-in-Chief. His wife knew that it was a dangerous post, but as a princess she valued his high honour. It meant that he might build a palace for them and have many servants and slaves. At first they had one sorrow because although they had a happy sexual relationship, there were as yet no children. However, eventually Tezalco found herself pregnant. At last they were to have a child. When it proved to be a girl they felt no disappointment. On the fourth day she was named Tecuichpo, and Montezuma consulted her horoscope in the book of fate and found to his surprise that she would have many husbands and would be filled with good fortune. How such a break with Aztec custom could come about was beyond him.

With power and influence Montezuma was able to have a small palace built on a hill slope overlooking Tula. This was his dream world, a place near the palace of his ancestors. It was two full days' marching to get there and in those bare plains it was of little use as a summer refuge. The main summer palace was near Cholula in the forests

Gourd drinking cup, lacquered red inside and with yellow sacred symbols still faintly discernible on the black lacquered exterior.

The silver mounts are of Spanish origin in the style of the early 16th century. This is probably a drinking vessel of Montezuma.

beyond the mountains and volcanoes. There indeed was a place of refuge from the overheated summer. The air was heavier, but the flowers spread scent and colour everywhere. Birds were brighter and the sky was often deep blue even in the rainy season. Near Cholula was peace and beauty. Only war could call Montezuma away from his family in that simple summer palace. For him it was a delight to be near the temple of Quetzalcoatl, his great ancestor. Sometimes he ascended the stairways and crossed sacred courtyards to the houses of the priests where he was always welcome. There, sitting with his companions, he was free to talk of the nature of the gods and the mysteries of their manifestations. He envied their peace, but as he rose in rank he realized that he must also suffer as an earthly king, just as Quetzalcoatl did. Maybe one day the god would return as he had promised. There were days ahead when such should be a possibility. Once more in his lifetime he knew there would be the conjunction of days which would bring about the gateway of time through which the god might appear. He knew that he himself would not be the coming divinity, for he, as a great army leader, must be the servant of the Blue Hummingbird. How he envied the sanctity of the priests which brought them close to the gods and lifted them to ecstasy. But as he had a double destiny he made the best of it. In the palace he would play with

127

tequihua

tequihua

tequihua

tequihua

mezquita

tianguez

lugar de
mercado/ casa

casa

casa

tequihua

esta partida
es el pu del
aji q̃ de atras
contengo q̃ fue
en plaza de
guerra por ser
rebelde al ge
nero de mex/
las figuras delos
tequihua/ significa
ser enbiados por
el s. de mex̃ a este
pueblo y a los qpaseen de rio descultamete
batalla/ y esten los guerreros ypiaticos/ del pu y
esto tres son vasallos del cacique

mexicano

todelas

valiente

valiente

valiente

tlacateca tl̃

tlaxcalcalcotl̃

qujtzicuoipamatl̃

the children, and laugh with real happiness. There in the family was his real refuge from the battles and the storm of events, his protection against some monstrous cyclone that was impending. Sometimes he went away alone except for a few servants to burn incense and pray in Tula, proud and yet half afraid of the ancestors who had fallen victims to Blue Hummingbird. Very occasionally in that mysterious place of sadness he was disturbed by the fact that he could see right through Mexico. He knew it was part of some larger scheme, that there were empty places in his heart where unfathomable mysteries lurked. He could never explain it even to himself.

But he was never absent from Cactus Rock for long because at any time he might need to come to the Council, or receive news that his uncle had decreed that the army should march. Then he would hasten back to the lakeside palace in Cactus Rock which was now his home. To return there he must travel now on other men's feet, because the Commander must be suitably carried by teams of bearers, while he sat upright under his canopies of feathers. He carried his arms, and the shield showing the coils of a warrior's fate which represented the contrast between victory and the pit of destruction. This journey took a full day because he was carried by relays of runners. As they reached the last trail from the northern hills they saw the great lake, surrounded by towns. Far away to the south were the volcanoes with their white hoods. Across the lake ran the great causeway and several subsidiary roads leading to the white and red houses, and the great courtyards in which stood temples and palaces. Such was the beauty of Cactus Rock that it was never forgotten by anyone who had seen it in the days of its splendour.

Between the towns the Commander was escorted by soldiers. When he reached the lake they spread mats before him as he strode through the mud to the gold-plated eagle-canoe. The paddlers began a chant as they passed along under bridges in the causeways and into the outskirts of the city where new houses were being built on the newly reclaimed areas. Everywhere cypresses draped with moss guarded the growing fringes of the town. People on the paths beside the canal stopped to see who was moving so quickly. Some stopped and bowed, touching the earth and putting a little dust on their foreheads as they recognized the sign of the great man in the canoe. He was a popular commander, well regarded because he was wise and just. Eventually the canoe turned into a narrower passage between houses near the great temple. They pulled up at the steps to his palace and were welcomed by the family who stood and bowed their heads until he had passed beyond the curtains which did duty for doors in Cactus Rock.

Opposite The Council of Four, including Montezuma, decide on war. After a battle around the market place *(tianguez)* they destroy the enemy temple. Below: the great war leaders of the Aztec nation. They are led by the army commander whose shield is now preserved in Stuttgart. *Codex Mendoza*.

Overleaf The Valley of Mexico today. When the Spaniards first saw it from this point the air was clear and the whole of the flat area was occupied by the Lake of the Moon in which stood the shining city of Cactus Rock with other cities around the shores.

The reason for one particular return from Tula was a new one. Ahuitzotl was planning to rebuild parts of Cactus Rock, and the army was required to assist in clearing old buildings and bringing new stones for reconstruction. The stone was to come as tribute from several cities, and the army would have to provide escorts for the teams of labourers dragging stones over rollers along the paths to Cactus Rock. The nobles were called to the palace of the Great Speaker and there they stood around the plans which were drawn on sheets of soft maguey paper. Cloths were brought in to show the routes for the transport of stones. Estimates of numbers of men needed were discussed and the scribes recorded them on rolls. Montezuma was able to check their work easily for he was one of the best trained of the Mexican rulers. He was glad to participate in this plan to beautify the city, and happy too that it was linked with the opening of the new wells the previous year in towns to the south of the lake. He knew that Ahuitzotl wished to draw the whole city into closer unity so that the towns with the new water supply, though still with independent councils, were becoming almost lakeside suburbs of Cactus Rock (they are now suburbs of Mexico City). It all combined to make Cactus Rock a more glorious place, befitting its historical claim to be the successor of Tula.

Left Lady Precious Green, seated in a more mature aspect. She is the wife of Tlaloc, Lord of all waters, and herself has command of whirlpools and sudden storms.

Opposite The Quetzalcoatl of Tula. Excavated from the burnt palace at Toltec Tula. This image is made from a mosaic of shell. One of the traditional palaces of Quetzalcoatl was known as the House of Shell. 7th to 9th century.

Overleaf The flower gardens of Cactus Rock still flourish at Xochimilco. The rich soil taken from the bottom of the canals in the ancient lake bed forms a top dressing which produces fine crops. The streets of Cactus Rock were originally similar canals.

While the work was still in its early stages another strange portent occurred. Suddenly the volume of water from the new wells to the south of the lake increased. Streams overflowed, the water became hot and steamed. Then there were earth tremors, the water of the great lake became a milky white and the small whirlpools through which the lake drained its surplus water were now spinning and raging as if Lady Precious Green was dancing in a frenzy. The powers of earth and water were disturbed. The lake rose as if it intended to destroy the growing island of Cactus Rock in its waters. Great waves rose without the help of the wind and hurled themselves on the causeway which served as an embankment protecting the city from storm waves. The wall was breached in several places and the waters surged through the suburbs. Many foundations were undermined and the houses collapsed. The disturbance lasted less than a month. Suddenly the winds rose from the mountains and blew over the raging lake, they mounted high and burst in a tremendous thunderstorm. When the storm died down the lake had returned to normal, except that the waves came lapping through the breached wall into the city.

There were prayers and special sacrifices, for people were not sure which of the gods had caused this strange windless storm. They thought that it must have come from the water deities, Tlaloc and his wife Lady Precious Green: but they were the specially loved deities of Ahuitzotl himself. Perhaps the storm was a magical blessing and the city would arise even more wonderful when the repairs were made. Ahuitzotl made no comment, but he came personally to the broken walls and rolled great stone blocks with his own hands to patch the breaches. Then came a time of organizing the regular labour gangs of the people of Cactus Rock. Each section of the town gave its quota of men and food, while from all around towns and villages sent contributions. Some were sent from admiration, some from fear, but the redesigning of large parts of Cactus Rock was well under way. About this time, in the town of Painalla, a town in Soconusco, a baby girl was born. She was the daughter of the town chief, the first child of her mother. The land where she was born was Mexican but far from Cactus Rock. The child was born on a day *Ce Malinalli* (which means One, Grass of Penance) which doomed her to an association with dark magic. But there were other circumstances, such as the name of the year and the ascendance of the evening star, which showed that she would come into disastrous conflict with Blue Hummingbird. It was accordingly decided by the priests that such an ill-omened child must be destroyed. However, her mother loved her and secretly changed her for the dead child of a slave girl. The real Ce Malinalli was brought up in Soconusco and later sent to live safely among the Maya peoples. There she was well liked and was attached to the court of a Maya leader who ruled this corner of the swampy mouth of the Usumacinta river.

Opposite Golden pendant representing the sun god in his radiant disc flying through the heavens.

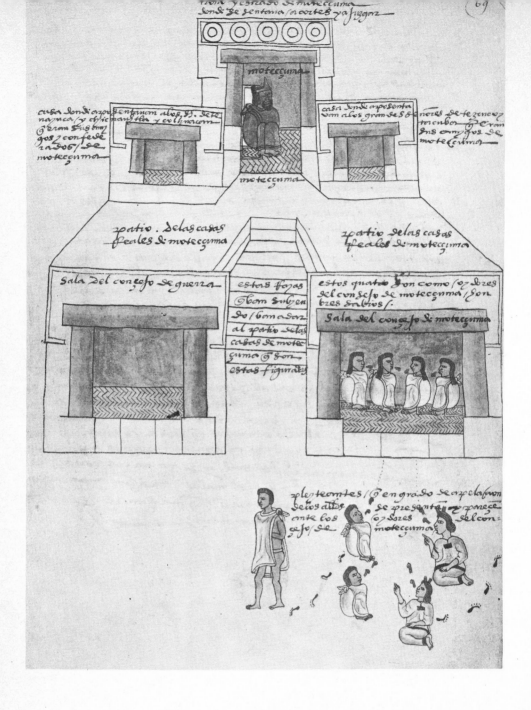

Above The Palace of Montezuma. The Great
Speaker sits above as final Lord of Appeal.
Below: his four judges discuss the legal
implications of a matrimonial suit in dispute
in the courtyard. *Codex Mendoza.*

Opposite left Pottery vase in the form of a
warrior's head, wearing the barred face paint
of Blue Hummingbird. Aztec polychrome,
16th century.

Opposite right Painted pottery jug, for cacao.
Aztec, after 1507.

But the people of Painalla knew nothing of this; and when the messengers came from Mexico for the annual tribute, they quite willingly sent a group of labourers to help in the carting of stones on the paths to Cactus Rock.

The great city was now growing very populous indeed. More than a million inhabitants were kept busy and cared for, but to do this successfully meant great increases in the tribute demanded from subject provinces. It was impossible to cultivate the land around the lake more intensively because agricultural methods in those days demanded that two fields out of every three should lie fallow to regain their fertility. So it was necessary for the welfare of the Aztecs to obtain vast quantities of tribute from the conquered cities. The limitations of the convoys of merchants trading by a primitive system of barter prevented the importation of great quantities of food by means of trade. In fact the merchants were concerned more with the exchange of prestige and luxury products. The trade in the market for fruit and grain was merely local. People could add to the household menu there by simple exchange, perhaps of pottery or cloth for extra fruit. Hence the arrival of trains of tributaries bringing their loads of grain, cloth and meat was more important than the jewels and feathers which made such a splendid show. Once a year and in any special time of disaster the Great Speaker sat in public at the doorway to the palace, and supervised the distribution of foodstuffs and clothing to the people. Exact records were kept by the scribes, and the amount of reserves and the expected income to the stores were always precisely known.

This became more important after the flood disaster in Cactus Rock. There was want, and there was work. So the stores were opened to give food while people went to work, each at his trade, to help the rebuilding. Rafts of wicker were made and covered with stones so that they sank in the lake mud as foundations for more mats above

water which were covered with fertile soil dredged from the lake bed. On each garden patch made in this way a wooden hut was built, which would be replaced with a stone house once all had settled down firmly. The walls across the lake were straightened and strengthened.

The subject nations were far from peaceful at the beginning of the sixteenth century. In particular in the northeast the Huaxteca had not settled down. They were treated too often as if they were slaves, and they resented it. But Montezuma himself felt especially grieved when the people and priests of Cholula revolted. They controlled the holy house of Quetzalcoatl and he was deeply reluctant to attack a place to which he was so attached. However, as an Aztec prince of the highest rank, he could not but be gratified when the victims were brought to the sacrificial stone as an offering of the defeated rebels.

Montezuma was now a person of great importance. He had overall control of the army, and so in the course of any year he could expect to be away on at least one campaign to bring new towns into subjection or to punish those who revolted. His home was now a considerable palace, peopled with a large household of slaves and officials. There was still the small palace at Tula as a refuge for meditation, and he was still expected to act as a sacrificing priest of high rank at all festivals for the military orders. The rise in social rank entitled him to take more wives, and he chose the princess Acatlan, Beside the Reeds, so named because of her gentleness like the soft breezes swaying the reeds. To Montezuma she was important because she was of impeccable Toltec descent. The beautiful Tezalco and Acatlan remained for the rest of Montezuma's life the only wives who had the honour of being 'married on the mat'. Tezalco and her children were not disturbed by the advent of another wife. It was proof that her husband had attained the highest rank, unlike the common people who were restricted to one wife alone. The two households were in one palace, but each wife had her own servants and rooms so that it was possible for them to be on friendly terms.

The whole palace quarter of the city was rather like a centre for one enormous extended family. The cousins of Montezuma were numerous, and his brothers and sisters were very dear to him. In fact some of them were to influence his destiny in no uncertain manner, but in the year 1502 all seemed settled and the endemic wars were accepted as natural events. The people of Cactus Rock were busy refurbishing their beautiful city. Every twentieth day there came a festival of sacrifice and processional dances. Song was everywhere.

But suddenly and unexpectedly a great disaster happened. The lord Great Speaker Ahuitzotl went in his carrying throne one day to inspect the work on the great storm barrier on the lake. He walked with the architects discussing the works, and, as he ventured to the edge, his golden sandal slipped on a stone. He fell only the height of a man but those who rushed to him saw that he had struck the back of his head against the angle of a great stone. He murmured a little when they came to lift him and bear him to the palace. In three days a great cry went up: the lord Ahuitzotl was dead.

At once plans were made for his funeral: the stone casket engraved with his name was filled with his ashes and fragments of cremated bones. It was a grand ceremony, solemn and beautiful, and the Aztecs lamented their brave fierce king who had loved women and music so dearly. The family council was again called; again, hundreds of speeches were made. At forty-one Montezuma might have considered himself too old for power but the choice was not his to make, and the family council of the Aztec nation chose him to be Great Speaker and to wear the turquoise mitre. Thus the way was opened for his dream of another Tula and an empire of Toltec glory to come.

Opposite The stone lid of the bone-box which contained the ashes of the Great Speaker Ahuitzotl. The carving gives his name.

8

THE MIGHTY LORD

THE CHANGE IN MONTEZUMA'S way of life was total. He was now an elected ruler, at the same time an autocrat and, as it were, the chairman of the Council of Four who were the supreme rulers of the country. Even in the Council he was the chief authority. All his training had fitted him to rule and he knew that from his birth he had been predestined to this fate. As a war leader he had seen all the Mexican lands, as a priest he had held high position and was revered as a great philosopher and seer, and as a leader responsible for military logistics he knew of the regulations of merchants and markets throughout Anahuac. The Great Speaker of the all-conquering Aztecs was now conscious of a wider responsibility. He was in truth a descendant of the god-king Quetzalcoatl and felt his duty now lay in protecting his people, in promoting their happiness and ancient culture, in encouraging trade and in unifying commands throughout the country. He was now ruler of a multi-national state, and accordingly increased the corps of interpreters attached to his palace. He listened to the complaints of the oppressed, and sent messengers to make contact with outlying peoples. But because of his assumption of Toltec royal status he was necessarily the more angered at any defiance of his authority. Hence a number of punitive expeditions against towns which had rejected Aztec rule were conducted with a cold ruthlessness which made him many enemies.

In his home life also everything altered. His two wives and children were as dear to him as ever, but they now had to prepare to live in a new palace, and to admit new women to the household. The chronicles talk of a thousand wives, but probably we should say some hundreds of princesses were given a rank as subsidiary wives to the Great Speaker. This was not only the custom, of which Ahuitzotl had made an outstanding example, but also a matter of diplomacy, so that every family and tribe of any importance had a blood relative in the Aztec ruling family. What this meant to the religious and priestly Montezuma is not clear. All was within proper conformity to Aztec customary law, which gave the Great Speaker an unlimited number of wives

Opposite A young fertility goddess, from the Totonac people of Vera Cruz. Note the headcloth arranged to protect the neck, and the topless dress which also indicated the heat of the Gulf Coast of Mexico.

yet imposed the most puritanical standards of monogamy on the mass of the people. Even the great nobles were not allowed more than three wives, but the ruler was not only forced to add a vast harem to his family but also was regarded as a kind of earthly divinity who dispensed life to his people. It is quite clear that Montezuma made use of these women, since we hear of the palace filled with children of all ages. Yet the junior wives were never promoted to become the Wives of the Mat. The first wives of the great ruler remained the first ladies of the whole extended *imperium*.

As ever, the priestly Montezuma kept up many of the penitential customs of his youth. He fasted, and every morning sacrificed quails at sunrise; at great festivals he slew a victim as sacrificing priest. His new duties as Great Speaker included a watch on the skies, and at sunset, midnight and sunrise he was to be found alone on the roof of his palace observing the signs of the future in the heavens. The simple prophecies derived from the calendar were no longer sufficient for the leader of the nation. The only great augurs were the high priests whose two gods dwelt in solitary splendour in the two houses at the top of the great temple pyramid. But they had auguries of magic on the one hand and fertility on the other. Montezuma was the proper recipient of historical warnings from the gods. He therefore watched their planets and stars marching slowly through the world of night. The stars marked their habitations in the sky, the planets showed the gods moving through the houses of fate. Where was there a cloud? What was to be seen of the zodiacal light? How was faithful Popocatepetl behaving? Where were the shooting stars darting? Look for the burning meteor, did it mean the same as the long-tailed slow comet?

All these things were noted, and probably Montezuma would know them so well that he hardly needed the words in his mind to classify them. It is too easy to say that Montezuma's policy was just an empirical reliance on astrology but there is evidence that it was indeed closely linked with star watching. In particular the rhythm of the planet Venus was of vital importance to Montezuma because he believed quite sincerely that Venus as morning star was the heavenly heart of his earthly ancestor the divine lord Quetzalcoatl. There can be no doubt that Montezuma was skilled in reading the crystal ball of the heavens. It appears that there was much truth in his deductions, but one must always remember that a great part of such study is the development of a receptive state of mind in which the promptings of the unconscious are rationalized. In his own world Montezuma was considered a wise man and one with prophetic gifts which were of great value to his nation. One may say that he was regarded as the ideal of a noble ruler by his own people and that in their fear and reverence for the Great Speaker there was mingled not a little love.

There was good reason for the affection in which Montezuma was held by his people. He realized that his world of magic was intimately connected with real life. Public welfare was the purpose of his astrology. Study must always link events in the sky with the happenings on earth, so that the great man, in assuming more and more autocracy, was putting himself into a position where he was arbiter of fate for the nation. This was not for selfish glory, for Montezuma's nature was gentle and affec-

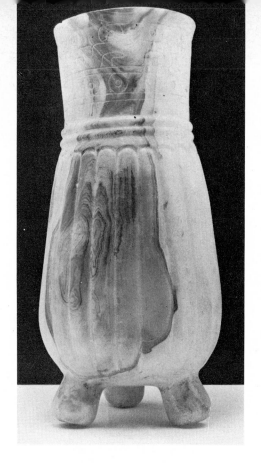

A vase for cacao, carved from calcite. Aztec, 16th century.

Colossal stone head of a man. Aztec work of the 16th century, found in Vera Cruz.

tionate, that of a self-effacing philosopher. It was his office which gave him prominence. For instance, he encouraged the market and merchants in his city of Cactus Rock, because he saw the Pleiades, the market in the sky, beside the great river of light, the shining serpent of the milky way. He felt that if Aztec trade were nurtured throughout Anahuac, the caravans of bearers would tread the roads like the stardust across the heavens. In fact, this wish of Montezuma was fulfilled. In the past the cocoa bean had been scarce and small hampers of four hundred beans had been used as a form of currency, but under his rule trade with the Maya peoples increased and for the first time since the days of the Toltecs the cocoa bean was openly sold in the markets of Cactus Rock. There was public rejoicing on this occasion for the whole nation was elated at regaining the prestigious position of the Toltecs. It was a kind of seal on their overlordship in the country. They knew that they were not in fact Toltec, and that only their chiefs had acquired Toltec blood by political marriages, but they remembered the stories of the past greatness of the people of Tula. All was now justified; the Aztec Great Speaker had acquired the prestige of an emperor, though he still consulted his fellows in the supreme council. Fate was building up Montezuma into greatness such as had not been seen in Anahuac for five centuries. But his studies had warned him that even the great founder ruler, the divine Quetzalcoatl of Tula, had fallen from glory and departed with only his personal followers into the eastern seas. Thus the glory of Montezuma was from the beginning mixed with a measure of sadness.

The customary year of withdrawal for a Great Speaker was a boon to Montezuma. For that period he was housed in the temple courtyard in the traditional holy place into which the uninitiated did not venture to step. Hence it was a refuge for him. As priest he was able to conduct his religious duties, and as war leader he was given peace to plan his campaigns. The two functions of life for Montezuma were united in the temple. Meanwhile ground was cleared to the north of the temple for a new palace. Squares were laid out, and the foundation mounds were piled so that all the buildings were based some ten feet above ground level and entered by steep stairways in the Aztec style. They were arranged around courtyards, long narrow rooms roofed with great beams of cedar, lit only by the fierce sunlight reflected through the doorways. Some of the courtyards were covered over by brilliantly coloured cotton awnings and were a riot of colour, others were places of flowers traversed by stone pathways which led by pleasant basins of water where lilies grew. There were no doors in this complex, for the Aztecs numbered no thieves in their tribe. Few would commit the infamy which led first to the loss of a hand and after that to an ignominious public execution. No barriers were needed, for the law was a sufficient warning. At the front of the palace there was an open courtyard surrounded on three sides by a shady colonnade. At the far end there were rooms on a raised platform, and beyond them rose a further platform ascended by a stairway to the room in which Montezuma would sit each morning as supreme judge of his people.

The rooms below him were occupied by the five judges, in effect the Lords of Appeal. All members of the tribe had access to this tribunal if the judges in the district courts and the markets had not satisfied them that justice was done. Anyone, man or woman, could appeal to the high court and to the Great Speaker himself. The judges wore white cloaks and demi-mitres of turquoise, the Great Speaker sat on a throne of basket-work in his blue robe and turquoise demi-mitre. It was there that he met his people and listened to their problems. They might not approach him except through the judges, but if there was any dispute his was the casting vote. Unlike the old Aztec Speakers Montezuma was not looked directly in the face. One must approach him with a hand lifted before the eyes, and the other touching the ground. Even the great nobles put on a coarse cloak of agave fibre before the Great Speaker. They made themselves seem like slaves in his presence. But his justice was precise and clear. He was most careful about this aspect of his rule, because it was the law of the people that an unjust judge was a criminal of the worst kind. He himself had ordered the restitution of property seized on uncertain judgments and had seen to it that those few judges who had deliberately acted unjustly were strangled in public.

A descendant of Montezuma, Don Alvaro Tezozomoc, tells us of an occasion when Montezuma left his summer palace in the mountains, disguised as a simple

Above Huge bowl for sacrificial hearts in the form of an ocelot, carved in basalt. This stood in a hall in the temple courtyard where the Aztec Great Speakers spent the first year of their rule.

Right Montezuma seated upon the *icpalli* (basket-work throne) addresses his Council. Sahagun's *Historia de las Cosas de Nueva España*.

nobleman, without his special head-dress or cloak. He went into the woods, seeking solitude, and heard the sound of chopping. He came near and saw a *macegual*, a small farmer of the district, cutting some dead wood in the forest which was part of the land of the palace. The man knew well that he might be maimed or even killed for breaking into the preserve of the Great Speaker. He was terrified at discovery but put a bold face on the matter. After all his discoverer seemed but a man of lesser rank. When asked why he was cutting the wood he simply said his family needed firewood, and that he was tired of the exactions of taxes and the work service that was required of him. His captor encouraged him to continue and he disclosed that his troubles were due to the boundaries of the forest encroaching further and further outwards, and he blamed this Great Speaker Montezuma for being overbearing in his power. In any case in the old days, he said, the local people had a right to cut dead wood for their own use. The nobleman thought for a moment and then told him that he seemed an honest man and commanded him to come the next day to the palace. The man saw then that his interlocutor was wearing a very splendid crystal lip-plug and was obviously a person of importance. Trembling, he gave his word, saying that he expected little justice from so merciless a judge.

Next day he came to the court and gave his name (which was Xochitlacotzin) to a young man. Soon he was summoned to enter and stand at the foot of the staircase. There he stood appalled when he saw descending a tall slender man in the blue cloak of the Great Speaker. He covered his eyes and bowed, putting dust over his head, and trembling. Suddenly he recognized the soft clear voice he had heard the previous day. Although in a state of terror, he steeled himself and bowed deeply before the great lord. Then he replied to Montezuma's questions in the same way that he had answered them the previous day. Montezuma then touched him and told him kindly to remain without fear. Soon the rule of ceremony was resumed. The official interpreter came forward and spoke the words of the Great Speaker. (In the court of Montezuma there were always at least twenty such interpreters, for even to his own subjects he did not speak directly.) To him the farmer gave words of thanks which were transmitted to the ruler. Gifts of clothing and jewels for his family were laid at his feet. Then new commands were issued and the farmer understood that he was to be honoured in some way. He was cast on a matting seat and held as he struggled to conceal the pain as his lower lip and the septum of his nose were cut through. In spite of the raw agony a lip plug and nose jewel were inserted. Then he was clothed in a new blanket, great bunches of feathers were hung from his shoulders and the priests came to paint his face. By that time the elders of Atzcapotzalco had arrived on the scene. Xochitlacotzin, his face swollen from the fresh wounds, was presented to them as the new town chief, and

Opposite Xiuhtecuhtli (Lord of Fire). Statue of a god from Cactus Rock. It retains its original coating of stucco and much of the surface painting. The disc cut in the chest once held a piece of jade, the heart of the god.

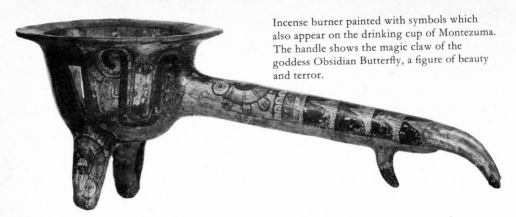

Incense burner painted with symbols which also appear on the drinking cup of Montezuma. The handle shows the magic claw of the goddess Obsidian Butterfly, a figure of beauty and terror.

when they heard his story they accepted him, feeling that one who had won such favour from the Great Speaker would always be prominent in the councils of Mexico. He went away once again, putting his old poor cloak over his shoulders as he bowed low before the Great Speaker and scattered dust on his own head.

Such a story reflects a facet of Montezuma as a great and much revered ruler. He used the seclusion of his first year to minister to his Toltec plans. All the former palace slaves and servants were found new positions, and every office where the holder would come into contact with Montezuma and his immediate family was filled by a noble of Toltec descent. This was a kind of palace revolution and seems only to have heightened the position of the Great Speaker in the eyes of the people. He intended to restore the glory of Mexico as it was in ancient times and this arbitrary development of an already nascent caste system was a step towards this aim. In addition he recognized that the merchant with his trains of porters was a valuable asset to the nation, and this was a step forward from the previous use of the trader as an *agent provocateur* who by his death might start a profitable war. In the arts, the last phase of Aztec art, under the rule of Montezuma, was the most interesting. The daring and geometric perfection of the great calendar stone is amazing when one considers that it was hammered from porphyry by means of stone tools. There are also a few stone heads and a painted statue of the fire god which show that Aztec artists could achieve realism. Possibly this was one of the rare moments in history where the art of portraiture became a reality. The glory of Montezuma's Mexico seems in reality to have eclipsed the lost beauty of ancient Tula.

As to the size of his city, every estimate differs. On festival days, with people coming in from the surrounding towns and villages, there were probably over a million individuals in the city. The growth had been phenomenal, though it was speeded by the success of the Aztec armies in extracting plunder from cities and tribes far afield in Anahuac.

Such a predatory *imperium* was bound to become more consolidated in time, perhaps as a federation of states under Aztec leadership, but the Aztecs had no Hiawatha to unite them in the way adopted by the otherwise far less civilized Iroquois federation.

They had only the distant tradition of Toltec high chiefs of great centralized power, even though there seems to be some evidence that the Toltec hegemony may have ruled a loose federation of peoples which broke up under the political stresses following a mésalliance of the ninth and last king. Alas! Montezuma knew that he was the ninth Speaker of the Aztec people. But he knew too that from a religious point of view he was in a different position. Though he might have been heir to Quetzalcoatl, the earthly god of Toltec power, he was the official servant on behalf of the Aztecs of the god Blue Hummingbird, who was a form of the infinitely powerful Lord of this World, Smoking Mirror, who had tempted the Toltecs to their downfall. Within Montezuma himself was the duality which had undone the Quetzalcoatls of Tula. The Codex now known as *Codex Laud* showed that the temptation of Quetzalcoatl had

The great chiefs make an agreement for peace
by ceremonially making fire.

been organized by the witch-goddess Tlazolteotl. Montezuma did not know that far away in Soconusco was a baby girl, already beginning to struggle to her feet, dedicated by the day of her birth to that same goddess and with the dreadful magical mission of overthrowing Blue Hummingbird. Neither could he have seen over the eastern sea into which Quetzalcoatl had sailed long ago when his heart flew up towards the sun in AD 753. There, a great distance away lay Spain where in the very year of Montezuma's accession an amorous young man of seventeen went climbing up an old wall to get to his sweetheart's window. Alas, unlike Romeo, he fell from the romantic assignment and a good deal of the wall fell with him. He was slightly lame ever after and he missed the boat which should have taken him to Cuba. For two more years Hernando Cortes had to stay in Spain before he could set sail for Santo Domingo in the Caribbean.

However, in this year of 1502 Montezuma was concerned with coming into his full power. His first action on being chosen was to climb the hundred and fourteen steps up to the house of Blue Hummingbird. There he bowed low, touching the earth and placing a little dust on his head in token of his submission before the great tribal protector spirit. Then as a priest he entered the holy of holies and offered burning copal incense for the pleasure of the monstrous black idol of the god. It was the white sweet-scented incense of adoration. Then going out he waved the incense holder as a sign of blessing towards the nobles of the *calpulli* from whom he had been chosen. Still as a priest he descended to the house where he was to be quartered for the first year of his reign, and offered more incense before the great white marble ocelot. Only then was he installed on the high backed, basket-work throne, where he was invested with the turquoise demi-mitre, the fire-stone diadem, and the brilliant blue, royal cloak knotted on one shoulder. The priest of the gods had become also the war leader of his nation.

His first problem was to obtain prisoners to be sacrificed to Blue Hummingbird and to the Rain God, Tlaloc, who shared his temple. (One would protect the armies of the nation, the other make the fields fruitful.) The allied cities of Tezcoco and Tlacopan were called in. Their Speakers assented in council and the combined armies marched northwards, to the region just north of the modern State of Mexico. They set out at the moment when the morning star rose above the horizon, indicating that they went as messengers of Quetzalcoatl. Messengers were sent two days march ahead of

Opposite The Aztec temple at Tenayuca seen across an agave (maguey) plantation. The Mexican agave was used as a source of strong fibre, but also its sap was fermented to make the mildly intoxicating pulque. The discovery of this drink was made by the goddess Mayauel.

Overleaf left The feather shield of Ahuitzotl who dedicated the great temple. The shield with the water-beast *(ahuitzotl)* was made of light cane, faced with paper covered with hummingbird feathers. The outlines of the design are made of thin gold strips.

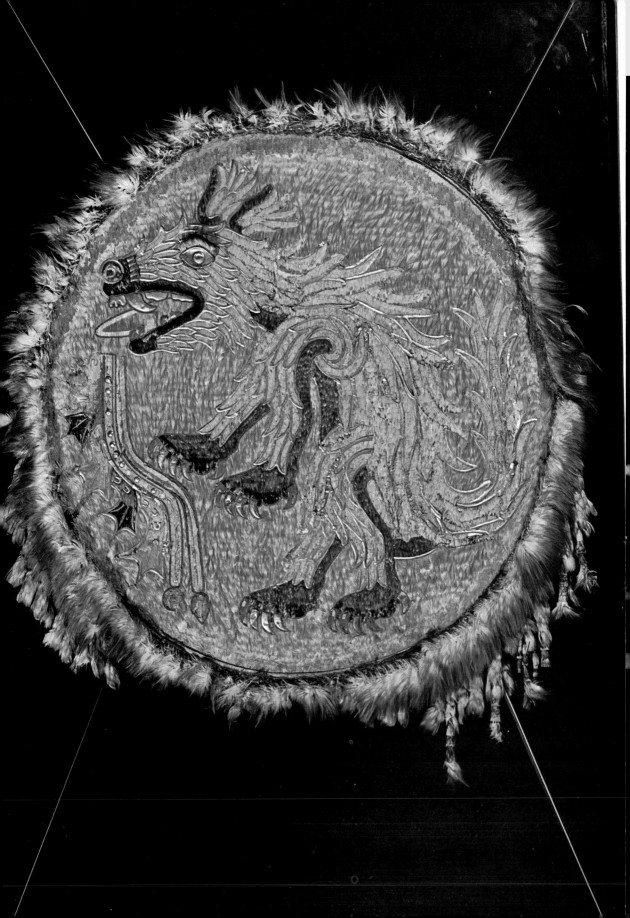

the warriors to ensure that provisions were made available, for this was really a presentation parade for the new Great Speaker. Montezuma was carried in a splendid palanquin, covered with feathers and gold. He wore his most sumptuous accoutrements and carried the shield of an army commander. His loincloth, mantle and crown were all of turquoise, his bracelets, earplugs and even his sandals were of gold, while in his lower lip he wore the crystal lip-plug in which was a single blue feather. His eagle head-dress was in the form of a bird with backswept wings of precious quetzal feathers. Surrounded by the greatest war leaders of the nation, this slender man of forty-one, with a slight beard and black-painted priestly face, looked like the divine ruler of the Toltecs, more splendid than any of his predecessors on the Mexican throne for five centuries. Everywhere people flocked out to meet their new ruler, with deep obeisances and songs of joy. They saw nothing but a distant figure, because as he came near they bowed low and shaded their eyes in symbolic respect for his divine brilliance. The power and the glory of the Aztecs were parading before the whole tribe.

Presents were heaped upon the leaders: food and refreshments for the soldiers, jewels and robes for the nobles, and marvellous garments and cloth for the Great Speaker. So in glory they marched to war. It was a short war against the peoples of Nopalla and Icpactepec. Montezuma personally ordered that in this first campaign enemies were not to be slain if it was possible to capture them to be slaves. The more important captives were to be taken back as sacrificial victims, and there were many of them, led along with ropes around their wrists and necks.

The return to Mexico was even more tumultuous. For Montezuma himself it was symbolic. He had employed all the honourable traditional tactics, divided his army into three sections, made an agreed assignment of the place of battle and faced the enemy with his Eagle warriors, while outflanking him by the Ocelot fighters. The number of prisoners taken and kept after the peace conference was gratifyingly high. Those to be sacrificed could expect a glorious fate, those to be enslaved were the more sad. In fact, it is likely that the concept of enslaving enemies was new to Mexican warfare. Domestic slaves seem usually to have been purchased from their families in return for food in times of famine. However, slavery was not a very important feature of Aztec society since at that period the development of a class of slave-owning nobles was not far advanced. It is likely that this departure of Montezuma towards capturing people as slaves had reference to his employment of nobles to do all the work of personal service for him as Great Speaker of the nation. There must have been quarters for slaves who performed menial tasks for the noble servants. Montezuma was changing the

Opposite above Featherwork disc with symbol of a whirlpool, possibly relating to the Goddess Chalchihuitlicue (Lady Precious Green). Aztec, early 16th century.

Previous page Featherwork fan decorated with the symbol of the soul butterfly. From the treasure of Montezuma given to Cortes in 1519.

Opposite below The shield of an Aztec army commander. Part of the treasure of Montezuma. The symbol indicates the hazards of war and the rainbow glory of the sun. Hummingbird feathers on cane.

balance of Aztec Mexico, and this was the result of his attempt to recreate what he believed were conditions under the greatest rulers of the Toltecs.

It was in the second year of Montezuma, when he was established in his new palace, that a great festival was held. It was called 'the second bringing of stones from Malinalco'. It was exactly a hundred and forty years after the ancestors had first brought stones for the first temple to Blue Hummingbird from the same place, where the local people were famed workers in stone. Montezuma had the stones brought for a great religious festival as he and all his people commemorated that ancient time when the first stone building was erected amid the reed cabins in the marshes. They marvelled at the changes which had come, bringing them greatness and dominion and vast stores of wealth. Blue Hummingbird had in very truth given his people dominion over Anahuac, the land between the two oceans. Yet there were still enclaves to be conquered; the prophesied greatness was not yet complete. Montezuma knew that he must continue marching with his armies.

In that year, when the cold north wind swept the country in the winter, there was a fall of heavy snow in Tlachquiauco in the Mixtec highlands. Such falls were infrequent, and the people regarded them as a presage of misfortune and hunger. The reason was that their carefully planted maize hills might be frozen and the young plants destroyed. However, the storm had at least provided water and the worse danger of drought was for this year dispelled. The year was 11 *acatl* (1503), and it was a little disturbing that the crops should be threatened in a year expected to produce plenty of fertilizing rain. However, the general state of the nation remained good.

As the year 12 *tecpatl* opened (February 1504 in our calendar) the merchants arrived back from the Maya country with their bearers carrying many hundreds of hampers of cocoa beans. There was great rejoicing at this auspicious occasion. But Montezuma feared, from reading the books of fate, that this year would be one of drought. To avert such a calamity he dedicated a splendid new temple to Cinteotl, the spirit of the maize crop. Men and women were slain at the spring festival, when in honour of the sprouting of the seed grain, victims were roasted and skinned alive, drugged so that they were barely conscious, in honour of the flayed god who symbolized the new maize plant bursting out of the golden skin of the old seed. Then, at the feast of the young corn, bare-breasted women were slain, beheaded and skinned as young girls danced, flaunting their breasts as a promise of food to come. There was much rejoicing and as the harvest began people ran singing through the streets pelting each other with turkey-egg shells filled with maize flour. But still Montezuma received no news that his piety had turned the footsteps of fate. They had danced and sung for the maize, they had suffered and wept for the rains. Blood had been poured out for the earth and the black incense had risen to the clouds, but somewhere in the land beyond the world there was a sullen anger. From all quarters of Anahuac messengers talked of blue skies and late heat, but none brought word of the rain spirits bringing their clouds across the mountains. Even the summer thunderstorms came from scattered clouds. It seemed that the coming year 12 *tecpatl* 'the year of the stone knife' would indeed be stony and cruel. The inherent ill-fortune of the year seemed to intensify to the point where bad luck was presaged without omens. At night as the Great Speaker ascended the roof of his new palace, the stars looked on him with cold eyes and the planets were strangely unfriendly. It was as if an old friend whom one consulted lovingly night after night had turned away his face. The shooting stars seemed strongest from the east as if some threat waited there. Montezuma could not know that in that year of cold-hearted drought a caravel had unloaded its crew of brave young adventurers on the island of Santo Domingo, and among them was young Hernando Cortes. However, for that year the Mexicans had food, though barely enough.

The result of the drought was fully experienced in the following year 13 *calli* (1505). Then the fields were not renewed, the seed corn was dry and parched and no life seemed to arise in the country. Montezuma pleaded with the gods, he did not spare his own blood and lacerated himself to offer his pain with the suffering of his people. But the gods were unmoved. The great powers of nature remained silent. His beloved Quetzal-coatl came as a wind, sweeping the paths in February, but although much dry soil was blown away no rains followed. Tlaloc remained obstinately upon his mountain tops. Dust devils spun up from the dry hot ground. People said the Lady Precious Green, spouse of Tlaloc, was reduced like a little bird to taking a dust bath instead of spinning whirlpools in the waters. And there was no food. Montezuma wisely opened the storehouses of the army and the palace to help the people, but it was not sufficient. He sent messengers and an army to the mouth of the River Panuco, where among the swamps the Huaxtec people were able to grow food. But even the thousands of packs of maize brought in were not enough for the inhabitants of the great city of Cactus Rock. The fields were taken over by starving birds and insects, the dust blew over the dead, and thousands of the living Aztecs left for distant lands, mostly in the Maya country where food could be found. Many of them became serfs or sold themselves into slavery.

Whatever Montezuma may have personally thought he accepted the will of the gods. It would have been perfectly possible for such a great ruler to have commanded some extension of the aqueducts like the one his ancestors had made to bring fresh water into Cactus Rock from Chapultepec. It would have been possible to occupy more land at one time by using fertilizers of natural humus instead of continuing with the traditional methods of the slash and burn cultivation of *milpas*, by which each patch of land was occupied for a few years and then left fallow for twice as long to recover fertility. Thus three patches were needed to feed each family. But the idea of fertilization never entered the Aztec mind. Events ran in pre-ordained cycles, and the magnitude of glory or disaster was simply dependent upon the will of the divine powers.

In the following year there was at last some rain and people planted crops with hope, though they knew that they might not all live to harvest the crop. But a strange thing happened. By some biological survival instinct the numbers of rats and mice increased enormously and the hordes of hungry animals invaded the plantations. It

Above The feast of Tlacaxipehualiztli (the flaying of men) celebrated each February to promote the growth of maize. A young warrior wearing the skin of his defeated enemy dances in the streets. Sahagun's *Historia de la Cosas de Nueva España*.

Right Turquoise encrusted double-headed serpent. Worn as a breastplate by the High Priest of Tlaloc the water god. One of the treasures sent to Cortes by Montezuma.

Opposite right The lady Chalchihuitlicue, spouse of Tlaloc. The young goddess of storms and beauty. This figure retains much of the stucco surface.

was the year 1 *tochtli* (1506) in which crops should indeed have been threatened by birds and animal pests. The situation was so bad that people had to sit out in the *milpas* at night with blazing torches to frighten the animals. Everybody in that over-crowded land thought rat meat a delicacy, so a plague which threatened famine was also a means of survival.

However, the gods who had inflicted such suffering were finally appeased by the sacrifices of warriors. The priests knew that the divine power emanating from the gods did not always follow a sequence that men could understand. It mattered little what humans achieved if the gods did not co-operate, so that the return of rains and the coming of the rats were seen as a return to a proper alliance between man and the gods. The army was in good heart again, and when the great and powerful city of Uexotzinco once again refused to send any tribute to Cactus Rock, it made an excuse

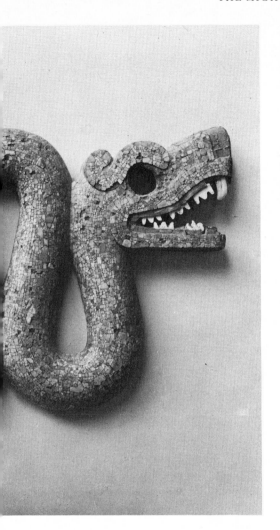

for a war. As was to be expected, the Tlaxcalans in their hill towns linked with Uexotzinco. They took every opportunity of fighting the Aztecs, not just to capture victims, but to express their resentment of the way in which the Aztecs preserved Tlaxcala almost as if it was a hunting reserve to supply humans for the table of the gods. The town of Atlixco came into the war against the Aztecs but it went badly for the allies. Eight thousand Mexicans met six thousand warriors and inflicted a heavy defeat on them. Prisoners were brought to Cactus Rock and sacrifices were made.

It was very important to Montezuma that the year 1506 should be successful and happy, because this year marked the end of an Aztec era of fifty-two years. The previous era was coming to its conclusion and in the following days a new period of time would be opening with the year 2 *acatl* and the great ceremony of New Fire. The waning of the great famine marked the ending of the old days, and gave a hope of

Figure of a warrior wearing the skin of his
sacrificed captive for the festival
Tlacaxipecualiztli. On the back is the date
2 *acatl* (1507), the year in which New Fire was
made in Cactus Rock for the last time.

better times to come.

The days immediately before the great ceremony of the new calendar were hard
for the people of Mexico. They fasted for twelve days. All old clothing was destroyed,
all pottery was smashed and thrown into pits. The past was coming to an end and little
things of everyday life went with it. The great monuments were left untouched, but
soon everything would be repainted. There was a general twelve days' fast, and no
household in the country lit their fire or ate other than maize gruel and water. Montezuma and the Council suffered as much as the simplest *tlalmaitl* (labourer). There was
no exemption from the religious rule of the period. It is heart-breaking to think of the
masses of exquisite feather-work, embroidery and fine pottery which was destroyed
at the beginning of the fast. It was the same in every palace. All the ephemeral things
were destroyed, and even the Great Speaker fasted on maize and water. To him it was
less hardship because of the austerity of his training. People tried to stay indoors in
those days. All women wore masks of green dough to symbolize maize awaiting a
new season. Pregnant women were afraid that their babies might be born during the

twelve days and then the child would turn into a mouse, or some magical monster. So they hid in the great basket-work vessels where maize was stored. The men of the household took turns of sentry duty so that for the twelve days a twenty-four hour patrol of fully-armed men guarded every house against the incursions of the spirits of darkness: those who waited for the ending of the sun to destroy the world. No one wore ornaments, all offered blood from legs and ears to propitiate the powers of darkness. The black side of the gods might become manifest at any time.

As the twelve days came to an end an air of hopeful expectancy mixed with dread spread around the dusty and lonely city. All who could moved out towards Star Hill, a promontory overlooking the lake where there was a very ancient temple of the Fire God. This was the place where the star-watchers would make the observations of the stars to determine whether the world had come to its end or whether the sun would rise once more in the morning. Those who were free thronged across the causeways and made their way towards the holy hill. Canoes crossed the lake in great flotillas. But in Cactus Rock the women still hid and the heads of the household kept their guard.

At the top of Star Hill beside the temple were the priests of the fire, painted black except for their faces, which were painted yellow from the nose upwards and red below. The fire priest himself, wearing his rayed head-dress, sat in front of the altar watching the passage of the stars cross the zenith. Around him were priests, including the astronomer-priest Montezuma.

This was no great festival. This last night of the fast was the night of decision. There was a possibility that it might be the last night of our world. On one of these occasions it was believed that the stars would stop moving around the earth, the sun would not rise in the morning, and the Olin Tonatiuh (Earth-tremor Sun) would meet its ordained fate. All would crash into ruin: palaces, temples, mountains and even the very clouds would shatter into chaos; perhaps one human couple might be spared, as history related had happened in the four previous endings of the sun, or perhaps all life would end. That was the doom for which they were watching. Montezuma and the high priests were less uncertain; they believed that a thousand years remained, or, according to some, fifteen centuries. But none was totally certain on that November night that the world would continue in existence. Then more than ever they thought of the earth as the jewel in the hands of the great Duality, the creator of life who was beyond world and gods and men, yet who was present at every conception of a human soul. Now those souls were awaiting His pleasure.

The silent company at the temple top watched. The Pleiades had passed overhead. Then the people were fixed in awe as the 'Firesticks' with Aldebaran approached the zenith. Aldebaran reached the line and passed. The victim on the altar was slain at once and the heart thrown to the fire-god's image with deep reverence. Then the High Priest placed two sticks together over the wounded breast and made a tiny fire which was in moments fanned into a blaze. Pine rods were taken as torches and the watching crowds seeing the light burst into song. Life was reprieved; drums and trumpets

Typical Aztec features on a stone head.

sounded; all was well for another fifty-two rounds of the sun to be lived by mankind. Montezuma, who knew something of the changing of fate, was happy and sad together. For him another period of uncertainty was opened. He knew he should not live to see another tying-up of years, for only the young children were likely to see the ceremony a second time.

Below the hill he could see the runners taking the new fire to the temples in Cactus Rock. Then, like a rain of stars, other runners came from the temples. To every house, whether palace or hut, they carried torches to bring new fire to every home in the great city. Life began again, the women and children discarded their masks, and came out of hiding, and the men relaxed their guard, because the powers of darkness were defeated and family life would go on.

As the sun rose, the shell trumpets sounded joyfully from every temple. Blood was offered from ears and legs by all the population and the rising brightness in the east was acclaimed. Light, love, sacrifice, all were there. Life would go on.

9

THE CLOUDS OF FATE

THE NEW BUNDLE OF YEARS (the Aztec time unit of fifty-two years) opened with good news for the Aztecs. The alliance between Tlaxcala and Uexotzinco was broken. There had been a long boundary dispute between the two groups because the Tlaxcalans included the sources of rivers flowing down to the town of Uexotzinco within their territory, and in times of drought the city had suffered from loss of water. Then, during the famine, hungry highlanders had descended to plunder the grain stores of the town, because the towns-people had not been inclined to help their erstwhile allies. Montezuma planned an attack on Tlaxcala. It was well organized and successful, and the subsequent treaty left Tlaxcalan lands intact, although many prisoners were taken to offer to the gods through the coming year. In particular, a Tlaxcalan war leader, Tlahuicole, was seized and bound. He had been intended as one of the combat sacrifices in honour of Blue Hummingbird, but although armed only with a plain wooden club he had slain four warriors whose clubs were edged with obsidian blades. He had broken them with masterly strokes, shattering shoulders, and breaking spines. It was rare that anyone survived this form of sacrifice, but in the midst of the carnage around him Tlahuicole remained calm, although bleeding from many slashes. He still insisted that he had a right to be sacrificed, though Montezuma, in honour of a brave enemy, offered him freedom, but there could be no answer to his argument: he was captured and should therefore be sacrificed. Anything else would deprive him of the glory of dancing with the sun in the sky. So he, too, was bent over the stone, and as his flesh split under the knife, his heart was stilled, and his soul sought its destiny.

After his victory over Tlaxcala, Montezuma was free to negotiate a peace with the people of Uexotzinco and Cholula, and the great city of Quetzalcoatl the god was once more at peace with Cactus Rock. It was a good omen.

On 20 July 1506, there came an eclipse of the sun, and it was followed by an earthquake. The making of New Fire had not altered the destructive pattern of fate. After the first victories of the new era a terrible disaster followed. A Mexican army was in the mountainous headwaters of the river Atoyac when a severe storm overtook them and the rising torrents drowned the valleys. Eighteen hundred men died there. Mourning and sacrifices followed. Then came a greater mystery. In 1509 a light was seen in the eastern sky. It rose every night as the sun set, and was described and drawn

Opposite The pyramid of the New Fire, basalt about 6 feet high. This monument marks the transition from the year 1 rabbit to the beginning of a new cycle of time with year 2 reed (1507). At the top, the god Blue Hummingbird on the left and Montezuma on the right offer blood to the image of the Sun. Aztec.

Above Honour to a great warrior. Sacrifice by combat. The captive with a wooden club is faced by Ocelot warriors armed with obsidian-edged clubs. Sahagun's *Historia de las Cosas de Nueva España.*

as if it were a triangular area of zodiacal light, a great fire with sparks running through it. Obviously something most unusual was happening. It was the more terrifying in that it persisted; accounts vary as to whether it shimmered there in the sky for one or for four years. It was something unusual on a world scale. Perhaps some unknown eruption of a volcano was responsible, but the light did not drift at all but remained in the eastern sky. Perhaps some strange meteor was circulating with the earth. But in Mexico no one had any comfort. Even fifty years later the event was remembered and described to Father Sahagun who published a drawing of it. It was something mysterious and really terrifying to the population. People waited under its glow and wondered.

A political event in the first year of its appearance shows that Montezuma could act with grim ruthlessness. The Zulantlaca people rebelled against the tax gatherers, and they were exterminated. Montezuma's other name, Xocoyotzin, means that kind of ruthless personality in a prince, and also indicates a certain sense of gloom.

In 1511 Montezuma interfered in the affairs of other tribes, and attacked the Tlachquiauca people because they had made a raid to plunder the tribute of Calixtla-huaca. It was the more important because the tribute was intended for Cactus Rock, but it indicated that the Aztecs were increasingly policing a developing empire. The changes were many but small and the results helped to cover over the tragic disasters in the earlier years of the reign.

It must have been obvious to Montezuma that he was not always succeeding in pleasing the two diverse gods who were most closely linked with his life. That winter the water god Tlaloc again showed displeasure: there were severe snowstorms in the mountains. However, Blue Hummingbird must have been pleased for every campaign in 1511 and 1512 was a success. But in 1512 there were three earthquakes. The situation was difficult, for these tremors were always regarded as signs that the earth was restive, and were reminders that the present sun must come to an end in the midst of a cosmic earthquake.

It was about this period that the first 'ugly ones' (the Europeans) came into sight of Mexico. They were in canoes so big that they looked like houses and which had white wings that caught the wind and looked like the wings of sea birds but much larger. Some of these strange creatures came along the coast of Yucatan. In some places the crews gave presents; in others the people tried to oppose them, but then the ugly ones took tubes and unleashed lighting with clouds of stinking smoke. A few of them were captured by the Maya warriors, and one of them was dressed all in black like a Mexican priest. Two of these floating houses passed along the coasts of Quintana Roo, where maybe the girl Ce Malinalli saw them and wondered.

This expedition was chronicled in Spain by the historiographer, Peter Martyr de Angleria, in his account of the trading adventure of the one-time companions of Columbus, Solis and Pinzón. He published a map which, before the 'discovery' of Mexico, showed that those bold navigators had traced nearly all the coasts of the Mexican Gulf round to California. Although the account says that the navigators sailed south, their list of place names and names of noblemen shows that in fact they sailed along the Maya coasts and then visited and traded with people on the coasts of Mexico itself. Sometimes they did good trade; sometimes they had to fight to get water, but they discovered that this was a land rich in gold. It seems that the voyagers tried to falsify their compass bearings to discourage future competitors in this rich area of trade, but the map gives them away, and to us the Maya names make all clear.

It is surprising to find that the Mexican annals and even the more detailed histories given to the later Spanish invaders make no mention of this voyage. But the event seems to have been echoed in a number of visions recorded in Cactus Rock; in the strange stories of the Princess Papantzin, and in the visions of Montezuma.

Papantzin (Butterfly Princess) was a younger sister of Montezuma; she was

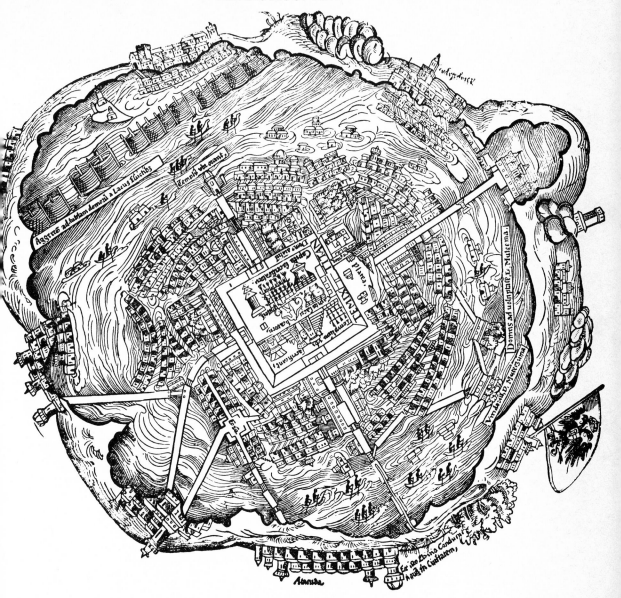

A map of Mexico, based on Cortes' description. From Cortes' letters published in Nuremberg, 1524.

married and had children of her own. One day she died. On the fourth day people going near the grave found the stones had been pushed aside and saw the somewhat dazed princess sitting up. We do not know why she was buried. It was not usual except in the case of the drowned or those suffering from dropsy. Was the body laid in a temporary grave before cremation? The story as we have it does not seem quite right in view of Aztec custom. However, the princess is said to have told her brother of a terrible vision she had had: of the appearance of strange beings dressed in grey

169

stone and with horrible bearded stony faces. They swept up from the sea and slew armies, eventually burning the city of Cactus Rock. One wonders if there was a core of truth in this story.

The fact remains that in about 1512 Montezuma was deeply disturbed. He was more gloomy and more taciturn than usual and was himself subject to a series of visions. While there is no known Mexican account of the voyage of Solis and Pinzón along the coast, messengers from the coastal commanders must have been sent to Tenochtitlan. Such a fantastically strange sight as bearded men of extreme ugliness coming to trade from wooden, winged houses floating on the sea must have been an occasion for sending messengers and probably drawings to Montezuma. This may well have provided the basis of the fantasies of the great ruler of Mexico. But although it is amazing that no tradition of the actual voyage seems to have survived, the visions of coming disaster which appeared to Montezuma are described minutely. They mostly concern apparitions, of which many were seen by other people. One apparition of a wailing woman with a fleshless face was seen by many. She was a common harbinger of misfortune referred to in many legends; one of those unfortunate mothers who had died in childbirth. When not engaged in seeing the sun down the evening sky, these sisters, the 'Princesses', might appear on earth to bring tidings of misfortune to people who had not shared the unhappy fate of early death without reward. The apparition prophesying unknown woes would appear at wells where women would go to draw water, but who would rush home weeping with empty pitchers because the girl with beautiful hair sitting at the well had turned her face towards them and they had seen a skull. Then there were the freaks, the twisted humpbacks who were regarded as beings to be sacrificed to ameliorate the effects of solar eclipses, the people with extra limbs, even the monstrous two-headed men. They appeared in unusual numbers as portents of some cosmic catastrophe. One group of them was apprehended and brought before Montezuma. They were placed in a hall, and the Great Speaker entered, prepared for sights to which he was accustomed, since he collected freaks and cripples and treated them well until the time came for them to be sacrificed to the sun when it was in danger. But this time no sooner had he entered the room and seen them than they disappeared. The soothsayers whom he had called were nonplussed. They could offer no interpretation and the Great Speaker had some of them sacrificed. He appears to have had a presentiment that the visionary cripples were shown him as a warning of a coming eclipse of some kind.

Montezuma was appalled. The gods had shown displeasure, but the power of the Aztecs had recently seemed to increase. Their armies advanced with fewer losses. The traders prospered and with them the well-being of the Aztecs. Markets were full, and the wave of famine seemed to have abated. The Rain God was still somewhat hostile, perhaps because he shared the magnificent pyramid with Blue Hummingbird, yet was not given the same splendid sacrifices. The trouble might of course be due to the whim of Tlaloc's wife, the young and tantalizing Lady Precious Green, who brought about prosperity or loss, administered whirlpools and sudden storms, and whose nature was

A soothsayer interprets the terrible omens of disaster seen in Mexico. Sahagun's *Historia de las Cosas de Nueva España*.

Stone figure of a Tlaloque (rain spirit), floating as a thundercloud over Mexico, ready to spill his bowl of fertilizing water. Aztec, early 16th century.

very changeable. However, Montezuma seems to have paid little heed to the fertility gods, except to give them the respect and feasts which were their due. Over all there seemed to hang this mystery of his own inner duality. He was the priest of Quetzalcoatl, and the warrior of Blue Hummingbird; they were of equal importance to him and to his people, for the one brought splendour and victory to his people, the Aztecs, the other brought wisdom and beauty. Long ago Quetzalcoatl had been driven from supreme power by the followers of Blue Hummingbird. It was known that one day he would return, and there would be another reversal of fate, such as occurred when Huemac the last Toltec Great Speaker saw the ruin of his great powers. One day and in one year, Quetzalcoatl would return, and that was the day 9 *tecpatl* in the year 1 *acatl*. This date came once in every period of fifty-two years, and this period would fall in six years time in 1518. The return might of course be in any subsequent bundle of years, but Montezuma was sure that the omens meant that Quetzalcoatl would return on this coming date to claim his right to resume his rule in Mexico. Montezuma was divided within himself. He could neither fight for Blue Hummingbird, nor abdicate to become the dedicated servant of Quetzalcoatl. The dilemma was a spiritual tearing apart, a kind of bitter crucifixion on the cross of fate.

Reports tell that at this time there was a great magician living in the ruins of Tula who conversed with the dead, a shaman of immense knowledge, named Huemac.

Montezuma himself was a learned astronomer-priest but he now sought the help of the inspired shaman whose life was devoted to suffering for the gods. Montezuma called upon this man to conjure up the spirit of his namesake, Montezuma's ancestor and last lord of the Toltecs.

Alone in Tula they called upon the gods, offering incense and awaiting their pleasure. At last Huemac appeared before them as a young and beautiful man, dressed in the sumptuous regalia of Blue Hummingbird and adorned with the flowers and glory of this world. He did not speak but moved silently away, turning back once and then again away, moving stiffly as if he were carved in grey stone and leaving an unutterable sadness behind. Montezuma realized that like Huemac, the last of the Toltec rulers, he stood at the changing of time and nothing would avail against fate – no sacrifices, no wars, neither cruelty nor joyfulness would alter his predestined end. Montezuma went silently away. He knew well that in his human personality there would be rages

Montezuma promotes two successful warriors to the highest military rank. They are given ear-tassels of plumage, ear and lip plugs and fine cloaks. Sahagun's *Historia de las Cosas de Nueva España*.

and pain, but also power and heroism. He was still the living servant of two gods, and therein lay fate.

In the year 1512 there were three earthquakes and in the winter snow fell; but the region of Soconusco was seized by the Aztecs, who exacted its usual tribute of victims and goods. Beyond the eastern sea Hernando Cortes was now fighting in Cuba against the almost defenceless Taino tribesmen. There he found a little gold but still had no conception of what lay further over the waters. It is unlikely that Solis and Pinzón had called at Cuba to talk of their new commercial discoveries. So the Mexican Great Speaker and the young Spanish nobleman moved on their separate courses, and only Montezuma had a foretaste of what was to come.

In 1513 the armies conquered another tribe and brought home victims for sacrifice and much wealth as tribute. But this year also yielded poor crops and there was a drought. In the following two years all went well. The military expeditions succeeded, and Blue Hummingbird was not short of human hearts for his sustenance. The crops prospered and distant tributes all reached Cactus Rock. The people of Uexotzinco sent a gift to Montezuma: a series of beautiful necklaces of gold with jade and turquoise inlays. Even the rain gods relented and springs trickled merrily down the mountain slopes to nourish the fields as they passed on to the rivers and the inland lake where innumerable water fowl shared the waters with the fishes and frogs. The fishermen in their canoes brought in a daily harvest to market. Some of them used nets to trap birds as well; others scooped up edible weed. Lady Precious Green received her annual present of pottery vases decorated with her image, each holding a cluster of fresh human hearts. The priests danced for her, imitating the movements and calls of her water fowl as they splashed in the water. They were rewarded by the massing of the rain clouds along the western mountains. In the city trade was brisk. The chief of the market place with his servants presided over the transactions. Sometimes he would intervene in disputes; sometimes he was consulted about proper exchange values of merchandise.

The quiet splash of paddles sounded occasionally as a canoe laden with merchandise came to the quays. Among the houses bordering the canals there were knots of people talking. Some called to their friends from the roofs, under the coloured cotton awnings, or laughed under the dappled shadows cast by the *ahuehuete* trees. As the quarters of the day passed the shell trumpets called from the temples, and occasionally the sound of drums announced some ceremony. Only once in twenty days did the people flock to the courtyards for the great ceremonies. Otherwise the days of the year brought work and prosperity. People felt that the beloved Great Speaker Montezuma had brought blessings on the land. Sometimes they listened to the dance music coming from the palace quarter, but few saw into the palace, past the cotton-covered openings in the wall or under the awnings high above street level. Sometimes they saw important visitors welcomed by the guards; sometimes the Great Speaker himself would appear. Then people crouched in reverence before him, afraid to look on his semi-divine visage. Often the warriors accompanying their chief would dispense

Montezuma on the roof of his palace observes an ominous comet. From Diego Duran's *Historia de los Indios de Nueva Hispaña*.

The annual distribution of clothing and food to needy citizens, supervized by Montezuma. Sahagun's *Historia de las Cosas de Nueva España*.

gifts in the shape of trinkets and cloth to the people they passed.

The great occasion of food-giving took place in the spring, the time of scarcity. Rows of squatting warriors at the palace gateway formed a guard round some of the great nobles and at the centre stood a great throne, a high-backed cushion-seat of jaguar skin, on which sat the Great Speaker of the nation. On his head was the great eagle head-dress made of precious quetzal feathers and his body shone with jewels of polished turquoise and gold. The people shielded their faces from such glory and crawled forward with hands extended to receive the bounty of dried maize and other foods from the palace storehouses. Among the nobles children played and sang, just as long ago Montezuma himself had done on such occasions. Priests, painted black, offered to the gods the white copal and black rubber incense as a prayer for the rains to come. The symbolic meaning of this ceremony was that mankind and the gods were united in the offering of food from one to the other through the organization of this nearly theocratic state. Montezuma was the focus: he gave the bounty of the gods to the people, and, presiding at the great ceremonies, he gave the bounty of human hearts offered by his people to the gods. Here the Great Speaker was much more than just the Chairman of the Council of Four; he was the mediator between gods and men, speaking to the gods of the needs of the people, and to the people of the hunger of the gods for life.

Sometimes Montezuma was seen within the city, when he was carried in his magnificent golden litter on the way to a military expedition. Sometimes he was seen in the distance as a gorgeous figure ascending the temple stairways towards the sky to superintend sacrifices as the man second only to the high priests. But the great leader who had made Cactus Rock as glorious as the half-fabulous Tula of the Toltecs was in reality not often able to go among the people. His duties lay within the palace where he held office surrounded by noblemen and interpreters.

In those days the wave of fear was mostly forgotten in Mexico, especially by those with little responsibility. But for Montezuma the prophecies were ever present at the back of his mind. He was at the height of glory, the glory which Blue Hummingbird had promised the ancestors more than four centuries before. Here was this great tribe of the Mexica ruling the land, glorious with the tributes which had been gathered. None dare say any word against the Aztecs for fear that the armies would descend to tear their towns apart. They were not loved, but they were obeyed. The whole land was there for the Aztecs to enjoy, in their beautiful Cactus Rock.

Montezuma with perhaps a few of the prophets understood that the prophecy, in reaching fulfilment, was to become its own destruction. Once the appointed symbol of change should be displayed, there would be no holding the ruin. It was not long now, the fateful day when the power of the priestly Quetzalcoatl should prevail. Montezuma hoped it might perhaps be postponed. Perhaps the prophecy would not be complete while Tlaxcala and the western Yopis remained outside the Aztec rule ... perhaps, perhaps.

At about this time the poets, the painters of thought, sang in praise of Montezuma:

> Fire and water flowering amid flames
> Butterflies of the House of Shields!
> Mohtecuzoma in Mexico
> Wields javelins spreading the painted thoughts
> From the precious books of the Gods.
> Our food, our fleshly hearts, are exchanged
> With the gods in sacrifice.

As a picture of Montezuma, the learned chief who through his knowledge of the books sent armies to conquer and bring back treasure to Mexico and food for his gods, this could hardly be bettered.

In the year 1515 fine carved stones were moved into Cactus Rock for the third time. Great was the glory and great the praise of Montezuma. Conquests were made, and booty and victims were brought back. But at this time, Montezuma's old friend

Above The Spaniards return towards Mexico after the defeat of Narvaez. On the right, Doña Marina and Cortes, and the Negro slave who introduced the smallpox to Mexico. Tlaxcalan porters carry loads, and the papal banner flies overhead. *Codex Azcatitlan.*

Opposite Stone carving of a young Aztec offering a melon at a festival. Early 16th century.

Nezahualpilli, Lord of Tezcoco, a partner with Cactus Rock in the alliance, died, heaped with honours, worn with years and still respected in our own day for his great wisdom. Montezuma no doubt grieved at the death of his friend, from whom he seems to have learnt much of the complex art of Mexican poetry. But the people of Tezcoco now needed a new lord, and the council recommended a prince of great brilliance, young Ixtlilxochitl, whose name means Vanilla Flower. But Montezuma insisted that in spite of the close family ties the weakness of youth weighed too heavily against him. By his diplomacy, in which the power of the Aztec armies was perhaps not openly mentioned, Montezuma persuaded the Tezcocan council to elect his friend Cacama to be the Great Speaker. Cacama was not young, and he had a very proper respect for the power of his great neighbour, but the Tezcocans were not fully persuaded to take Cacama to their hearts as their leader. With the connivance of many important people young Ixtlilxochitl took to the hills, to live as a hunted exile.

Montezuma now had control of his greatest ally. He worried little about Tlacopan. That valiant little town had always supported the Aztecs and was not likely to cause disputes in the council of the triple-alliance of cities because it controlled only a fifth of the voting power. Meanwhile the exiled Ixtlilxochitl was awaiting the day when he could return to Tezcoco as of right. It came about in a far stranger way than he had ever imagined. In fact his defection proved a vital prop for the returning Cortes Quetzalcoatl in the coming crisis.

In effect, the prophecy of the greatness of Cactus Rock was now much closer to realization. Not just a partner in a triumvirate but undisputed leader of all the towns of the valley, Cactus Rock had become alone the seat of an imperial power.

In 1517 the people of Uexotzinco rebelled against an oppressive Mexican tax collector. They regretted deeply their former gifts to Montezuma. However, they were to suffer a swift vengeance. The Aztec armies marched, challenged, and fought the arranged battle. Uexotzinco was hardly a city any more. The punishments were severe, and in the next year the victims were sacrificed. Hardly were their hearts cold when a messenger came from the coast to the palace.

On the coast of the Gulf of Mexico great wooden houses with white wings had been sighted and in them were strange and ugly men with black beards. From one of the floating houses a small canoe with strange long paddles had set out, in which were men of whom some seemed to be wearing grey stone clothing. Grey stone, like the stone Montezuma had seen in his vision of Huemac. The men cruised a while before returning to the great wooden house. Montezuma now knew the worst. The visions would come again, and then the reality. The monsters who would accompany Quetzalcoatl on his return were surely coming, and it was nearing the day when the god himself was expected. Time was about to change. The Great Speaker was ashen and trembling.

IO

VISIONS AND REALITY

THREE TIMES REPORTS CAME to Montezuma of the strange men from the sea. He heard of them landing and fighting with grey swords which were more deadly than the Aztec obsidian-edged clubs. He heard of the mysterious *tepuztli* which released thunder and lightning while it cast thunderbolts which could smash forest trees at a stroke as if a typhoon had struck them. The men possessed strange deer without horns, on whose backs they rode and charged against the people, slaying them with spears. The people were not lacking in courage but these monsters from some unknown world inspired absolute terror.

Montezuma was faced with a grave crisis. He knew that the gods might assume the shape of men, and he was aware that Quetzalcoatl, whom he expected, had been a man, both priest and king, in ancient Tula. But there was magic in these present happenings. The strangers had been driven away under certain astrological influences, at other times they had been invincible. They had insisted as Quetzalcoatl would have that the images of many of the gods should be removed, and that human sacrifices should stop. Instead they demanded that only flowers and fruit should be offered to strange deities, a man hanging on a wooden cross of the four directions like a victim slain at the crossroads for magic, and a woman with a child. The strangers seemed to think that these were the only gods. In their name they had great power, for they marched and slaughtered wherever they went. However, they brought strange and precious things with them: green crystal and clear crystal beads, which they exchanged for bronze choppers and gold bells. Nothing happened without it being reported to Montezuma. All the stories brought by traders from the Maya country were repeated in Cactus Rock. A gloom settled over the country because this strange series of happenings was unaccountable. No one knew whence these unknown ugly creatures came. They were obviously human, but perhaps they were the companions of Quetzalcoatl, preparing for his expected arrival on the birthday of the god-priest. More weight was given to this idea because among the strangers there had been seen one or two *papas* (priests)

Opposite Quetzalcoatl as the planet Venus setting in the jaws of earth. The serpent's tongue is the stone-knife of sacrifice, and from its mouth flows the *atl-tlachinolli*, symbol of war.

Above Jade figure of Quetzalcoatl on the disc of the sun. Possibly a reference to the transit of Venus in 1508. Aztec, early 16th century.

Above right Montezuma meditates whether he should seek death in the subterranean chambers at Mitla, or face the oncoming Cortes. Sahagun's *Historia de las Cosas de Nueva España*.

Opposite The guardians of the Toltecs. Gigantic stone figures of Toltec warriors forming part of a ruined colonnade before the main temple in ancient Tollan (Tula, Hidalgo), but now assembled on top of the pyramid. The breast ornaments show they were members of the Xiuh (firebird) clan. 9th century.

in long black gowns, but, unlike Aztec priests, the tops of their heads were shaven and their ears were not slashed for blood sacrifice. The strange beings were not gentle. Their ferocity knew no bounds: they killed the people before them and made no attempt to take prisoners for sacrifice. They made hoarse shouting and not whistling as they attacked. They seemed almost invincible, and it was clear that magic must be used if they were to be brought within the control of Mexico.

Montezuma, however, fell into deep depression and seemed unable to rouse himself into action. He could not bring himself to touch any of the hundred dishes presented to him at every meal. Only a little drink passed his lips from the gourd cup which was dedicated to Blue Hummingbird. Pride, however, finally came to his aid. He was unwilling to hand over power voluntarily and he decided therefore to delay the victory while he was still ruler. Despite this decision he was tortured by doubts whether he should resign his powers and enter the ancient portals of the land of the dead, the passageway to the underground halls of Mitla. He retired awhile from the palace and stayed trembling among the ruins of Tula. There courage returned – the last Quetzalcoatl, Huemac, whom he had seen was not afraid of his fate. He, Monte-

zuma, must also face destiny and do what he could for Mexico. He knew this would be in vain and that he must temporize when the day came.

This day would be soon, but meanwhile a miraculous bird had been found by some fishermen on the lake. They had spread their bird nets and caught a great grey crane, the symbol of the Aztecs, whose young men wore two crane feathers in their hair when they set out to conquer their neighbours. On one side of the bird's head was the black smoking mirror of Tezcatlipoca, the great god of this world. So the fishermen took the wondrous creature and brought it in their net to the palace. They crawled in with downcast eyes before the great lord, and stammered out their story. Instead of an interpreter repeating the words of the great one they heard his own calm voice speaking in beautiful Nahuatl, for he was a poet and had the gift of words. They were to go away with gifts of fine cotton, and leave the bird with the Great Speaker. Trembling at his graciousness to such lowly persons, they crawled away backwards, collected their reward and hastened in their canoe to their house beside the lake.

When Montezuma saw the bird, he sat silently, for he knew well that it was a messenger from the great god whose southern form was Blue Hummingbird. He had now assumed the form of the Aztec crane, a reminder of his promise in the long ago days to give the Aztecs dominion over the lands between the waters. Then the messenger bird bent towards the lord Montezuma so that he could gaze into the mirror. There he saw the stars in the heaven and on each side equally balanced were the stars of the Great Bear and of Cassiopoeia. As he watched the magical obsidian mirror, the scene changed to daytime over the sea and a sandy beach. Up from the waters came the strange bearded men on their hornless deer. They advanced and before them came fire and destruction. In horror at what he knew to be true he demanded the clairvoyant priests be called to see the bird and interpret the visions he was seeing. They hastened to him for they revered him as the holy priest more than the great war leader. They threw themselves in obeisance at his feet but the great lord, sitting bolt upright upon his throne, was staring before him at something which he could no longer see. The bird had disappeared. Montezuma recounted his vision to them and they fell into debate, making speeches suggesting various explanations but unable to speak the truth about the apparition, for they feared to tell the mighty lord, he of the strong arm, about the downfall of Mexico. He was disturbed by them but realizing their deliberate foolishness he called the guards to cast them all out, which was done with such violence that some of them were fatally injured.

But wonders were not to end, for even as the reports of the second appearance of

Opposite The Bimilek vase: carved stone vessel for ceremonial offerings, perhaps of blood, to the gods. The head of one of the underworld deities is surrounded by hair representing the water of war. The whole vase is covered by figures from Aztec mythology. Part of the treasure of Montezuma.

the strangers and of their landing and defeat in Tabasco reached him, Montezuma was confronted by other strangely real apparitions. People had been astonished to find strangers wandering in the city. They were not ordinary strangers but hunchbacks, cripples and men with two heads. They were rounded up and brought in nets to Montezuma. He beheld them, and understood the message in his heart, but again he wanted the advice of the ecstatic prophets. From their hearts would come words to clear the situation. But they were again frightened of the truth and unable to follow the magical path of inspiration, so that when they came all the strange men disappeared as if they had never been. The great lord, dejected and forlorn, sat facing the apparition of his fate, for it seemed to him that these creatures were the ones who had accompanied Quetzalcoatl when he left Mexico. Some had died of the cold in the mountain passes, some were slain by the great winds casting trees upon them and some had been destroyed falling into ravines. Quetzalcoatl had wept for them, his last companions, before he set off to his fate on the serpent raft sailing into the sunrise. Now they were the messengers of his return. But the prophets who could have helped merely bowed and drawled before him, chanting his praises and making muddled attempts to explain things away. He had them all killed.

There was now little repose for the Great Speaker of the Aztec nation. He was sure that the strange *acalli* (water houses) bringing the ugly strangers were the harbingers of the return of Quetzalcoatl. But the resources of the priests were totally inadequate to interpret the real meanings. Only a few dared tell the bad tidings that they had discovered from the sacred painted books. The days of the Aztec rule were numbered, and a new people would come to dominate Anahuac. There was nothing incongruous to the Aztec mind in the mortality of those strangers who had been slain among the Maya and in Tabasco. Gods were mortal, and the legends told of the destruction of the servants of the gods.

The strange appearance of the men from the sunrise reminded the Great Speaker of the story of the ugly visage which the first Quetzalcoatl had often concealed behind his masks. The legends said that his face was like a rock, a great rugged stone, and some stories suggested that under the sacred face-paint shown in the books there was a visage like whitish stone. However, that might be because the god was the morning star and he was expected to be of a light colour and bearded with rays. Was the new-comer, like Quetzalcoatl, at once an ascetic and a lascivious being with a very large penis? The behaviour of his heralds was very like that. There were stories of *papas* in black and the worship of strange images to which offerings of flowers and fruit were made instead of human victims. This was indeed like Quetzalcoatl. Then the warriors were savage, and with their long black beards they were like the thunder clouds blown by Quetzalcoatl in the spring when he was clearing the paths for the rains. Their sexual prowess was known to be remarkable. The strange warriors not only took plenty of

Opposite Figure of a warrior god in protective coat. Possibly a figure of Blue Hummingbird.

girls as gifts from the chiefs who submitted to them, but were also given to rape on a scale unknown in Mexican warfare. All the signs were that the wonderful lord of the morning star was about to return and to assume power in Mexico over the worshippers of Blue Hummingbird. Once again 'the Precious Twin' would rule over Mexico as once he had ruled from Tula. Once again his picture-symbol, the quetzal-feathered serpent, might be seen in the land. This was all clear to Montezuma and his greatest advisers. They recalled a prophecy of the wise Nezahualcoyotl of Tezcoco that the end of the gods was not far distant. They wondered, for the new year would soon dawn, and its name was *ce acatl*, the year of the planet morning star which was also named *ce acatl*, or One Reed.

As the date grew nearer, depression increased in Mexico. The army was not ordered out on raids to bring in more tribute. The Great Speaker was obviously distressed and often remained incommunicado or burst into sudden furies. He had never been a soft man, but he had usually been of a predictable nature, but now even the higher officials trembled, and the royal wives were unable to bring solace to him. Some strange anxiety had made him impotent. But he never lost his love for the children, was never lacking in gentleness towards them.

News came that other *acalli* had been sighted along the Maya coasts. There were stories of battles and also of trading. This was the fourth such visit of the houses on the water. Spies described the fighting and also the trading. They brought pictures of many strange things including the giant deer which were ridden by men dressed in the grey stone. Montezuma alerted his intelligence service, the Ocelot warriors, and sent messengers to all the coastal towns. They should be ready for the fourth series of visitors who were divine beings and therefore would bring the completion of the mystery. If they were the expected deities they were to be treated as *tecuhtli*, or great lords, given gifts and be persuaded to stay on the coasts. His mind was becoming more clear about what Smoking Mirror would desire of the Aztecs. It was apparent that the Morning Star must be held back to allow the tribal god of the Aztecs to hold his place. It was fated that change must come, but to delay the incoming deity was now all important.

On the eve of the new year a ragged stranger arrived at the palace. He was tired and lame, and because he was only a small farmer whose presence would normally have been forbidden, the guards seized him. But so strange was his story of the events on the coast that Montezuma was informed and the stranger was taken before the Great Speaker. He was not lacking in courtesy, and duly kissed the ground before the feet of the great chief. Then he told of the great wooden mountain which had appeared, of pale men with black beards who were dressed in strange colours, some in red and some in blue, a few in black. Their ship spoke with thunder. Montezuma knew well enough that the story was true, but how could the man have reached the palace almost at the time that the ships had come before the Totonac town of Cempoalla? He saw that the stranger was mutilated, he had lost the toes of one foot and his ears. However, he had him put in a cage like a victim for sacrifice and called his council. They debated the matter and agreed that this night would determine the issue. At sunset the priests would add another rod to the Bundle of Years in the temple, and the year *ce acatl* would begin. The strange messenger was sent for, and it was no surprise to Montezuma that the man seemed to have dematerialized. He was not in the secure cage, neither was he to be found within the palace. The Great Speaker knew that the gods had spoken. At once he sent a high-ranking nobleman post haste to the coast.

The next move was to call the jewellers. The best craftsmen in Cactus Rock were summoned before the Great Speaker, who ordered them to make a set of jewellery for neck, ears, wrists and ankles, to be sent to the gods. The gold was to be ornamented by inset jewels of particular significance, including quetzal-green jade. For a few days the craftsmen worked continuously, then they sent one of the palace hunchbacks who served the Great Speaker with a message that Montezuma would be welcome in their workshop to inspect the new jewels. The Great Speaker found them perfect in every respect but he warned the jewellers that nothing was to be said about this special work when they returned to their homes. If they broke silence their houses and all their families would be destroyed. They went away well-rewarded and silent. The jewels of jade and turquoise were carefully packed.

Messengers from the coasts reported the progress of the great water houses. Montezuma sent Cuitlalpitoc, a high official, to survey the scene and to join the local Aztec commander, Pinotl. They climbed a tree and silently watched the people walking about in the big ship. They saw them lower a small boat and noted that they fished with rod and line as well as nets. Then the Aztec officials returned quickly to Cactus Rock to report.

News of the movement of the strangers was now coming in continuously. The eve of the new year was come and the ceremonies were prepared when the word came that the strangers were nearing the Totonac coasts. Immediately a party of messengers, with noblemen taking the prepared gifts, was sent to be in readiness to approach the gods and make offerings to them.

When this important mission arrived the Spaniards had already landed. They found a friendly population and exchanged most desirable glass beads for what was locally regarded as base gold of little worth; so both parties were happy. But the news that reached Montezuma was that the strangers had first landed on shore on the new year's day *ce acatl*. To clinch the matter there was a description of their leader, a man of strange pale colour with black beard and hair. He had landed in black tights and gloves, like the black paint worn by priests, and by Quetzalcoatl himself. He wore a body covering with a chain of gold from which was suspended a white shell cameo: the wind-jewel of Quetzalcoatl; and on his head was the flat topped Huaxtec hat of a type always worn by Quetzalcoatl. It was obvious that the god had arrived. Montezuma was glad that his messengers had been laden with special treasures.

He had taken the insignia and masks of the gods from the temples. There was the dress of Tezcatlipoca, Lord of Fate, the masks and dress of Tlaloc, Lord of the Rains,

Portrait of Don Hernando Cortes shortly after
the fall of Mexico.

and of his consort the beautiful storm goddess, but chiefly the quetzal-feather head-dress, the turquoise masks and the costume of Quetzalcoatl. The treasures were of vast importance and could only have been taken with the permission of the High Priest. Everything was arranged to receive the gods and show them that they had been honoured during the five centuries that Quetzalcoatl had been absent from Mexico. There were books also, showing the stories of the gods, and in particular the magnificent book of the previous lives of Quetzalcoatl. Such a gift could only be made to a god, for no human had any right to handle these things outside the palace and temple. They were worn by the impersonators of the gods in the great ceremonies, and had never before been allowed outside the temple precincts of Cactus Rock.

The envoys came to the coast and with great fear met the strange stony-faced gods. They bowed and kissed the ground. Hernando Cortes Quetzalcoatl received them with courtesy. He decided that they should first meet him at sea on the ship, and with some trepidation they ascended the rope ladder to the deck. They made speeches to the god, and he replied to them; a young man in the black robe of a priest spoke again in Maya to a beautiful eighteen-year-old girl dressed in the most respectable Aztec fashion. She spoke the words to them in high-class Nahuatl, their own language, so a two-way conversation was possible through the girl, whose name was Ce Malinalli, and the Maya-speaking junior god whose name was Aguilar.

The messengers approached the god with his permission and dressed him in the robes of Quetzalcoatl – the mask of two serpents, the quetzal-feather head-dress with the golden beak and the great red and black loincloth. They judged by his stuffed codpiece that the penis beneath was probably worthy of the god. They placed the golden sandals on his feet and the red and black cloak on his shoulders. Cortes accepted all the gifts with quiet dignity. Then they were asked why there was so little gold. They were seized and tied up, while the strangers took a ball of stone and put it in an iron tube. Then the tube spat sulphurous smoke, and the stone hurtled across the waves and struck a palm tree which exploded into fragments. The crash was of thunder and lightning. This was indeed a god, and they fell back fainting in terror. The god motioned for them to be set free from the chains, and gave them some wondrous shining and translucent jewels to take back to Cactus Rock. They saw a soldier wearing an iron helmet, and told Cortes that they had seen a similar helmet worn on their god Blue Hummingbird in Mexico. They offered him two slaves to be killed but the strangers were horrified and would not allow it. They gave them the iron helmet to show to Montezuma and asked for it to be returned full of gold dust. But also they showed them their gods, the woman god with the baby boy, and the man god on a wooden cross naked and tortured like Xipe Totec, Lord of Spring. They saw the new gods eat, but they were too terrified to take more than a morsel of bread. They were sent below, but in the night they slipped away and swam ashore, more frightened at the strange things they had seen than of the sharks.

Calling on their servants, they hastened back to Cactus Rock. There they came to report at the palace, and were taken to the temple courtyard. Montezuma awaited

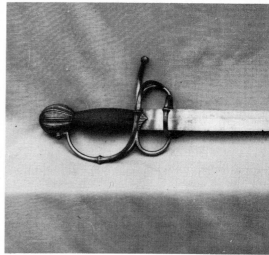

Hernando Cortes receives the messengers of
Montezuma bearing gifts. The feather fan is
probably the one now in Vienna. Sahagun's
Historia de las Cosas de Nueva España.

The sword of Hernando Cortes.

quietly, outwardly impassive yet in an internal agony of suspense. The messengers
had seen the gods and spoken with them face to face and they were therefore too holy to
speak to. Two young warriors were brought in. The priests stretched them over the
stone and lifted their hearts towards the gods. Then the messengers were sprinkled
with the fresh blood. So having been given this little share of the offering made to the
divine ones they were made normal again and might hold conversation with the Great
Speaker without any danger to him.

They described the gods to him, telling of several of them having long yellow hair
and great shiny golden beards. They talked of Quetzalcoatl, of his soft skin and black
hair, of his preference for black clothing. They noted that he seemed a small man
among his followers, gentle and slight, but with a glance of fire and a strength of will
in giving command that none dare resist. They told of the grey stone which proved
to be a metal, harder than bronze and duller than silver, and to prove their point they
showed the helmet which was like the casque of Blue Hummingbird. They described
the loaves of sweetened bread which were eaten on the ship; the deer as high as a small
native house; the huge and fierce dogs; the power over the lightnings and their utter
ruthlessness in battle. This was a changed Quetzalcoatl, no longer the divine refugee
from sin, but a warrior come back to defy the might of Blue Hummingbird. Montezuma knew well that Cortes Quetzalcoatl would win, and he himself must face the
final destruction. He was sick at heart.

Meanwhile, on the coast Cortes Quetzalcoatl was surrounded by his men and
cared for by the beautiful young girl whom the native peoples called Malintzin,

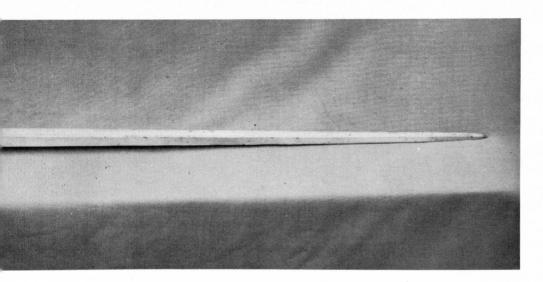

'princess of suffering'. (Malinalli was the grass passed through a hole dug in the tongue when making an offering to acknowledge sin. One thread of the grass was passed through the bloody hole and knotted as each evil deed was counted.) Truly Malintzin or Ce Malinalli was the bringer of misfortune. There was no doubt that this young woman was fated to play a great part in the defeat of the Aztecs, and it seems that she knew it well. It was Malintzin who had dressed Cortes for his landing without telling him that wearing black velvet was the mark of a god. She had held back his desire to land immediately on arrival so that he landed in full daylight on the magical day of the beginning of the year *ce acatl*. She was a young woman in love with the stranger who she knew would be a conqueror. Much wisdom was in her graceful head as she pondered on the magic significance of the expedition which Cortes would never know. Meanwhile she studied hard with Aguilar who spoke Maya, so that she rapidly learned to speak Spanish without the need of any other interpreter. She had been presented to Cortes as a source of sexual pleasure. This to her people was a good thing, as graceful and proper as a gift of jewels and food. So for her there was no trace of shame in calming her master by caresses and love. She was like the young goddess who in the past had seduced Quetzalcoatl, but this time seduction was not necessary. If this was the returned god she found that her love gave him no destruction, but renewed strength and purpose. His penis was the instrument of life as natural as his liking for fine clothes and good food. A god or a man, for Ce Malinalli he was very much of a man and her witch-goddess protectress danced in her loins.

Montezuma must have heard of this girl from his informants. Maybe he worked out her fortunes from the magic books. However, he treated her with quiet courtesy when they met. He must have wondered at the sexual aspect of this new incarnation of Quetzalcoatl, who had formerly been an ascetic, but he probably decided that it was natural that after a life of abstinence and suffering such as he himself had endured while a boy, the god should come back to take his fill of delight as he assumed his power to rule in Mexico.

It was not long before he heard with painful shock that the god was inciting the coastal Totonacs, conquered only a few years before, to throw off the dominion of Mexico and to seize the ambassadors sent from Cactus Rock. The god had started a campaign against the people of Blue Hummingbird. He tried magic and sent a deputation to visit Cortes Quetzalcoatl which included prophets and enchanters. They secretly worked their rituals, danced and made magic signs, but the strangers' incomprehension of the ceremonies gave the impression that they were impervious to magic. Other more powerful enchanters were sent, but on their way they were met by a beautiful young man dressed with eight cords tied across his chest. He was intoxicated, raving and singing, and at every turn coming across their path to stop them. At last they sat down hoping he would become calm and let them pass. But he grew taller and spoke to them. He said that they would not be able to work magic against the 'grey faces'. Then he told them to look back, and they saw a vision of the city of Cactus Rock in flames. And again he spoke to them words of lamentation for the Aztecs. Then the young man vanished and so they knew it was the great Smoking Mirror who had stopped their adventure, and they knew their doom was sealed.

Montezuma fell into a rage when he heard of this for it opened wide the division within his own soul. The glory of the Aztecs was about to depart, but in spite of his terror he had determined that their honour should remain untarnished. He would fight as best he could. The weapons on his side must come from Smoking Mirror, the powerful form of the god who manifested himself to the Aztecs as Blue Hummingbird. The protector of the Aztecs had hitherto aided them to fulfil his plan. Now would he desert them? Montezuma knew this deity was a deity of youth, and therefore not reliable. This was the trickster who gave glory with one hand and death with the other. So Montezuma made many sacrifices to the god, and sought for more magic to distract the oncoming Quetzalcoatl. When the morning star was in the sky, then Cortes Quetzalcoatl could not be opposed, but when the evil twin of Quetzalcoatl shone in the evening sky as Xolotl, then was the time to try destructive magic.

One notes that although Cortes imprisoned the Aztec tribute collectors at Cempoalla, he also released them later with friendly messages to Montezuma. Cortes in this was a clever and diplomatic commander.

The Spanish camp was established at Villa Rica de Vera Cruz. Trade went well with the Totonacs, and after the first shocks Montezuma left them strictly in peace. The morning star was conquering.

The peace still continued with the Aztecs when the Spaniards travelled to the mountains and encountered the Tlaxcalans. There were bitter battles with combined forces of Otomi and Tlaxcalans. The Tlaxcalans had been kept as a source of victims for Aztec sacrifices. Now they trusted no one and were ready to fight at the least excuse. Their Council of Four had not fallen under the domination of a single chief as had the Aztec Council under Montezuma. But the blind old man, Xicotencatl the

Elder, was respected most among them, and he wanted the battles to continue. Three other fights followed, and the Spaniards were hard put to it to survive. The cold and the thin air of the mountains weakened them, and many men and horses died in battle. The Spaniards were not gods to the Tlaxcalans, and their situation was precarious. Then suddenly the attacks ceased. The Spaniards were sent bread and turkeys and invited to a peace conference. Both sides had learned to respect each other as brave warriors, but the real reason for the truce was that the Tlaxcalans had finally decided that the gods had willed the Spaniards' advance. They had been tested from the four directions to discover if the strangers were protected by one or other of the patron gods and every time they had survived and inflicted great losses on their opponents. In addition the Tlaxcalans saw the chance, if they joined up with these new people, of taking revenge for all their young men who had been dragged away to be fattened, sacrificed and eaten by the Aztecs. They were a poor, practical people who were more likely to take a political advantage when it presented itself than to seek out auguries and magic. An alliance between Tlaxcala and the Spaniards was therefore concluded. Some of the Tlaxcalan nobles became Christians and gave princesses of their most respected families to mate with the Spaniards. Then Cortes decided to march again. The Tlaxcalans persuaded him to march on Cholula, their ancient foe, a great city long independent, but now under Aztec dominion. Montezuma and Ce Malinalli, now called Doña Marina, knew well that this was the holy city of Quetzalcoatl. It was important that Cortes should visit his former home and see the immense pyramid in which his jade image was worshipped as Lord of the Breath of Life. But he was himself to have a quite different experience.

As the force approached Cholula, a deputation of priests and nobles came from the city to meet Cortes. They were well informed on the events in Tlaxcala and came to beg that the Tlaxcalans should not be allowed inside the city. They explained that there had been war between the two peoples for so long that they feared the Tlaxcalans would attack them and devour their children. Cortes felt it would be good policy to conciliate the powerful city which had only a few years earlier accepted the overlordship of Montezuma. He therefore persuaded his allies to form a great camp in the fields outside the town, where there was flat ground and where they could not be attacked by stealth. The Cholulans soon sent out of the city many slaves carrying supplies of food and drink to the Indian warriors whom they had learned to fear in past battles.

The Spaniards entered the city, with the mounted knights leading, and the escort of Cortes in the centre. As always Cortes dressed for the special occasion in black velvet, and was accompanied by Father Olmedo carrying the Christian crucifix. But the Cempoallan nobles with Cortes soon noticed signs of something being wrong. The city was strangely quiet. In some side streets they noticed barricades, and the houses had defences placed around the parapets as if to conceal warriors who might cast stones and spears on an enemy in the streets. Nevertheless the great ceremonial welcome continued. Gifts were exchanged and long speeches of welcome were delivered by the great nobles. Cortes was settled with his Spaniards in a palace with a

Above Cortes is given food by the Tlaxcalans at the town of Yliyocan. Doña Marina interprets. From *Lienzo de Tlaxcala*, ed. *Antiguedades Mexicanos*, 1892.

Below The chiefs of Tlaxcala having accepted the new religion attend Mass. Father Olmedo gives the sacrament, Cortes holds the cross. From *Lienzo de Tlaxcala*.

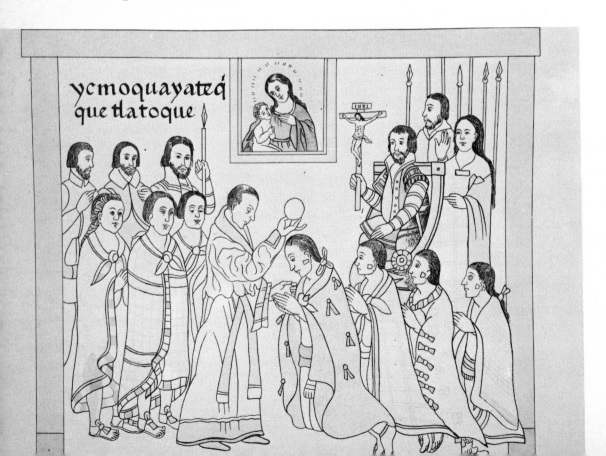

Quitlauhtique

Above The peace agreement between Cortes and the Tlaxcalans. Doña Marina interprets. From *Lienzo de Tlaxcala*.

Below Cortes is met by the Lords of Tlaxcala bearing gifts of girls, jewels and clothing. From maguey paper copy of *Lienzo de Tlaxcala*.

courtyard where the horses could be stabled and fed. So many people thronged around to obtain a glimpse of the strange fighting deer that they became an embarrassment.

It fell to Doña Marina to reveal the plot against Cortes. An elderly noblewoman, who had realized from Doña Marina's accent that she was of noble birth, thought that a kindness to her might start a friendship through which the young lady might be persuaded to marry her son. So she invited the young princess to her home, where she warned Marina that she was in danger and asked her to leave the Spanish quarters to live with her so that she might escape when the strangers were destroyed.

As the conversation developed Marina became more interested and promised to return the next day. She came, bringing a small bundle of personal possessions as if she were going to stay. But she had, she told them, forgotten some jewels and hurried back to fetch them. There she found Cortes and warned him of all that was planned against him. She knew well from her own destiny that the planned attack must fail, and that Cortes would act, as a returning god should, by sweeping all opposition away. Cortes acted by seizing the chief priests of Quetzalcoatl. They confessed to the plot with such unusual facility that one wonders if Doña Marina had persuaded them that Cortes was indeed a reincarnation of their beloved Quetzalcoatl. However, in spite of the discovery of the plot there was some stone throwing one morning, and some military personnel were seen digging pits to trap horses in the streets. Cortes decided to attack.

Streets were swept clear of people, anyone seen was slain, houses were burnt, and the warriors cut down at any point where they gathered. The destruction was heavy and the surrender abject. Cortes Quetzalcoatl was taken up the innumerable staircases of the temple pyramid and here he revealed himself not as the returned god, but as the bearer of a new deity. He asked the priests to prepare a new clean shrine in which he could set up an image of the Mother and Child whom the Spaniards worshipped. It was seen that he obeyed another power which he acknowledged was greater than his own. The priests complied and the work was done.

During the fighting a Mexican army had lain in wait in the hilly ground just north of the city. There by orders of Montezuma they had awaited an uprising in the city which should be the signal for them to attack. But their generals had been told of the exact day of attack and would not stir first. It looked as if they were waiting for the appearance of the Evening Star, the enemy of Quetzalcoatl. But they waited too long. Their armies melted away and apart from a few skirmishes there was nothing to hinder the Spaniards as they advanced towards the col between the snow-capped volcanoes before them which protected the road to Cactus Rock.

The hardships of the advance were immense. The road was a footpath which ascended into the pine forests and skirted great rocks and gullies down the mountain-side. The Spaniards were by now used to the thin air at an altitude nearly two miles above the sea level of their original settlement at Vera Cruz. Nevertheless, the clouds and drizzling rain added to the cold of the ascent. Even under such circumstances a small party of them climbed above the oratories where the mountain spirits were wor-

The fight at Cholula, and the assault on the
temple of Quetzalcoatl. From
Lienzo de Tlaxcala.

shipped. They reached the snow crest of Popocatepetl and descended into the crater
in search of sulphur, which they needed to make more gunpowder. They found the
crater a veritable inferno. Amid great columns of rock and endless caves and crevasses
there were smaller craters in full activity ejecting steam and rock. Even in Cactus Rock
people had noticed that their volcano was more active than usual. However, in spite
of the terrors of hell all around them, the adventurers came back with their indispensable load. One was injured and died on the return journey, but all the local people, the
Tlaxcalans and the hundreds of porters from Cholula were now convinced that the
strangers were beings of superhuman power.

When the path began to descend they were met by a party of elegantly dressed
Aztecs with a supply of food. They came to bring formal greetings to Cortes from the
Great Speaker of the nation. Their courtesy was profound and their dress proclaimed
their high rank, but Doña Marina in translating their words warned Cortes to be very
suspicious. They did not speak well, but used a dialect common to the lower social

Above The Spaniards are met by the Aztec
messengers at the pass between the volcanoes.
Sahagun's *Historia de las Cosas de Nueva España*.

Opposite The jade figure of Xolotl, the evening
star, and evil twin of Quetzalcoatl. Probably
from the treasure of Montezuma. In front the
god is a skeleton with the sun eagle on his
loincloth. At the back is the feathered serpent
of the green earth with the sun under the
earth at night.

orders. They were dressed in borrowed finery and were no real nobles. Cortes had them seized and the gifts inspected. The packages of meat among the food had been cut from the limbs of young men. It was meat from a sacrifice to Blue Hummingbird. The impersonators were tied together and sent back to Mexico with a message that Cortes had detected these impostors who pretended to have been sent from Montezuma. Nevertheless it was quite clear to the Spaniards that these were a party of enchanters sent to use black magic against Cortes Quetzalcoatl. The thought in Montezuma's mind must have been that if the lord Quetzalcoatl and his followers ate the meat which was now filled with the spiritual power of Blue Hummingbird they would be destroyed by the conflict within their own souls. In the beautiful lonely palace in Cactus Rock Montezuma concluded that the strangers had indeed divine protection and that undoubtedly Cortes must be an incarnation of Quetzalcoatl returning to avenge his expulsion five centuries before. It is also clear from this planned assault by magic that Montezuma had rejected his own dedication to Quetzalcoatl, father of all priesthood. The strain on his personality must have been enormous. The gods had clashed within the man and he was aware that he must face his future defeats alone. But one last effort was to be made to test the strangers.

As they came in sight of that wonderful Lake of the Moon which embraced Cactus Rock, another embassy arrived, with a young nobleman arrayed like the Great Speaker in a mass of gold and turquoise. He walked delicately and carried a bouquet of flowers. It was said by his followers that this was Montezuma come to welcome the gods. But already Cortes, through his interpreter, had enquired about the person of Montezuma and expected a man of middle age with a slight beard. This was no such man, but a young cousin of the Great Speaker. So he was told directly that he was not Montezuma, but was treated kindly and sent back with a message that the soldier of His Majesty Charles v of Spain would welcome a meeting with the great Lord Montezuma. Thus it was clear that Cortes knew whom he was going to meet. A kind of divine prescience was attributed to him.

The weary cavalcade of Castillians with their allies and burden-bearers continued on the march. As they did so they gazed over the lake with its ring of white cities like a circuit of pearls around the most wonderful jewel of all, the city of Cactus Rock. It shone on the blue-grey lake, a city far larger than any city of Spain, with great areas of houses set among tree-lined canals. Causeways of grey rock led to it, and in two areas great pyramidal temples rose clustered together as if reaching to the sky. The white plaster glistened like silver in the sun, and here and there one could see the bright colours, and the glittering gold pillars on the temple tops. By now the Spaniards knew only too well what the dark red streams flowing down the steps of the temples meant,

Opposite Quetzalcoatl on a carved stone monument in Vera Cruz. This Totonac carving is probably of the 9th century, and displays the traditional symbols of the god, including the wind-jewel.

Montezuma and the nobles weep at hearing of
the magical powers of the Spaniards.
Sahagun's *Historia de las Cosas de Nueva España*.

and many of them felt the chill in their hearts as they thought that they too might be
drained of blood at the slaughter stones.

But now all seemed peaceful. They descended towards the city where they were
met by a deputation of nobles who offered them food and displayed every courtesy.
They were conducted to the shores of the lake and given quarters in the splendid town
of Ixtapalapan. Here they saw an Aztec palace for the first time, and marvelled at the
painted walls, the cedarwood beams, the rich hangings and the simple furnishings.
There were gardens of flowers, waterfalls and pools, courtyards filled with the scent
of flowers and copal incense, and cool dark rooms screened by curtains.

The night was spent in preparing for the morrow. The Spaniards were busy fur-
bishing their accoutrements, polishing rusty armour, seeing to the few guns they had,
and bringing the bows and crossbows into good order. The horses had to be fed and
groomed. Over all there was an air of excitement. The next day they would enter the
city of Cactus Rock, the mysterious and wonderful centre of a great power which they
had seen as an oppressive empire, and a source of the most bloodthirsty excesses in
religious sacrifice of which they had ever heard. Even in the gardens of this beautiful
palace where the wild beasts were kept there were human bones and half-devoured
entrails to be seen. There was a beauty and a horror in this strange land. The Spanish

The meeting of Cortes and Montezuma, with Doña Marina interpreting. Sahagun's *Historia de las Cosas de Nueva España*.

Tonatiuh (Lord of Fate) the Sun God, in turquoise mosaic on wood. Aztec, early 16th century.

soldiers knew they would be in danger when they crossed the lake on those narrow causeways, so they made their preparations bravely.

The morning dawned splendidly, the sun shone over the lake and glittered on the waves. The trumpets sounded and the Spanish host, few but strong in heart, gathered for the great adventure. They knelt in a courtyard on which was a stone table where Father Olmedo celebrated Holy Mass. All had found some time the previous day to confess their sinfulness, and now they felt clean and ready to face death at the hands of any heathen forces which might attack. Then after a light meal of tortillas with gravy, they assembled, their armour shining, and Cortes Quetzalcoatl conspicuous in his well-brushed black velvet and fashionable hat. Ever at his side was Doña Marina, ready to speak for him to the great Montezuma. The few horsemen rode proudly with lances erect. Behind them trotted the long files of porters, and then a few Spaniards came as a rearguard with the regiments of Tlaxcalan warriors. It was a splendid sight, and it struck terror into many an Aztec heart. Not only did the men clad in grey iron really look like strange divinities, but also the despised Tlaxcalans marched with them looking from side to side as if they were deciding which of the people they would kill and devour. The Aztecs thought of them as horrible savages and were prepared to fight them at the least excuse. As the Spaniards advanced towards the causeway they all felt some fear, for on either side of the trackway there were thousands of canoes with Aztec warriors and their families in festal array. However, the small band advanced in proud independence. Cortes was greeted with deep obeisances. He did not know that the people were saluting a god.

It was not far to the spot where two causeways joined to make one large raised street crossing direct to Cactus Rock. Coming along this street they saw a glorious procession of nobles and warriors glistening in featherwork and golden ornaments. On the backs of many were great symbolic decorations of featherwork. Those in front carried nosegays of flowers, and they marched with drooping heads because of the one who was following. They marched to music, and such a sound was never heard in Spain, for there were drums and trumpets, rattles and conch shells, whistles and ocarinas, playing a powerful rhythm. And there in the midst was a golden palanquin carried on the shoulders of four great nobles dressed in loincloths and cloaks of blue with blue diadems in front of their featherwork crowns. They wore sandals of jaguar skins, and stepped gently with downcast faces. The golden palanquin was screened but one could just discern the upright figure sitting within.

Cortes stopped, the palanquin was halted and lowered. Two mighty kings stood beside it and extended their hands. Now hands decorated with gold came out and rested on their shoulders. Thus, with his arms supported by the two kings who were the confederates of the Aztec tribe, came Montezuma before Cortes.

Each gazed steadily at the other. Then bowing a little and speaking with his usual calm quiet voice the Great Speaker of the nation welcomed the god from the sunrise. Doña Marina translated and saw that Montezuma recognized that she was a princess in her own right. She also translated Cortes' words of welcome and promises of friendship. Then, after a few words of command, the two processions moved side by side with Cortes riding beside the golden palanquin back to Cactus Rock. The meeting was accomplished some seven moons after the first landing of the strangers from the sunrise.

II

PREPARATIONS FOR SACRIFICE

THE DECISION TO INVITE Cortes Quetzalcoatl to Cactus Rock was not the decision of Montezuma alone. He had called a general council of the national leaders of the city and also of the confederated cities of Tlacopan and Tezcoco. The concensus was that the strange beings must be allowed into the city. The behaviour of Cortes was altogether consistent with the interpretations put forward by Montezuma. But it appears that some of the nobles, particularly his nephew Cacama, Lord of Tezcoco, had doubts about the divinity of the stony-faced foreigners. Probably there was a double motive in the invitation, as there was in subsequent relations between the Aztecs and Spaniards. To that extent Montezuma was already losing ground among his own people. He must have felt the subversion of the Totonacs as keenly as any of his nobles, but he was still buoyed up by his inner conviction that this was the working of pre-ordained forces altering the formation of history. To him it was a reversal of the tragedy of Tula. Montezuma did not live to see the outcome, the destruction, and the pestilences which were to follow the ruin of Cactus Rock just as they followed the fall of Tula of the Toltecs. The foresight granted him in the visions, and the warnings given by Blue Hummingbird to his messengers were unequivocal guides to his actions. He must face fate with all the bravery that a warrior-priest of the Aztecs could summon to his aid.

Thus the welcome to Cortes Quetzalcoatl was a willing acceptance of fate. It was with the greatest courtesy that the visitor was taken to the old palace of Axayacatl. There was accommodation for him and for the notable warriors in the elevated central buildings, and for the soldiers in the many rooms around the courtyards of the building. However, the Tlaxcalans were offered nothing but the open courtyards. The Mexicans despised them as barbarians fit only for slavery and sacrifice, yet at the same time they feared their violence, so they were shown no courtesy nor given any assistance.

Montezuma led Cortes by the hand through the labyrinth of halls and courtyards and personally made sure that the palace was ready to be used by the visitors. He was subdued and courteous, as became one who welcomed a returning deity, or at least the messenger of the gods. Cortes was astonished at the luxury, which was far beyond anything had imagined. The halls were paved with polished stones, the walls hung with featherwork, and the ceilings of scented cedar wood were carved and gilded with a profusion of mythological designs and sculpture.

As soon as the Great Speaker left in his golden palanquin to cross the square to his own palace, Cortes gave commands to his men. A constant watch was to be kept, guards were to be posted at every vantage point, and a relief system arranged so that everyone could get some rest. They had seen the crowd of a million Aztecs who had watched them enter the city, and they had noticed the unwillingness of the people to welcome the Tlaxcalans. Cortes had also noted well the adoration paid to Montezuma. People lining the canals and roads had all bowed with their faces to the ground as the Great Speaker passed. The canals of the city had bridges, but like those of the causeways they were made of loose planks which could easily be removed. Their welcome had been warm, but he had had experience of Aztec professions of friendship. He was certain that they had deliberately walked into a place of terrible danger. The sacrificial stone was as close to them as the banquet of delicate fruit.

Sleep was not easy for the Spaniards that night, especially at midnight when the calls of shell trumpets from the temples echoed around the city to call the priests to their duty and to inform the people that all was well in the heavens.

The following morning Montezuma decided to bring Cortes to visit his palace. The journey skirted the sacred serpent-wall of the great temple. He showed his guest into the palace, with its halls and gardens. It was so magnificent that Cortes himself, when writing to Charles v, said of it that there was nothing like it in Spain. Its colours and its variety of courtyards astonished the eye. On the flat roofs there were gardens of flowers and coloured awnings to give shade. It was like a dream palace, not least in its attendant houris. Many of the lesser wives of the Great Speaker were there with their children. Numerous girls waited on them, and all had been chosen for their beauty and grace. A number of other servants shocked the strangers: these were the cripples and hunchbacks of the court who were the royal clowns and messengers until the time came for them to be sacrificed at an eclipse of the sun or moon. Meanwhile they were fed and cared for as if they were of noble family. There were priests in the palace for the offering of sacrifices and incense; they were also ready to open the books of fate when asked for advice. The strangers shrank from them for they smelt of the clotted blood which matted their long black hair. Some of them had hair so long that the gruesome locks reached to their ankles. It was no strange sight to Cortes, but somehow in that beautiful palace it was more than usually shocking to the Spaniards.

Everywhere that Cortes went Doña Marina went with him. It was necessary for the interpreting to be so exact that mistakes would be avoided, and now it was more than ever essential that she should take part in what was to be a diplomatic discussion. Montezuma took her presence in good part and he trusted her, as a young Aztec of excellent family, to represent his ideas fairly to the strange Cortes Quetzalcoatl. To him and to all Mexicans she was Malintzin, Princess Malinalli. Montezuma would have also realized at once that she was by her birth dedicated to the goddess Tlazolteotl, Devourer of Filth, who could devour sin. Thus within the realm of Aztec magic the girl presaged both pain and healing through pain. Montezuma addressed Cortes also

Vase polished from a block of obsidian
(natural volcanic glass) representing a monkey
carrying a load. Aztec, 16th century.

as Malintzin, or Prince of Suffering. If Doña Marina had translated it for him he would
have accepted it as a Christian symbol, for Cortes was a devout Christian within the
cultural framework of his age. But to Montezuma the reference was to Quetzalcoatl,
the ascetic priest.

During their talks Cortes tried to explain that he was an emissary from a great prince
beyond the seas who had sent him to bring the Mexican peoples to a knowledge of the
true religion and to whom they should give obedience and tribute. Montezuma was
somewhat confused at the god calling himself an emissary. From the short description
of Christianity given by Cortes he might well have deduced that Cortes Quetzalcoatl
meant that he was the messenger of the supreme deity, The Two, who was male and
female at once, and who created everything, including the gods. The symbols of the
Christians, the man on the cross of the four directions, and the woman with the child,
might well have led to this interpretation in an educated Aztec priest like Montezuma.
He agreed that he would willingly arrange for tributes to be sent regularly to the great
king beyond the waters, and that someone should come back each year to collect the

tribute. Perhaps Cortes by now had knowledge of the Aztec system of tribute which was paid only for as long as the overlord could enforce payment. Certainly this was in the mind of the Great Speaker. Montezuma and Cortes reached agreement quite easily, although nothing was written down, and everything seemed strange and foreign to both parties. To Montezuma there was a confirmation of the earliest reports he had received of the Spaniards: that they were greedy for gold. This was strange, for the Aztecs thought of the beautiful soft metal as the excrement of the gods. Cortes was well on the way to losing his divinity in the eyes of Montezuma. But worse was to come.

The strangers wanted to visit the great temple. Montezuma thought it proper that they should, but the priests who were called in consultation were at first unwilling because of the ungodly nature of the visitors. At length they agreed, and a selected party was escorted to the staircase ascending to heaven. The skull rack was an object of dislike to the strangers. They had visions of their own heads rotting there, and were not aware that it was the glory of the Aztecs that those tens of thousands of men had been offered to the divine powers; then up more than a hundred feet to the heights above the city, where the view from the huge platform at the top of the pyramid commanded the whole of the Valley of Mexico. In the clear air the lake and all the surrounding mountains were visible, right to the great snow-capped volcanoes. At that season after the freshening rains it was a world of unbelievable beauty. But on the top of the platform were two great houses of stone with wooden upper storeys, all richly painted and ornamented with gold and feathers. Here were the twin deities of Mexico, on one side Blue Hummingbird, on the other the fertility god Tlaloc, lord of all waters. In front of each was a sacrificial stone with fresh blood on it.

They entered the house of Blue Hummingbird. It was dark except for the light reflected from the polished pavement outside. Dimly they discerned a monstrous image of the god carrying throwing-darts each twice the height of a man. He was dressed in the finery of an Aztec warrior, with the addition of a black stone mirror in his head-dress, and one foot made of a plume of hummingbird feathers. It was a terrible being with his blue and black-barred mask that confronted Cortes. Beside him stood his deputy, the Little Black One, all made of obsidian, as big as a man and glistening in the dark. The walls of the chamber were plated with gold and had rich hangings, but they were coated with a thick layer of dried blood, which smelt dreadfully of death and corruption. In front of the glorious divinity was his food, a bowl containing an offering of three freshly-cut human hearts. The priests in their black robes and black stinking hair danced around them waving long-handled bowls from which the white smoke of copal incense ascended. The Spaniards drew back from their unwelcome attentions, and hurried out into the fresh air. Cortes wanted a place

Opposite The skull rack for sacrificial victims had long been a display of military trophies. This Yucatec Toltec carving from Chichen Itza dates from the 12th century.

cleared for a Christian cross to be erected, and the horrible idol thrown down, but Father Olmedo, the missionary priest, persuaded him to wait. It was too soon to impose so many new ideas on the Great Speaker who was at least well-intentioned. But Cortes threatened to destroy the idol if more people were slain before it. Montezuma was terribly shocked. In the past, in spite of the rivalry between Quetzalcoatl and Blue Hummingbird, the two gods had been of equal power and equally balanced between their roles of creation and destruction. But here was Cortes Quetzalcoatl demanding that his rival be destroyed, that the protector of the Aztecs should be dethroned. To Montezuma this was a terrible moment of sacrilege.

The Great Speaker hurried the Spaniards away from the holy place, but the priests had understood from the translation by Doña Marina and they were incensed at the blasphemy against their god. All they believed in, all that the ancestors had taught, was being denied. The god who had appeared to his favoured subjects was now called a force of destruction. Doom had been prophesied, and there was now little doubt that it would work itself out with terror worthy of the god.

Montezuma himself was beginning to feel a desperate anxiety. He knew that events were still following the path laid down in the books. He continued to act according to his training with courtesy to the Spaniards. But he had begun to believe the things they said about themselves. Quetzalcoatl was returning but he was a different Quetzalcoatl; yet he was in human form just as the priest-king of the Toltecs had been. The end of an era was here. Subject people had been subverted and even the savage Tlaxcalans had entered Cactus Rock. So Montezuma began to intrigue, watching the stars for his fortunes, counting the days of the planet Venus as morning star and as evening star. The circular House of Fear which was the home of the god Quetzalcoatl in Cactus Rock was the place where it would be possible to delay the god by magic. It had been the custom to kill one nobleman of Toltec descent each year in this temple but now the Spaniards passing the portal in the shape of a gaping rattlesnake noticed with horror that the place ran with blood. To them it was just another horrible Mexican sacrifice. To the Aztecs it was out of character, a defiance of the Lord of the Morning Star for death had been meted out in the house of the Lord of the Breath of Life.

While Cortes and his entourage were in Cactus Rock, trouble began back in Vera Cruz with a sudden request from an Aztec noble, Chief Smoky Eagle, to meet the Spanish garrison at the camp. A group of four Spaniards was sent to escort them to the garrison but Smoky Eagle promptly attacked them. Two were slain and two escaped. The Camp Commandant, Juan de Escalante, set out on a punitive mission and ran into an ambush. After bitter fighting the Aztecs were finally driven back, but eight Spaniards were killed in the battle, and two days later Juan de Escalante died of his wounds. From now on the Spanish line of communication with the sea was threatened. Then a messenger arrived at Cactus Rock with a covered gift for Montezuma. After the proper obeisances he unwrapped a human head, a Spanish head with a white face and a bushy black beard. It was horrible to see and Montezuma turned away in disgust and ordered the thing to be burnt. Soon afterwards news of the tragedy reached Cortes

Montezuma is taken to the Palace of Axayacatl.
Sahagun's *Historia de las Cosas de Nueva España.*

and he realized that he could not be safe while this kind of plotting was going on among the Aztec nobles. It was only too possible that a serious attack on Vera Cruz could destroy the little settlement, that the causeways in Cactus Rock might be breached and the Spaniards cut off so that any who escaped from Cactus Rock would be hunted down without any hope of reaching the sea.

A week after reaching the city, Cortes made a decision which involved desperate risk: it was to take a prisoner. He felt that he must act and act quickly even if there was a risk of a general insurrection of the people. No doubt he felt that the Aztecs would respond to a captive Montezuma in the same way that European peasants would submit if their king were seized. The Spaniards had no knowledge of the Aztec manner of choosing a sovereign Great Speaker by election. It did not enter their heads that a captive chief might be deposed.

So the Spaniards asked for an interview with the Great Speaker. When this was granted all the great captains of the Spanish party marched in fully armed. Courteously they addressed Montezuma, speaking first of trivialities and then inviting him to leave his own palace and to stay as their guest in the old palace of Axayacatl. Montezuma returned no answer to this until finally, angered at his silence, the Spaniards accused him of planning the attack at Vera Cruz. They said that he only simulated goodwill to them while all the time planning their destruction. The Great Speaker knew that he was trapped. He had no real hope of emerging alive from such a captivity, for even if there was a successful insurrection he knew that the Spaniards would slay him at the threat of danger. However, he must comply while he still could hold off the final act of the drama, so putting a good face on the matter he ordered his retinue to bring his two wives, some servants and many personal treasures to accompany him while he went with his friends to stay in the old palace.

Montezuma was installed in great state but given little freedom in the palace on the western side of the great temple. He was not obviously under duress but armed Spanish noblemen were always in attendance. They thought he would be powerless while they were around him. He did, however, acquire a friend in Orteguilla, a young page boy, who learned from the great Aztec king enough Nahuatl to converse with him in his native tongue. This boy later became a monk and related his experiences of this time.

The Spaniards behaved with courtesy and deference to the Great Speaker, never passing before him without bowing and raising their hats. On his part Montezuma was very kind to them. For the least kindness he would give chains of gold. It seemed that he was delighted with their company and happiest when he was able to please them with some attractive present. Thus began half a year of a most extraordinary situation. The Spaniards, a tiny minority in a crowded city which could be cut off from the mainland at a minute's notice, held in their power the man whom they believed to be the supreme head of the Aztec nation. He was held as a hostage and yet treated as a friend. For his part Montezuma was calm. He knew that another head of the Council of Four would be chosen as the Great Speaker if he was killed. But meanwhile he kept up his state, and gave and received orders as freely as ever, always directing his policy to preserving the interests of his nation and its gods. Undoubtedly he must by now have realized the mortal nature of the Spaniards, but nevertheless they were still the emissaries of a greater being beyond the sea towards the sunrise. They had power in themselves and their equipment which was beyond anything known to the Aztecs, yet in many ways they were hardly civilized. The astonishing thing was their terrible greed for gold which they did not seek for its beauty in jewels, but as metal. Montezuma found that they melted the jewels down into ingots just for ease in carrying. To him it seemed insane. He was ready to flatter them, however, for in that way he could enlarge his freedom. When he found that they had discovered the inner room in which the treasures of his uncle had been stored, he openly invited them to enter and with a magnificent gesture he abandoned the whole hoard to them. To some he gave special ornaments, but Cortes Quetzalcoatl, now called Malintzin, ordered it to be sorted and most of the gold to be melted down. The treasure of featherwork and arms was bundled up with the crates of gold and transported to Villa Rica de Vera Cruz to send to the unknown great one, the Emperor Charles v. The only piece of it known today is the feather shield of Ahuitzotl still in the Habsburg capital in Vienna.

These gifts may have been presented to a god, or they may have been the contemptuous abandonment of a treasure into the hands of people who could not appreciate their true worth. In any case the Spaniards seized on them avidly, and began to quarrel among themselves about them, until Cortes reminded them that the proper 'royal fifth' and a gift beyond it must be put aside for His Majesty the Emperor as required by Spanish law. Of the remainder, the beautiful golden collars and birds of silver and gold became gambling stakes.

The pain of Montezuma's captivity was cruelly increased when the warrior chief Smoky Eagle and his followers were brought as prisoners to Mexico. With a refinement of irony the Spaniards freed them before they went before Montezuma. They crawled before their master and, as was the rule in that noble court, Smoky Eagle covered his fine robes with a coarse maguey-fibre cloak and kissed the ground before his sovereign's feet. The Spaniards repeated their accusation that Montezuma had ordered the attack on the garrison at Vera Cruz. Montezuma absolutely denied it. He trembled for the prisoners, but thought it better that a few should die so that he could preserve his palace contacts with the other warrior chiefs of the Aztecs. So he had to accept a sentence unheard of in Mexico: that the conspirators should be chained to posts and surrounded with fire until they had been consumed in the flames. It is said that some of them, shocked at their fate, accused Montezuma of having commanded the attack. He resolutely denied this, but, fettered in chains, was obliged as a prisoner to watch the execution carried out. The fire was made of Aztec weapons found in the palace storehouses. None of the victims uttered a sound, for they were warriors who would go indeed as smoky eagles before their lord the Sun. When it was over, the ashes cleared away and all was peaceful again, Montezuma returned to his rooms and the Spaniards assumed that having seen what happened to his warriors he would never more enter into a plot.

It was quite clear to Montezuma now that he was doomed, and that he had been overtaken by a fate ordained at his birth. Whether he was responsible or not there were rumours spreading among the Aztec tribes-people that this was the truth and that Montezuma *was* doomed. The ninth Great Speaker of the Aztecs was to be the last, just as the ninth great Quetzalcoatl of the Toltecs had been the last.

Nevertheless, he had the sympathy of his people. Once his nephew Cacama burst into the palace, denounced Cortes to his face as a murderer and thief and threatened to bring the nation in revolt. It was only by consummate diplomacy that Montezuma persuaded the Spaniards that the young chief was without support even in his own city of Tezcoco. In fact, he went so far as to engineer the selection of a powerless junior chief to take over the control of the allied city.

Montezuma now sank into a mood of settled gloom which was very apparent to the Spaniards. His concern was not so much for himself as for his three daughters by his two official wives, and the other palace children. He thought it might be a help to them if his eldest daughter married Cortes, and one day he proposed this to the

Montezuma is put in irons as a captive.
Sahagun's *Historia de las Cosas de Nueva España*.

The Spaniards restrain Montezuma from
attending a festival. Sahagun's *Historia de las
Cosas de Nueva España*.

Spaniard. Cortes declined, explaining that he already had a wife in Cuba. Montezuma
then realized that the strangers followed the Aztec custom by which the noblemen
had official wives as well as others whose children could not inherit. However,
Montezuma entreated his conqueror to protect the children in the days of danger to
come. Cortes gave his word and kept it honourably. It was quite clear that Doña
Marina, who had to translate all this, was a junior wife of Cortes. Whether this conversation had any effect on her is not clear, but she was already obviously pregnant
with the child who was to become Don Martin Cortes.

Cortes was often entertained by the Great Speaker, and those Aztecs who objected
were always told by Montezuma that he remained in the old palace of his own free will.
This was partly diplomacy and perhaps partly true since it is clear that the two men
were on terms of friendship. The theological issues remained a complete barrier, yet
the discussions were friendly. The Spanish priest, Father Olmedo, was a reasonable
and kindly man who often dissuaded Cortes from an over-enthusiastic approach.

Yet beside the palace the great temple still stood, and once every twenty days the
drums and trumpets sounded for a festival·to one of the gods. Some of these were
dance festivals with flowers and music. Others were the occasions of human sacrifice.
However, there were few victims now that the warriors were no longer employed in
raiding outlying areas for prisoners.

It took much persuasion for the Great Speaker to be allowed to take his natural
part in the ceremonies. Probably Cortes never understood Montezuma's position as a
leading priest. However, he was allowed to go under guard with Cortes and he presided at a sacrifice which so horrified the Spanish warrior that he seized the Great

Speaker and demanded that the priests should be brought before them. During the fierce and even violent argument that followed Montezuma remained adamant that his temple must not be desecrated, and he was able to threaten a total revolt of the Aztec people if anything was done to disturb Blue Hummingbird. In the end, among the curses of the black-painted priests, it was agreed that the Spaniards should have an oratory in the house of Tlaloc, the water god. It was cleansed and limewashed and a Christian cross erected in it. A veteran Spaniard was stationed to guard this newly consecrated Christian chapel. What it meant to Montezuma is not clear. The cross to him was in any case probably associated with Tlaloc as the symbol of the four directions of the winds and the four kinds of rain, but many people must have felt in their hearts that the desecration of the holy image of Tlaloc would bring drought and starvation to Mexico.

Meanwhile, Cortes continued to insist that when ships came he would return to the lands beyond the sunrise with tribute from Cactus Rock and after that only return each year to collect tribute in the Aztec fashion.

Montezuma continued to await events. His relatives were allowed to come and go freely and through them he kept informed of events and retained some slight authority in the land. But he could not forget the chains with which he had been fettered when the Spaniards condemned and burnt Smoky Eagle. Then one day a messenger came with a sheet of painted cotton. Montezuma gazed and read hope there. The Spaniards noted that he seemed almost happy. After a decent interval he asked Cortes to come to him. He showed him a painting of the coast and a flotilla of Spanish ships, and told him that now the ship had come he could leave Mexico at his convenience with the tribute for the mysterious king beyond the waters. (Boats were now no mystery to Montezuma. The Spaniards had two little boats with guns on the lake, and he had been taken on sailing trips for hunting expeditions.)

To his surprise the Spaniard appeared visibly disturbed. Then a messenger arrived from the settlement at Vera Cruz with a letter for the Commander. Immediately Cortes called a council of war. An event he had feared had come about and Diego Velasquez, the Governor of Cuba, had sent an invasion force with instructions to arrest Cortes and take over Mexico. It was led by a nobleman, Narvaez, who was a kinsman of the Governor. To Cortes this was a threat to everything he had accomplished in Mexico. He must act rapidly and decisively. After a hurried council of war he decided that one-third of the Spaniards were to be left in Cactus Rock, and the remaining two-thirds were to march with him in battle order to Villa Rica de Vera Cruz in order to defend themselves from this fratricidal attack.

Montezuma pondered these matters. Was this new man an emissary from some other deity? Was Cortes Quetzalcoatl likely to suffer an eclipse, or to be overwhelmed by the dark power of the Evening Star, Xolotl? However, he could take no part in the events in the Totonac country where Vera Cruz was situated because it had revolted against him under the incitement of Cortes. All he could do was to sit and wait. But he knew that Cortes would have a very unpleasant journey because he would be travelling in late May and early June when rainstorms sweep the country and typhoons might overwhelm the coast. There was some hope that Tlaloc might avenge the insults to his image in the great temple.

After Cortes had departed from Cactus Rock the Great Speaker became on good terms with the new commander of the Spanish garrison. His name was Pedro de Alvarado, a gallant soldier, fierce and impetuous. He had been the first to seize hold of Montezuma when he had been forced to leave his palace, but he was a volatile man, quick to smile, and at first was friendly with all around him. The Mexicans admired his shining golden hair and beard and called him Tonatiuh, as if he were the sun god, and indeed his temperament suited the name. So at first things went well enough. It may be that Alvarado had some information about the messengers who came and went from Montezuma, but this is not certain. In any case, after a time he developed a belief that the position of the Spaniards was so precarious that the Aztecs, if they had any sense at all, would attack the garrison at the first opportunity. His sunny moods became fewer and he went around with a portentous frown, keeping the soldiers always in readiness for immediate action.

Above Narvaez is welcomed by some chiefs at Cempoalla. With him is the Negro who so deeply impressed the local people by his unusual colour. From Diego Duran's *Historia de los Indios de Nueva Hispaña.*

Opposite Fragments of sculptured rock, the scattered remains of the summer palace of Montezuma on the hill of Chapultepec, Mexico City.

Then late in April, near the Christian Easter and just over a year since the landing of the Spaniards, the Aztec nobles were due to hold their great festival for the glory of Blue Hummingbird. A young man was to be sacrificed on this occasion. He must be a brave warrior, and physically perfect. For a year he had been dressed and painted like the god. The Spaniards must often have seen him passing by, playing little tunes on the gilded bone flutes hanging from his neck, and dancing as he went, accompanied by his four beautiful young wives. Maybe they had heard that he was to die at the coming of the festival day. But what was of special interest to them was the bustle around the great square outside their quarters. The place was filling with warriors, all in their gorgeous featherwork costumes, and all armed with war clubs and shields, who were arriving for the dances in honour of the god. Among them were the war leaders of the nation, sorrowful because Montezuma was not with them. (Although he had often protested that he went of his own free will with Cortes Quetzalcoatl, no one of importance believed him, and no one now believed that the Spaniard was Quetzalcoatl. He had behaved in too irreligious a fashion. In fact, as many said, he had only claimed to be the messenger of some strange being beyond the sunrise.) So the warriors were ready to make the war dances before the god into occasions of hatred against the strangers in their midst.

Tonatiuh Alvarado was disturbed for everywhere he saw the gathering of high-ranking warriors. Being no Aztec, he had no clear idea of the reason for the ceremony. He felt threatened, and saw that here was a chance of destroying the leadership of the Mexican forces. He called his men together, and issued orders for the arquebusiers to occupy the tops of the palace walls, and for the rest to slip out and surround the square. When all was ready the gateways were opened and a whirlwind of steel was released as the horsemen charged the feather-clad warriors. There were shouts and screams of dismay. No quarter was given or asked. The beautiful feathers fell broken in the blood and entrails on the floor. Everywhere among the screaming could be heard the Spanish battle cry, 'Santiago, Santiago'. Then after a period of madness quiet fell on the square, and spread over the whole city. The Spaniards, well pleased with their slaughter of possible foes, sent a messenger to Cortes at Santa Cruz with news of the great victory, or rather the massacre, and this at a time when he most needed peace because of his own weakness against Narvaez.

Montezuma said nothing, but a deeper gloom settled on him. Messengers came and went away sadly. His relatives were encouraged to leave, and he seemed to be preparing himself to take leave of this world, although it was clear to him that he could not abandon the sacred books which had served so well in foretelling so many un-

Opposite The sun setting over the ruins of Tollan of the Toltecs, at Tula, Hidalgo. The ancient city was destroyed in a civil war near the end of the 10th century. It was five centuries later that Montezuma found it to be the home of his inspiration.

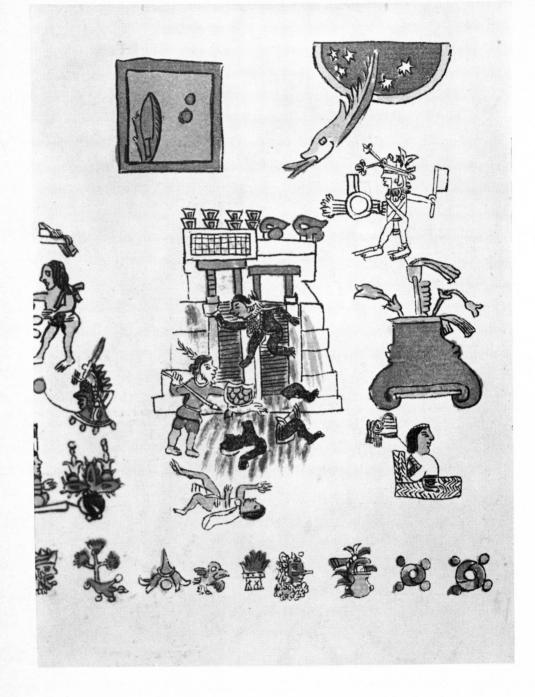

Alvarado massacres the Aztec nobles before
the great temple. *Codex Messicano-Vaticano 3738.*

believable events. It must by now have been obvious to him that Cortes was not a full reincarnation of Quetzalcoatl, but that he represented some related power. The whole matter was one of pre-ordained fate. It seemed to him that when his round of fifty-two years was completed the whole cycle of personal fate for him would be consummated. Probably he realized it must be by death. Meanwhile he, the Great Speaker for the Aztec nation, could neither rule nor speak effectively. His personal tragedy was felt keenly by the great nobles of his people. That is clear from their previous offers of rescue attempts which he had always declined. But after Tonatiuh Alvarado's massacre of the warriors the Aztecs could no longer remain passive.

Montezuma asked the Spaniards for an interview with his brother Cuitlahuac. What the discussion was about is not known. Nobody has reported its details, because Montezuma made sure of secrecy by asking his Spanish friends to let them talk in peace with only a guard of soldiers present. He knew that the soldiers would know a little Nahuatl, but not enough to follow a conversation, and he personally asked that the young page, Orteguilla, stay away. The events that followed suggest that he had been preparing for his own removal from the scene of misery, and that he either asked for or approved a meeting of the Great Council at which the Aztecs would decide on a course of action in the light of what he had said. It was perfectly clear that he would not be able to take part.

The parting with his brother was a sad one, for now Montezuma had few male relatives in that palace of restrictions. His daughters remained and some attendants, as well as the many slaves and helpers who cared for the Spaniards in such duties as cleaning and cooking. Something in Montezuma's mind had kept him steadily sending his relatives and friends on errands from which they were not expected to return to him. Some of the Spaniards felt this to be ominous but overt action against the great lord of the Aztecs was as yet far too dangerous a gamble. It would have given an immediate cue for an insurrection of the whole people, and there was no chance at that stage of any Spaniard surviving. Montezuma also persuaded the Spaniards to take no action against the priests and to allow them to continue their sacrifices. He explained in his diplomatic way that the love the common people felt for their protecting spirits would have made the imprisonment of the priests even more dangerous than attacking him personally. The Spaniards saw in his soft and gentle speech the submission of a defeated chieftain to their will, for they could have had no idea that the Mexican Indian would submit only before the fate decreed by the powers above. They saw in Monte-zuma the cowardly ruler trying to save his own position in spite of the downfall of his people, although they suspected that he must have been plotting something for a long time.

The news of the massacre had been a sad blow to Montezuma. Then came mes-sengers from the coast with news still more painful to bear. There had been a battle at Cempoalla in which Cortes had met the better-equipped and much larger force led by Narvaez and had defeated it in a single fight. For Montezuma the real terror was that the victory of Cortes had been won in a tropical storm, in which the torrential rain and flickering uncertainty caused by the lightning had been a major factor in bringing about the defeat of the newcomers. Tlaloc and his consort had been dancing and pouring out the waters and whirlwinds to assist Cortes. This was their revenge for being ousted from the shrine next to Blue Hummingbird on the great temple top. Cortes Quetzalcoatl was now marching back towards Cactus Rock with three times as many men as he had taken out, more horses, more weapons and more cannon. Whatever power was assisting the stranger was no friend of the Aztecs. It seemed that the vision given a year ago by Blue Hummingbird to the envoys from Mexico was being fulfilled. Montezuma hoped he would never see that dreadful day when his beautiful city would be consumed in flames.

In a strange way Montezuma was relieved to know that Cortes was returning, for now that he had accepted his fate, he felt almost eager that its consummation should not be too far distant. Meanwhile there was silence in the city. The Great Council of the nation was meeting and Montezuma knew well enough that he would be replaced as Great Speaker.

On the coast Cortes was organizing his newly-acquired levies and supervising the dismantling of the ships from which he had removed all the iron-work and blocks and tackle. Apparently he had some idea of preventing them from sailing away to Cuba and bringing new forces against him. However, he was soon to be pleased that he had the materials in readiness for another more immediate use.

At this point Mexican messengers arrived to spread the news that Cactus Rock was in turmoil and that the Spanish invaders were being driven out. The stories worried Cortes and he sent messengers with an urgent request for information. It was two weeks before the letter from Alvarado arrived and it brought frightening news. The Aztecs had risen to attack the old palace from all quarters. The Spanish garrison had resisted them, but they were in a desperate situation and the Aztecs were beginning to dig tunnels to undermine the walls. There were not enough Spaniards to prevent them. This rebellion was perhaps to be expected. Cortes had had no part in the slaughter on the festival of Blue Hummingbird, and he was angry at the rashness of Alvarado which had been certain to bring trouble upon them. Now it had happened and was even worse than he feared.

The Spaniards set out on their march to Cactus Rock immediately, but the journey took two weeks. As they neared the city they found no welcome from the surrounding villages. No opposition was offered them but no crowds came out to see them or to offer them provisions. What they needed they must search for and seize. Though there was no resistance the hatred of them was almost tangible. Messengers reached them from Alvarado with more heartening news: the attacks had ceased, but there was still a complete blockade of the palace. They needed reinforcements to improve their

Opposite Quetzalcoatl as morning star rising from the jaws of green earth. Sculptured in hard stone.

position and to seize food if possible. Another messenger, an Aztec, came from Montezuma. Presumably his badge of authority helped the two messengers through the blockade. The Great Speaker sent word that he had had no part in the troubles which had swept over the palace like a storm wave from the lake. He said that he had no longer any power to stop the revolt and that he welcomed the return of his friend Cortes and his new allies from across the sea.

Cortes had no choice but to advance. He could not leave his garrison to be slaughtered, nor could he ask for them to leave with Montezuma as a hostage. Nothing would do but to put a bold face on it and march to the city centre, strong in the knowledge that with the new troops he could hardly be defeated, even though the danger would be extreme. So on the midsummer feast of St John Baptist, 24 June 1520, Cortes entered Mexico for the second time. It was a sad journey; his companions were in danger, the city was sullen and completely silent. As he crossed the causeway he saw no canoes on the lake. The two sailing boats he had built and armed were not there and he knew already that the Mexicans had burnt them. So if the causeways were broken down retreat could not be by boat. A few smaller streets in the town already presented gaps in the roads where the timber bridges had been torn away. The threat was obvious. Its dangers were emphasized by the silence which hung over the previously gay city. No crowds in the market, no one on the roof tops, a few spirals of smoke to show that people were in the silent houses. What people? With what intent? They marched on. Even the great temple pyramid was lonely. There was no sign of the priests, and the curtains hung low over the gods' houses. The house in which the statues had been placed showed black smoke stains over the clean white plaster where the gods of the strangers had been burnt. Cortes promised himself a revenge against Blue Humming-bird.

The force marched across the great square, and then into the opening doorways of the old palace. There was great joy at the strange reunion. Grim old warriors met again and wept on each others' shoulders. The only exception to the rejoicing was Cortes who refused to speak to the hot-headed Tonatiuh Alvarado. However, the situation was so desperate that they had no time to quarrel. The only course lay in retrieving the error that had already been committed.

The food situation in the palace was not desperate but supplies would not last long, especially with the new army which had joined them. In ordinary times the store-rooms would have been full, waiting for the time when the people would come for their supplies of food to tide them over the last few days before the harvest. But this year hardly any tribute had been gathered. Revolts and the marching of armies had frightened the peasantry and everyone had hoarded what was possible from the crops. The Spaniards would not leave Montezuma to his peaceful despair. They railed at him and insulted him, calling him a useless dog, though, indeed, Cortes was still courteous. His messengers were heeded for old times' sake, but the supplies of food which were brought to the palace were placed at the gates and left without any message. They were not in great quantity and were poor in quality. The Spaniards would not have

Montezuma realizes he has been deposed.

The stoning of the deposed Great Speaker.

noticed this, but Montezuma knew well that he was being slighted. All things must be endured by him, however, for he knew that the end could not long be delayed.

The next morning proved him right. There was a roar of voices approaching, which turned into a great shouting and whistling of warriors as human waves of attackers surged up to the palace wall. They were mown down by the guns which Cortes had placed in specially cut embrasures, but to no avail; the attack continued, and the courtyard of the old palace was showered with sling stones falling from above and a deadly rain of arrows. The furious people had at last revolted under the leadership of Montezuma's younger brother, Cuitlahuac, and were doing what they could to destroy the hated strangers. Death was no stranger in that city and the warriors were not afraid. Their attack was partially successful, for they had fired some blazing arrows into the

air, and these set the wooden shacks inhabited by the Tlaxcalans into a blaze. Some of the huts were smashed down without too much difficulty to prevent the fire from spreading to the cedar roof-beams of the palace; but some of the timber supports of the defensive wall caught fire. Cortes saw that it would fall, and had cannon brought up to fire through the breach as the wall collapsed. The step was successful. The evening fell and the Aztecs withdrew for the night. A few bold spirits continued to throw stones intermittently all night, but they were too few in number to present a real danger. The respite allowed the invaders to pile back the stones of the broken wall into a reasonably useful defensive position, but there was little sleep for them that night.

Montezuma himself took no action and he remained in his room and servants brought him food.

On the next day the attack was resumed at first light. Here and there great war chiefs could be seen in their feather-work panoplies directing the assaults. There was some extra danger to the Spaniards from heavier stones and fire brands thrown from the

roofs of houses near the palace. Cortes decided to take a party of soldiers in armour on a sortie to clear the region closest to his base. The gates opened and as the Aztecs prepared to rush them they were swept down by a wave of grey steel. There was no holding them as they cleared the square. Nearby houses were set on fire and only the walls remained. But the next row of houses was a fortress which could not be reached until planks were found and placed across the gaps where bridges had been. Then the Spanish foray progressed slowly clearing the ground street by street. Great boulders came tumbling on them from the roofs. Some were unhorsed and the enemy tried to seize them and drag them away for sacrifice. There was horror in the air for the bearded ex-gods. At last when some three hundred houses had been burnt, Cortes began to fight his way back. He personally came to the rescue of many friends and followers. But for every step taken back by the Spaniards a step forward was taken by ever-increasing multitudes of warriors who believed that death for their gods was a pathway to the glories of heaven. A few Spaniards had been captured. For them there was no ceremonial death. They were dragged up the temple stairway and sliced open so that their hearts, still beating and spurting their life's blood, could be offered to the sun. Their companions saw all this, unable to help. Horror in fighting was a commonplace with them but they were sickened by this callous human sacrifice. It was terrible, too, because they were convinced that their friends were being offered to the devil himself.

There was little peace at night, and in the morning, in spite of a lull, the ominous murmur of whistles and beating of drums warned of another attack. Cortes and the leading Spaniards came to Montezuma. They asked him to try to save the lives of his countrymen by commanding the attacks to cease, but Montezuma saw it was their own lives that they feared for. He felt he could do nothing more for Cortes. Already his submission had led him to prison and loneliness. What more could he do, except to die? They begged him to go out and call a halt to the attacks. He asked why anyone in that Aztec nation in arms would believe him or accept any promise from faithless Spaniards. The time of the gods was here and man could not intervene. Yet he allowed their demands and entreaties to prevail. He took his turquoise-studded cloak, put on his turquoise crown and telling the Spaniards that he was already a nobody among his people he ascended to the parapet of the wall.

There was a total hush for a minute or two when the people saw him. Then a few voices called out that he was a coward and a traitor. A voice of greater authority spoke out and said that he had no more rule over them, for the Great Council had elected Cuitlahuac in his place. For a moment there was quiet again, and then a swishing sound as one, two, three stones came flying through the air. One stone struck the crown from his head, one struck his cheek and another his forehead. Without a word he fell to the ground, not apparently badly hurt but deeply shocked. Yet he had half expected this to happen. Only the crowd of the Aztecs was really hurt. They retired without a word, many of them weeping. The anger they had felt against the ex-Great Speaker

Opposite Montezuma dies, abandoned by his people.

Above The Spaniards cast out the cadavers of Montezuma and his cousin Itzcuauhtzin. Sahagun's *Historia de las Cosas de Nueva España.*

Below The dead Montezuma is carried away by the Aztecs. Sahagun's *Historia de las Cosas de Nueva España.*

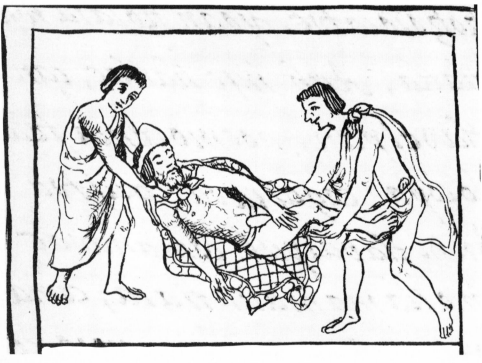

was somehow dissolved. He had become a victim offered to the spirit of Mexico's protector, Blue Hummingbird.

In great consternation the Spaniards hurried the wounded man back to his quarters in the heart of the palace. He would not lie down, but sat upright against a column. They brought medicines and bandages. But as soon as any bandage was in place he tore it away, slowly and deliberately. Orteguilla begged him to live but the emperor said nothing to his friend.

For three days the great Montezuma suffered stoically and silently, then on the fourth day he died. For three days and nights young Orteguilla wept and would not eat. Such was the greatest tribute to the dead man from one to whom he had never been a king.

The horoscope in the painted books for the day of his death was a strange one, as of one who had been drawn in two directions. It might have been a horoscope of his birth.

There are two accounts of the events that followed. The Spaniards say that they parleyed with the Aztec Great Speaker, Cuitlahuac, and gave Montezuma's body into his care with due honour. The Aztecs, on the other hand, say that at dead of night a doorway opened and the body of Montezuma and that of a nephew of his were cast out, and that Montezuma had been stabbed. The Spaniards talk of kindness and a vain attempt to convert Montezuma to Christianity. The Aztecs tell of Spanish chagrin and rage which turned to murder. Either would have been in character for the Spaniards.

We shall never know the truth now. Montezuma's nephew Itzcuautzin, Eagle Prince of Knives, had been in the palace visiting his uncle. Did he try to fight a way out? Certainly he was a brave young warrior, and had no love for cruel men from the eastern seas. There is no evidence to back up either story.

With deep grief and respect Itzcuautzin's body was taken to a courtyard for cremation. Montezuma's dead body was not honoured, but was put also on a pile of wood, of broken darts and spears. Then fire was brought to the pyres. The flames spread. From the brave Itzcuautzin there came white smoke, but the body of Montezuma had to suffer a last revenge by Tlaloc, the storm god. As it burnt, the corpse burst and generated great black clouds of sulphurous smoke as if in a terrible thunderstorm. People were horrified. But the burning continued until the whitened bone ash was all that was left. It was hurriedly pushed into a stone box and hastened away to an unmarked burial. There was no time to honour the dead in those terrible days of killing in Cactus Rock. The war would go on, not with any hope of a return of the Toltec glories, but to drive away the foreigners and their gods. The Aztecs would fight for victory and their national honour.

12
THE TOTALITY OF CHANGE

THE DEATH OF MONTEZUMA could not alter the fated outcome of the Spanish invasion. But at first things seemed to go badly for the strangers. The Spaniards knew that with the whole of the Aztec people in desperate revolt they had no chance of escape unless they could get away from Cactus Rock. Cortes tried to arrange parleys with the new Great Speaker, but to no avail. He offered a great bribe of stolen treasures for permission to leave in a week's time, and the Aztecs seemed prepared to accept this chance of recovering some of their lost heritage. Cortes, however, had no intention, in spite of his offer, of parting with the treasure. Nights were dark around Cactus Rock and the Spaniards knew that on the following night there was no moon. They waited for the next night to fall, then they muffled the horses' hooves and slipped out. Each man was laden with such of the treasures as he could carry. Newcomers loaded themselves with heavy gold, to their sorrow later. The cavalcade of Spaniards and Tlaxcalans was led by the bravest Spanish horsemen and more of these took up the rearguard, which was commanded by Tonatiuh Alvarado. In the centre were the women with a few older or wounded Spanish soldiers, and the great body of Tlaxcalan warriors. The cavalcade left fires burning in the palace so that all seemed normal as they slipped silently out into the streets.

They had passed over one bridge and were on the causeway across the lake, when a woman cried out, 'Mexicans, Mexicans, the evil ones are leaving.' Then trumpets sounded. Suddenly there was a splashing of thousands of paddles as canoes stormed across the lake. The bridges were pulled down, and the Spaniards were attacked from all sides. Few could have withstood such an onslaught. Warriors leaping from canoes tried to drag their enemies into the lake and drown them. Others harassed the rear, killing the wounded as they fell back. Some of the Mexican war leaders commanded forces which opposed the advancing van and saw to it that the losses were heavy.

As the Spanish party advanced to the gaps in the causeway they fought each step. Some fell into the waters, some scrambled or leapt fighting across the gap. Those following struggled through. Many were cut down, others dropped their loads in the marshy lake bed. The main body clambered across piles of dead and wounded, through

Opposite Skull of Mictlantecuhtli (Lord of the
Land of the Dead) carved in smoky quartz.

broken boxes of treasure and shattered spears. But the piles of dead increased; the Aztecs were not pausing to select prisoners for sacrifice.

Cortes and his warriors fought on and reached the end of the causeway. There they were joined by the survivors, some of the women including Doña Marina, and Doña Luisa, daughter of the Tlaxcalan commander, and last of all by a few scarred veterans led by Alvarado who had had what seemed a miraculous escape. As the attacks ceased they formed into a defensive ring, and Cortes wept as he saw that two-thirds of those who had left the besieged palace were now missing, mostly dead in the marshy lake. Under the great *ahuehuete* cypress where Cortes rested his troops he named the occasion 'the night of sorrow'. Among his sorrows was the news that one of Montezuma's daughters had been slain, so that he had not entirely kept his promise to protect them.

For a while the attacks were reduced to a continual harassment. The Aztec plan was to allow the Spaniards to continue on their march so that they could be massacred successfully in a suitable place. On the fourth day, as the Spaniards marched towards the hills, they saw a great army with war banners of feather-work, and glistening with gold and silver. This was the group which had come to destroy them. As was usual the Aztec army halted before the attack, and Cortes had time to note that in the centre in a golden palanquin the army commander was to be seen directing the movements of the Ocelot and Eagle warriors. Cortes called his horsemen to form up and to strike a path through the enemy and to kill or at least upset the commander. When the attack began, all the Spanish horsemen were wounded, but nevertheless the assault got through. The golden palanquin was upset, the commander trampled and wounded, and his golden standard was carried off by a Spanish horseman back to Cortes. Demoralization set in among the Aztecs, some warriors stood and fought, others scattered.

The Spaniards persisted in their attacks. Every sortie was a risk, but their desperate position demanded desperate bravery. The Tlaxcalans too were particularly bold. They kept good order in their advance, fighting steadily all the way. After all, they were on the road home to Tlaxcala and had everything to gain. So the strangers conquered the road from Otumba to Tlaxcala and found at least a respite from their disasters.

None of the Spaniards knew what would happen when they reached Tlaxcala. So many of the warriors had been killed that the towns would be filled with mourning. Cortes was often in council with his captains, but nothing could be decided. They simply hoped and prayed ... as they had all through their terrible ordeal.

They passed through the defensive wall of the Tlaxcalan state without opposition. Then they were met by a delegation of the four chiefs who ruled the land. There was

Opposite Xochipilli (Flower Prince), the god of
song and material pleasures. Seated on a plinth
he lifts his head to sing in true Aztec fashion.
Early 16th century Aztec work.

Opposite The monkey, Ozomatli, servant of Xochipilli. The monkey was thought of as a wildly erotic and irresponsible being. On his breast he wears the symbol of unbridled pleasure the Oyoualli, symbol of the vulva. Aztec, early 16th century.

Above After the retreat from Cactus Rock, Cortes is given succour by the Tlaxcalans. He sits between Doña Marina and the younger Xicotencatl who has succeeded his father as Speaker of the Tlaxcalans. From a maguey paper version of *Lienzo de Tlaxcala*.

weeping, but commendation too. The chiefs had watched the campaign and knew of the heroism of the Spaniards as well as the destruction of their old enemy, Montezuma. They had no regrets that they had allied themselves with Spain, and gave the Spaniards a practical welcome in the form of food, clothes and women.

Tlaxcala was a poor and harsh place compared to the luxurious wonders of Cactus Rock. But it was a haven in which recovery was soon well advanced. Cortes sent men to the coast to bring back what military stores were still left. The Totonacs had not raided the camps and remained friendly. Then more ships arrived from Cuba. The crews were persuaded to join the expedition and to bring their supplies of new arms, gunpowder, and armour to the aid of Cortes. So once more a well-equipped though small army from the strange world across the seas was ready to face the might of the Aztecs.

237

But there was another terrible ally of the Spanish invaders in Mexico: the smallpox. It had been brought by a Negro lieutenant in the army of Narvaez, and seemed to be a horrible evil spirit which afflicted its victims with red sores, and terrible pains. If they went to the sweat baths and then leapt into cold streams as they had done in the past for healing, they died only the more quickly. The terror spread and millions died. It was said that a quarter of the people were slain by the red demon, including the emperor Cuitlahuac. Cries to the gods were unavailing, for the gods had turned their faces from them when the great temple was desecrated.

Cuitlahuac being dead, the appointment of a new Great Speaker was an urgent matter. Some sought a brilliant mind, others wanted to choose only a warrior. But all were satisfied at the choice of Cuauhtemoctzin, Prince Falling Eagle. He was very young, then hardly twenty, but a brave fighter and of a brilliant intellect. If any of the Aztec chief family could destroy the strangers, young Falling Eagle could do so. (His name has a double meaning, implying both the eagle stooping to pluck its prey from the earth, and the eagle as the setting sun. Although the latter meaning was to prevail, no one was to question the heroism which the prince possessed and with which he inspired his people.)

The battle of the gods still continued, for the Mexican warriors still fought for Blue Hummingbird, and the Spaniards were still engaged in a Christian crusade. For the few people who understood there might have been a reconciliation which would have replaced the archetypal gods with a Christian solution to their problems but there were very few who understood and the outward faces of the two forms of belief were utterly irreconcilable. The sacrifice of the Divine in man was not seen to have any relationship with the sacrifice of man to the Divine.

A little more than a year from the first entry of the Spaniards into Cactus Rock, news came that Cortes was leaving Tlaxcala, and approaching some smaller fortified towns towards Tezcoco. The plan was not to assault Cactus Rock but to encircle it. In Tlaxcala shipwrights were finding timber, tools and men to turn forest trees into a series of strongly built, prefabricated brigantines which were to sail on the lake and carry the dreaded cannon to blast the Aztecs into surrender. But they could not know this and so both sides played a waiting game.

Now an event occurred which was to be disastrous for the Aztecs and provide the Spaniards with their greatest opportunity. It sprang originally from Montezuma's refusal to recognize Prince Ixlilxochtitl, nephew of Nezahualpilli, as Speaker of

Opposite A page from a 'Doctrina Cristiana' written after about 1550 in Testerian characters. The friars found that the Mexicans responded to written symbols, but they did not use the ancient system. A famous preacher named Tester (of Swiss origin) developed an accepted system of symbols to be used in teaching. This section deals with the matter of contrition in the sacrament of penance.

Tezcoco. The prince had gone into hiding and bided his time. Cuitlahuac had appointed a new Speaker for Tezcoco, who promptly murdered the young chief Cacama, previously appointed by Montezuma. Meanwhile, many Tezcocans still supported the exiled young Prince Ixtlilxochitl (Vanilla Flower). Thus Tezcoco was divided amongst itself.

When the Spaniards reached Tezcoco, the chief appointed by Cuitlahuac came out with an embassy, presented Cortes with a golden banner and invited him to enter the city. They did so, but warily, because the interview seemed too pat and there was no elaborate exchange of gifts. As they arrived they noticed that the people seemed to have gone into hiding. Then a flotilla of canoes was seen leaving with women and children. Next an outburst of warriors attacked and were defeated, and the Spaniards found themselves in an apparently deserted city in which they could be besieged and destroyed. However, great numbers of people came out of hiding, and another embassy arrived from the hills. This was led by the legitimate chief, Prince Vanilla Flower, who came to offer assistance to the enemies of the Aztecs who had dispossessed him. Thus another of Montezuma's errors of judgment came to the aid of the Spaniards. Ixtlilxochitl was ready to listen to the priests and teachers of the new religion. His submission and baptism were great victories for the new God. In addition, his city with its canals and access to the lake was vital for Cortes' project to use the brigantines.

Word was sent to Tlaxcala and thousands of porters set out on the long march surrounded by more thousands of warriors whom Cortes fondly hoped had become Christians. (Later he had often to reprimand and punish them for murder and cannibalism in the ancient tradition.) The great caravan of warriors and porters finally arrived safely in the valley of Mexico. There was great rejoicing, not least in Tezcoco where there was now sufficient force to repel any Aztec attack. Prince Vanilla Flower was baptized as a Christian, choosing the name of his supporter Hernando Cortes as his Christian name, though his own people continued to call him Vanilla Flower. He had always been popular and now he organized life in the city with so much justice that there was little likelihood of his people ever supporting the Aztecs again.

Now began a series of difficult campaigns in which the Spaniards lost many men and horses, but the Aztecs failed to break them. More than half the shores of the lakes were captured. Fortresses were stormed and Aztec armies driven back. Many cities were totally abandoned, because those of the people who had survived the plague had gone to other towns or to Cactus Rock. In other places the desperate Aztecs had oppressed the people, taking food and women indiscriminately, so that the nobles secretly sent to ask the Spaniards to deliver them.

On one occasion the Spaniards drove the Aztec armies from a city, but within hours Falling Eagle had sent a flotilla of ten thousand canoes to retake it. When the Spaniards hastened back they arrived to find their new allies had smashed the attacking Aztec force and were marching towards them with a great train of prisoners. Such was the power of the hatred aroused by past generations of Aztec oppression.

The Spaniards and their allies besiege Cactus
Rock. From *Lienzo de Tlaxcala*.

The Aztecs demanded from several towns a supply of maize grown on special
farms for the service of the gods. They sent warriors to collect it but the Spanish
caballeros went with armies of the local people to prevent the grain from reaching
Cactus Rock. At least half the food reserves of the Aztecs were thus cut off.

At Xochimilco, the busy market town at the end of the main causeway into Cactus
Rock, there were great battles, and the Spaniards were forced back twice before they
finally took the town. Here again the Aztecs attacked and retreated easily from canoes.
As one battle ended another one started. Cortes had sent an embassy of captured Aztec
nobles to offer Falling Eagle immediate peace and freedom if he would surrender. But
the noble Aztec was fighting for the life of the nation and for the honour of his gods
and refused any parley. The war must go on.

The Aztecs must have realized that they were effectively doomed when the first of

Prince Ixtlilxochitl (Vanilla Flower) assists the
Spaniards to build the brigantines on the lake.
Diego Duran's *Historia de los Indios de
Nueva Hispaña.*

the Spanish brigantines sailed out on to the lake. The two boats in which Montezuma
had sailed had already shown the possibilities of fast-moving craft armed with guns.
Now there was a flotilla of them ready to sweep up and destroy any group of canoes
coming from Cactus Rock. The end was in sight, but the Aztecs were not cowards.
They were prepared to fight to the last. The great drum sounded from the temple top
more than ever before. The sound was already known to the Spaniards. Now they
knew that some of their companions were being sliced open so that their hearts could
be lifted up to the lips of the terrible idol of Blue Hummingbird. They were determined that this abomination should cease.

The battle continued, long drawn out and severe. The Aztecs evolved a strategy of
luring the brigantines on to the sharp stakes hidden in the water, and then boarding
them. Death was all around and no fighting man on either side remained unwounded.
Cortes had had thirteen brigantines made, and they were now able to shield the three

columns of Spaniards fighting a way along the causeways. They were trapped and forced back into open gaps in the walls so often that it seemed at times that the Aztecs might succeed in destroying them all. The only way was to advance and smash any houses and fortifications and use the rubble to fill in the canals and gaps in the causeways. With bitter struggles the Spaniards advanced, and eventually reached the city. Twice more Cortes sent messengers through to Falling Eagle, but each time the heroic prince still refused a truce.

Much to his distress Cortes was forced to move into the beleaguered town, where there was now no fresh water and little food except for the flesh of sacrificial victims. The resistance was so fierce that each house must be destroyed as it was captured and the rubble thrown into the canals. The soldiers, under Sandoval, burst first into the quarter of the city where Falling Eagle had lived. They captured the great market squares and temples at Tlaltelolco and then drove slowly forward.

Cortes himself was pushed back but again drove forward, although he and every man in his command were wounded more than once. They poured hot oil into the cuts to cauterize them and after a short pause pushed on, desperately. At last as they broke into the main square of Cactus Rock, they saw a splendid canoe set out surrounded by a flotilla of other canoes filled with fighting men. The Spanish brigantines went after it. Cortes gave strict orders that if possible no one was to be killed or injured. He had seen too much of slaughter and had pity on the starving Aztec women and children who crawled from the ruins to beg for food and water before they died. It was a horror for both sides. So the brigantine, commanded by Juan Jaramillo, came up with the Aztec canoes. There was no fight. The starving and still glorious warriors finally surrendered at the order of Falling Eagle.

Cortes welcomed Falling Eagle with honour and proffered friendship. The young chief said he submitted though he would have preferred to die. But that was not to be. Cortes had forced his men to behave with unwilling clemency in the battle; now he was determined to be magnanimous. His only sign of victory as he sat at the gateway of the palace was a plume of shining quetzal feathers secured to his hat. It may well be that Doña Marina had arranged this symbol. It was, though Cortes never knew it, the symbol of royal power derived from Quetzalcoatl. To him it was simply an attribute of great chiefs. To the defeated Aztecs it was a symbol that it was not the man but the decree of fate that had conquered. Some of them must have hoped that now the victory was achieved the reign of a benevolent new god would commence.

Even while Falling Eagle arrived before Cortes, Spanish officers took a loaf of bread to the palace where the daughters of Montezuma anxiously awaited their fate. Although starving and weak, they yet retained their quiet bearing as noblewomen. Cortes went to visit them and welcomed them as the daughters of a much-valued friend. He was now secure in victory and could afford to be generous to the defeated. But soon dissensions arose among his own people, who were, as Montezuma had noted, hungry for gold. Very little treasure had been found either in the palace of Montezuma or in the rooms occupied by Falling Eagle. The treasures carried off by the Spaniards on the

yepolinhã mexica

Above Cortes receives the surrender of
Cuauhtemoctzin (Chief Falling Eagle) and
sends food to the daughters of Montezuma.
From *Lienzo de Tlaxcala*.

Opposite A page from the tribute lists of
Montezuma, copied into *Codex Mendoza*,
Bodleian Library, Oxford. This page shows the
tribute exacted from Soconusco, the home state
of Doña Marina. As befits a tropical region it
sends jaguar skins, feathers of tropical birds,
and bales of cacao beans. There are also jade
beads and crystal lip-plugs. On the left side
the towns paying the tribute are listed.

Overleaf Last refuge of the Toltec Itza princes,
the Maya-Toltec centre of Chichen Itza in
Yucatan. The Castillo, a temple to
Quetzalcoatl, seen from beside the serpent
columns of the Temple of the Warriors.
12th to 13th centuries.

noche triste and lost in the lake were never recovered. So far no trace has been found
of them. Most likely they were carried off in small quantities by Aztecs before the city
fell. However, the soldiers who had fought on land now accused those on the brigantines of having robbed the Aztecs and kept the plunder for themselves. Cortes ordered
all gold found in the camp to be seized, but even then it was a disappointingly small
amount.

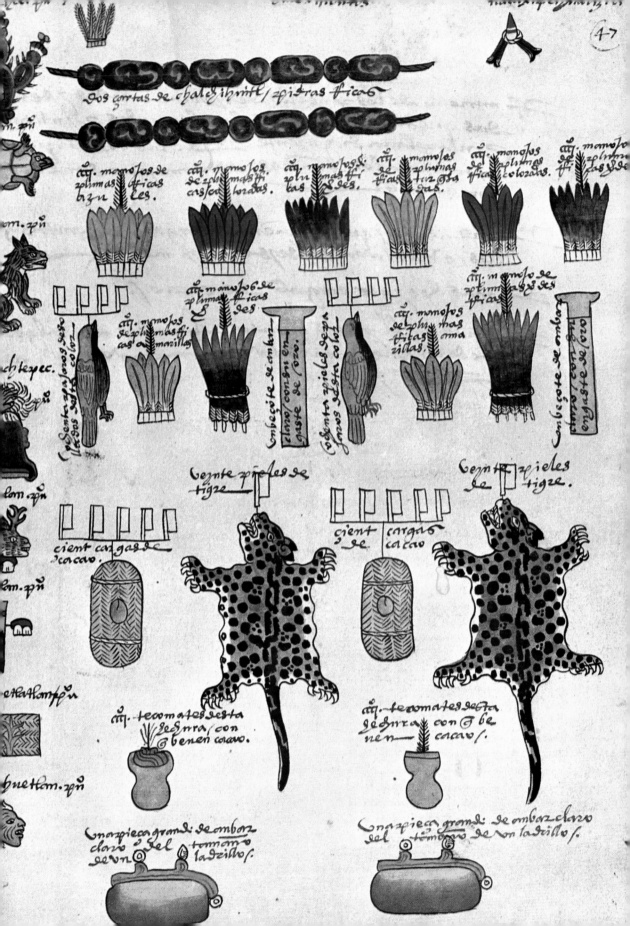

On the day before the end of the fighting a Spanish force had stormed the great temple pyramid of Blue Hummingbird. It was a glorious exploit and dangerous in the extreme. On the top platform they found some remains of their comrades who had been offered to the god. They found the skin of their faces, and their skulls, all cleaned and ready to be sent around to other towns to show that Spaniards were only mortal. But the blood-stained mess of the place with its bowls of hearts and remains of the butchery of dead bodies after sacrifice horrified them. There was little treasure there except for jade and turquoise. So in a spirit of utter loathing the Spaniards burnt down the glorious gilded and painted shrines of cedar wood. It was said that the conflagration joined a thunder storm, and that among the rushing flames the shape of Blue Hummingbird was seen hastening screaming into the storm. His terrible image had been cast down and smashed before being burnt.

The Spaniards and their allies were faced with the aftermath of that most ferocious struggle of war. The city was literally reduced to rubble which blocked all the canals. Amid the ruins the great pyramid temples of Tlaltelolco and Cactus Rock towered high and vacant. Among the rubble lay thousands of bodies of those who had died of hunger as well as the dead of the fighting. The air was chilly and wet, but a vast sweet stink of rotting flesh hung over the place. Cortes feared plague. He sent soldiers around to burn what they could of the ruins. There was not much wood left either. The men reported nothing of life, only swollen grotesque bodies and human heads rolling loose among the stones. So Cortes ordered abandonment of the ruins, and the soldiers, the Aztecs and the rescued civilians left Cactus Rock to the natural forces of decay.

The nadir of the city's fortunes had been reached. Nothing was left but a vast emptiness. The Spaniards who had seen Cactus Rock in its sunny beauty wept for what was gone. Cortes lamented the grim necessity, and the Aztecs mourned without hope. The towns-people were living on the gifts of strangers, and were without homes, often without families, and deserted by their gods. The tragedy of the city was greater than the tragedy of the wise Montezuma, for in its destruction lay the loss of an entire civilization. And now all that glory was a field of rubble scattered with the evidence of fleshly corruption. And this mess with its empty pyramids lay in the lake surrounded by mountains. The sky was clear for a while so that the beauty of the setting emphasized the loss of the jewel which had been its heart.

Ce Coatl Vei Calli

14 August 1521

By this date, which marked the downfall of Mexico, nearly a quarter of a million

Opposite The Gulf Coast of Mexico near Vera Cruz. This was the natural eastern limitation of Aztec power. It was also the western point where the Spaniards commenced the invasion of Mexico. By tradition it was also in this region that Quetzalcoatl after abandoning Mexico sailed into the sunrise.

A Mexican nobleman wearing a feather cloak.
From the *Trachtenbuch* of Christoph Weidetz.

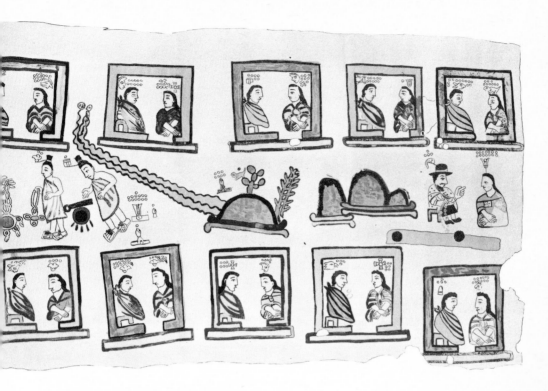

A page from *Codex Baranda*. Centre section:
the native warriors cast down their weapons.
They are forced to give treasures to the Spanish
conquerors. Later an Hispanicised chief is
married to a local heiress in the year of new
fire – 1559.

Aztecs had died after eighty days of heroic resistance.

After the fall of Cactus Rock, Doña Marina asked for an interview with Cortes. She resigned her position as his secretary and asked permission to marry a Spaniard named Don Juan Jaramillo, who had captured Falling Eagle and whom she loved. She had fulfilled the mission of her birth and the magic was concluded. Cortes gave her his friendly consent. After this she lived happily and had many children. Her home was in Painalla where she had been born. She made her mother happy and spread kindness around her. Nevertheless in Mexico even today the name Malintzin echoes a sense of betrayal and of the cruelty which marched beside her in the form of Cortes who was also called Malintzin.

When the fires in Mexico had all died out it was possible for people to re-enter the ruins and bury the sad heaps of human bones. All was left clean; but no one knew what would replace the city of Cactus Rock. The people were without hopes and without gods. They were looked upon as curiosities. Visiting chiefs from other parts

Aztec craftsmen quarry and carve stone for the new churches in Mexico. From Sahagun's *Historia de los Cosas de Nueva España*.

The Mexican house built for Hernando Cortes after the Conquest. From a 19th century print.

of Mexico came to give their submission to the Spaniards because of their obviously magic powers. Cortes had them taken on the sailing brigantines to tour the ruins. They were astonished by the boats and terrified by the sight of such destruction. A great and wonderful capital of an empire of terror had been razed to the ground. Some of those chiefs came from Michoacan, which is on the Pacific coast. Having made their peace with the Spaniards they conducted them on the long journey to their homeland and showed them the Pacific Ocean. Immediately on seeing the great ocean the Spaniards made a great cross of wood and marched into the sea to plant it, thus claiming it for His Catholic Majesty the King of Spain and for the Holy Church. The local people must have been astonished, but they accepted these things as they happened, for there was nothing else for them to do.

The soldiers, hungry for gold, demanded that Falling Eagle should be tortured so that he would reveal the hiding place of the Aztec treasure. Cortes was unable to persuade them otherwise. The principal captives were tied to the frames. Another chief on the rack groaned of the pain, but the silent Falling Eagle spoke to him, 'Do you

Fig. 9.

The aftermath of conquest. Year 11 *calli* (1529).
Nuñez de Guzman sets out to pacify the
Tarascans. His campaign was carried out with
exceptional cruelty. *Codex Telleriano Rememensis.*

think *I* am having a bath?' He said much gold had been thrown in the water. No more.
Cortes at length came in and released the prisoner. The only gold they found was one
huge golden sun which was in the pond in the gardens of Falling Eagle's palace.

Meanwhile what was to be done about Mexico? The whole country was at the feet
of Cortes. He was determined that it should be ruled by the laws and customs of Spain.
So he needed a capital. After much speculation and discussion with native Mexican
chiefs he came to the conclusion that a new Mexico City should be built on the site of
the ancient capital. There was ample manpower among the refugees and the men from
nearby towns. Thousands of them were mobilized to level the site and construct an
elegant sixteenth-century European town with wide roads, gardens, squares and, of
course, churches. Those first churches were built like fortresses, for safety's sake. No
one knew whether the Indian population would continue to accept the new world
which had opened all around them. Some things they found difficult indeed. When the
first cathedral building was going up it was decided to roof it with a barrel vault. The
stones were fitted very exactly over a wooden framing by the native stone masons.

Then when all was ready the Spaniards began to remove the timbers. The labourers thought it was a dastardly plot to kill them all and ran for their lives. Then after a while they saw the vault was standing firm. This was their first experience of the true arch and a great wonder to them. But they were skilled men proud of their ability, and soon they had equalled and even outstripped their Spanish instructors. With the help of the native artisans, the nameless non-noble Aztecs, a new city arose on the platform of ruined Tenochtitlan. The plan followed the ancient streets and the cathedral stood over the courtyard of the great pyramid of Blue Hummingbird. The city was a fine Renaissance town, but its carvings and decorations were all the work of Aztec artists. The great pyramid still stood for another generation. Then with the help of several hundred barrels of gunpowder the monument of a dreadful past was blown up. Today one can see a corner of the ancient building which has been excavated from the rubble. Enough remains to hint at the size and complex grandeur which was replaced by colonial Mexico.

However, as well as the artisans, the Spaniards controlled thousands of slaves. They were the people of towns which had opposed Cortes during the conquest. Branded on face and arms they were exploited unmercifully. Some of the Spaniards, though, alas, very few, were kindly masters and kept a happy household together. But for the most part the women were ill used, and the men beaten and driven to work.

Cortes had wished to establish in Mexico a kind of mixed culture in which his imported cattle and sheep, and the use of the wheeled cart, should expand the quality of life for the people in his care, especially on his enormous personal estates in Oaxaca. In some areas, where allegiance was taken by oath from the chiefs and a church established, life went on reasonably well. Or might have done if it had not been for the spread of the new diseases. Fever and smallpox were all around and although there was a slackening of epidemics it proved to be only a temporary respite. Soon the diseases returned with ever-increasing devastation. The population died in thousands upon thousands so that there was a shortage of labour which the landowners tried to cure by enforced levies and ever-increasing pressure upon the surviving Indians entrusted to their care. The loss of life in the plagues unwittingly brought from Europe was the main cause of the terrible depopulation and the catastrophic slide of the Mexicans into a state of miserable serfdom.

In addition, the introduction of the European feudal tradition led to much hardship for the Indians. Some of the Spanish expeditions were disasters for the population. Thousands were reduced to slavery. Violence was deliberately used to stimulate violence so that punishments could be inflicted. The main aim was to obtain any residual gold in the region and pick up slaves. Even in Mexico City there was oppression

Opposite above Contemporary portrait of Hernando Cortes, painted in Spain at the Court of Charles v. He is shown holding the coat of arms granted to him by the Emperor in July 1529 as Marques del Valle de Oaxaca. From the *Trachtenbuch* of Christoph Weidetz.

Opposite below Indians playing *tlachtli*, with a solid rubber ball. From Weidetz's *Trachtenbuch*.

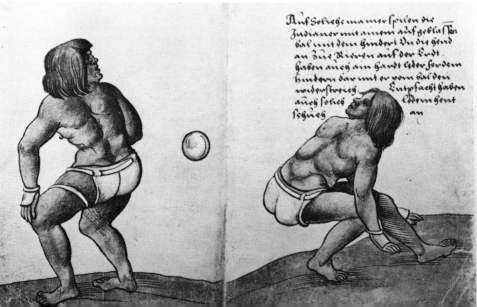

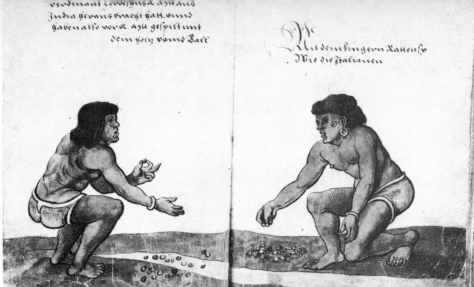

through the courts, and ever-increasing assessments for taxation in kind. One can still see in the British Museum the record of one small town, the 'Petition of the Indians of Tepetlaoztoc' (Cave in the Rocks) where the pictures show the local overseers beating and burning the towns-people to exact tribute, and the gradual loss of wealth which resulted. The gifts, once of jewels, deteriorated until the impoverished citizens could only pay with bundles of firewood and cases of frogs. But that such a 'Petition' could be made and considered in the courts shows that the intentions of the government were often good, though the practical application of regulations was more often thoroughly bad.

While all the business of social reorganization was continuing under the direction of Cortes he had heard that one of his lieutenants had seized land in southern Guatemala and was setting up a new dominion. Cortes could not tolerate this, so he prepared an expedition to cross the Maya country and confront the presumed rebels. On this expedition he determined to take with him a group of Aztec nobles, including Falling Eagle. It had been noted that Cortes had never allowed Falling Eagle to be far away from him; it seems that he was wise enough to know that the young Aztec Speaker, if an opportunity presented itself, would lead a revolt of the Aztecs. To persist in seeking a way to recover the freedom of the people from foreign domination was certainly in keeping with Aztec character.

The expedition encountered terrible difficulty from the terrain. As was usual in Cortes' expeditions in Mexico it was hampered by rain, almost as if the rain god Tlaloc was harassing him, and no doubt the Mexicans saw that as the explanation. The expedition found itself in a maze of tropical swamps with only a map given by some Maya traders to guide them. They came to the busy town of Acalan where they camped. One of the Indian mercenaries informed Cortes that the Aztec chiefs were plotting to kill him. Cortes acted promptly, had the suspects confined and brought to a court martial. The questioning was brief and biased and the prisoners were condemned to hang. So died the brave young Falling Eagle and his friends. He had always declared his innocence but the situation allowed no time for a fair trial.

After the incident they continued the march through the swamps which eventually gave way to forest. The rebel leader had died before the Spaniards arrived and they were able to reassert Cortes' authority peacefully and without bloodshed. When they planned to return, they were prevented by Cortes falling ill. He was suffering from fever and acute depression and was so ill that they tried to send him back by boat. Three times the storm gods struck and battered the boat. After much delay it was blown off course and landed in Cuba. Cortes' companions were very anxious to get him back to Mexico City because they had heard that the Governing Council, believing Cortes to have died in the forests, were asserting their authority with unnecessary brutality; there was danger of civil strife and Indian rebellion. Finally, after a long illness and a

Opposite above Indians gambling with pebbles. This game was also a means of divination. From Weidetz's *Trachtenbuch*.

Opposite below Drawing by Christoph Weidiez in 1529 of a Mexican warrior accompanying Cortes in Spain.

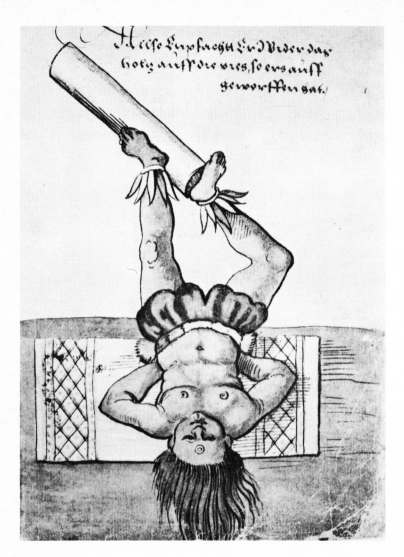

Above A Mexican foot-juggler performing in Spain. From Christopher Weidetz's *Trachtenbuch*.

Centre An Indian of high rank, with featherwork shade and a tame parrot. From the *Trachtenbuch*.

great deal of devoted care from his friends, Cortes recovered and set off back to Mexico.

The news of the returning conqueror was an occasion for fiesta. Triumphal arches were erected and flower petals scattered in his path. The Spaniards felt that this was the man who could bring order because he was above the factions in the city; the Indians felt that he was the rightful conqueror and that he had in fact been less cruel towards them than had the other Spaniards. However, he had no wish to return to Mexico City itself, but stayed awhile in Tezcoco. Then he went to his favourite residence, a palace

Above A young Indian woman. From the *Trachtenbuch*.

rather like a castle in Cuernavaca. There he lived in great state with his servants and Spanish gentlemen who served his food and obeyed the measured etiquette of his court. Nevertheless, he continued to acknowledge himself the servant of the Council of the Indies and of the Royal Commissioners in Mexico, and claimed jurisdiction only in his own estates.

In this period Cortes made his most notable contribution to Mexico. He taught the Indians to tend the oxen and sheep that he had imported, he brought sugar cane from Cuba, and laid the basis of a mixed economy by which Mexican agriculture could progress without losing its more ancient roots in the cultivation of maize, cotton, and native fruits. His finest estates were in Oaxaca, where he had achieved a good relationship with the native nobility. His favourite title was that of Lord of the Valley of Oaxaca. (Indeed, on his recall to Spain he was offered a title and he chose to be dubbed Marques del Valle de Oaxaca.)

Eventually the plotting of his enemies in Spain caused him to be recalled. These enemies included the Bishop of Burgos who had consistently opposed the preferment of the explorers, including Columbus, and of course the relatives of Diego Velasquez, Governor of Cuba. Cortes, however, received a hearing from the Emperor Charles v. He was vindicated and raised to his rank of marquis. He gained the friendship of the emperor who consulted him on the condition of the Indians in the American colonies; Cortes is said to have advised liberal reforms.

He had brought over a group of Zapotec Indian dancers and jugglers whose juggling acts and skill with rubber balls had never before been seen in Europe. They were seen and drawn by Christoph Weiditz, a well-known German artist, who depicted them, and Cortes himself, in his *Trachtenbuch*.

While in Spain Cortes married a second wife, a lady of the highest rank, and by the new marquessa he had three children. His first wife had died childless after a sudden illness about a year after her arrival in Mexico.

Cortes returned to Mexico and was very splendidly received. He was restless, however, and spent much energy and money on expeditions along the Pacific coasts. It was Cortes who was responsible for discovering the coasts of California. However, Tlaloc and his wife, the storm goddess, still obstructed his path and the saga of shipwreck and loss nearly ruined him.

Finally he was once more recalled to Spain where many envious foes tried to cause his downfall. His health was poor, his father had recently died and he found himself confronted with every kind of difficulty. This time too Charles v was cold towards him and the disputes were long and wearing. Cortes died in Spain in 1547 worn out with his troubles, an exhausted and unhappy man.

Cortes kept the promises that he had made to Montezuma. He had cared for all the royal children that he could trace. The three princesses married Spanish grandees; the eldest was given control of a city and great estates, and they, like many others of the Aztec nobility, became landowners of equal rank with the Spaniards. The aristocratic system of the Aztecs was well adapted for amalgamation with the developed feudalism surviving among the Spaniards. So the line of Montezuma continued, and in the years to come many important nobles in Mexico were of the Montezuma family. Their descendants still rejoice in the proud name of the last Great Speaker of the Mexicans.

Opposite Old Zapotec woman wearing the typical hand-woven dark-blue *rebozo* standing by the organ cactus fence of her home.

Mexico itself, however, did not prosper. The greed and oppression of the land-lords could not be prevented either by good laws or by religious exhortation. The depredations of plague were even worse. It is said that by 1600 the population of Mexico was only a fourth of what it was under Montezuma. The Spanish colonial system, with its iron-bound caste system, kept the Indians of the villages in a semi-serfdom not far removed from slavery. However, the nation survived and, although class was a barrier, race was not. So there arose a vigorous class of *mestizos* who could hold high office and aspire to a good life. The revolution of 1821 swept away much of the old feudalism, and then came a century of struggle, of dictators and heroes, of an invasion under Maximilian. From these tribulations arose President Juarez, and once more a Mexican Indian ruled Mexico. His liberal reforms were later subverted by the growth of great private estates and political intrigues for power. President Porfirio Diaz became the centre of an effete system which was finally overthrown. Now Mexican democracy moves forward, searching for a middle course among pressures from all around. The arts and sciences flourish, and above all the Aztecs are honoured in their own land. Falling Eagle is a national hero, and the elegant Nahuatl tongue is still the language of poetry. The Conquest is over and the Mexicans once more rule their own country. It may be that the dream of Montezuma of the return of Quetzalcoatl may one day be realized.

Opposite Mexican Indian woman hand-weaving a man's belt. The spinning and weaving are still performed in the pre-Columbian style.

Overleaf Zapotec girl carrying a gourd bowl and wearing a hand-woven *rebozo*.

SELECT BIBLIOGRAPHY

PRIMARY SOURCES

Codex Aubin ed. Eugene Goupil, Paris, 1893.

Codex Vindobonensis Mexico I, facsimile edition, Akademische Druck u. Verlagsanstalt, Graz, 1970.

Codex Xolotl. ed. Charles Dibble, Mexico, 1951.

De Acosta, Joseph. *Historia Natural y Moral de las Indias*, republished, Mexico, 1940.

De Sahagun, Bernardino. *Historia General de las Cosas de la Nueva España,* English-Nahuatl edition, Dibble and Anderson, School of American Research at Santa Fé, and the University of Utah, in progress.

De Salazar, Francisco Cervantes. *La Coronica de la Conquista de la Nueva España,* ed. Troncosco y Paso, Madrid, 1914.

Duran, Diego. *Historia de las Indias de Nueva España, e Islas de Terra Firma,* ed. Ramirez, 1867–80, Mexico.

Duran, Diego. *Historia Tolteca-Chichimeca,* edited with the *Anales de Cuauhtitlan* by H. Berlin, Mexico, 1947.

Diaz del Castillo, Bernal. *The True History of the Conquest of New Spain,* 5 vols., ed. A. P. Maudslay, Hakluyt Society, London, 1908; trans. J. M. Cohen (slightly abridged), *The Conquest of New Spain*, Penguin books, 1963.

Ixtlilxochitl, Fernando de Alva. *Obras Historicas*, Mexico, 1891–92.

Motolinia, Toribio de Benavente. *History of the Indians of New Spain*; trans. Foster, Berkeley, 1950.

Tezozomoc, Fernando Alvarado. *Cronica Mexicayotl*, ed. Leon, Mexico, 1948.

MORE RECENT WORKS

Beyer, German. *Mito y Simbolismo del Mexico Antiguo,* Mexico, 1965.

Burland, Cottie A. *Magic Books from Mexico,* King Penguin, London, 1953.

Burland, Cottie A. *The Gods of Mexico,* London and New York, 1967.

Caso, Alfonso. *The Aztecs, People of the Sun*, Oklahoma, 1958.

Joyce, Thomas Athol. *Mexican Archaeology*, London, 1914.

Nicholoson, Irene. *Firefly in the Night*, London, 1959.

Peterson, Frederick. *Ancient Mexico*, London, 1959.

Prescott, William H. *The Conquest of Mexico*, illustrated by Keith Henderson and edited by T. A. Joyce, London, 1922.

Leon Portilla, Miguel. *The Broken Spears, Aztec accounts of the Conquest*, London, 1962.

Soustelle, Jacques. *Daily Life of the Aztecs,* London, 1961.

Vaillant, George C. *The Aztecs of Mexico,* edited and annotated by Suzannah B. Vaillant, New York, 1962.

INDEX